W9-CJX-344

"RAW JOURNALISM. . . . A cold, harsh look at a cold, harsh system of justice . . . fascinating."
—*Philadelphia Bulletin*

"ILLUMINATING . . . James Mills, author of four previous best sellers on crime, tells this story graphically."
—*Tampa Tribune*

ON THE EDGE

"The intimate portraits Mills has created from his subjects supply an immediate and vivid indictment of defects and equivocations in U.S. justice."
—*Booklist*

"FASCINATING . . . GRIPPING . . . Mills details his portraits of the people who live in this world with a fine, sure hand."
—*Tulsa World*

BOOKS BY JAMES MILLS

Nonfiction
On the Edge
The Prosecutor
The Underground Empire

Fiction
One Just Man
Report to the Commissioner
The Panic in Needle Park

QUANTITY SALES

ON THE EDGE

James Mills

A DELL BOOK

Published by
Dell Publishing
a division of
The Bantam Doubleday Dell Publishing Group, Inc.
1 Dag Hammarskjold Plaza
New York, New York 10017

For my mother and father

Justice is people, after all. This book is about people: a detective, a judge, heroin addicts, a lawyer, a gangster, prisoners, a jail guard. Each has been close to the taking of life—suddenly on the street or slowly day by day, in prison. Each has lived on the edge.

—James Mills
1975

ON THE EDGE

ONE

EVERY EVENING GEORGE BARRETT KISSES HIS four sons good night, including the two oldest, who are seventeen and nineteen. It embarrasses the older boys to be kissed by their father, and he admits that it may seem "a little weird." But, he says, "I think that the way I live I may never see them again, and I don't want to be stretched out dying in a street some place wishing for one more chance to see my family and say good-by. So every time I kiss them it's like it's the last time I'll ever see them, and I'm kissing them good-by forever."

Forever can come very suddenly to Detective George Barrett. He is a hunter of men. And none of those he hunts—thieves, drug pushers, Murphy men, assault and robbery men, killers—wants to confront him on anything resembling even terms. Because when George Barrett hunts for a man, he invariably finds him; and when he finds him, the man is not always arrested, but he is always sorry he was found. George Barrett is a tough cop. His eyes, cold as gun metal, can be looked at but not into. His jaw is hard and square as a brick, and his thin lips are kept moist by nervous darting passes of his tongue. When he laughs, only his face and voice laugh. Inside, George Barrett does not laugh.

"I'm obsessed," he says, "with the idea that I've *got* to win—and these animals can smell it. No one's going to mess with me and win because I've been around, I've been up against the bad guys. These animals on Broadway? I'll eat them up. I've got the tools and I know how to use them. If I can't get the best of the guy with punches, I'll kick him, and if he's a better kicker than I am, I'll go with the stick or the jack, and if I have to, I'll use my gun."

To some people George Barrett is precisely what's wrong with law enforcement. To others he is all that can save it.

In late evening darkness he stands on New York City's West Fifty-second Street, the Sixteenth Precinct's northern border, and looks south into the flashing neon fireball of Times Square. This is Broadway, the Great White Way, the fabled street of dreams. Barrett calls it the sewer. Down it flows the worst America has to offer in the way of degenerates, perverts and lawbreakers—to Barrett, "germs."

Already on Broadway and on Seventh Avenue, down to the precinct's southern edge at Forty-second Street, the prostitutes are prowling. Murphy men (confidence men who pose as pimps, then vanish when they have the money) are hunting for their marks. Car boosters, working close to the curb and nodding as they pass each car to see what they can find inside, walk the side streets, always against the traffic to thwart detectives who might follow them in cars. From 8 P.M. to midnight they'll do their biggest business, hitting theatergoers' cars, most with out-of-state plates so the drivers won't be around to go to court if the thief is caught. No car lock can protect suitcases against the booster's screwdriver (to snap open fly windows on sedans) or his bent fork (stuck between the closed windows of a hardtop or convertible to flip up the lock button).

This early in the evening the Murphy men concentrate near the dance halls and discotheques, looking for men grown bold on beer. And looking with them are their more vicious cousins, the A&R men, assault and robbery specialists, muggers. The gypsy women, dotted around the precinct in little glass-fronted shops with dim lights, velvet chairs and phony flowers, sit seductively, moving occasionally to the doorway to invite some passer-by to taste the delicious intrigues of the back room. If the quarry enters, he will have his pocket picked, and by experts whose fingers can slip the 20s from the inside of a roll without disturbing the outside singles.

On Broadway, between Forty-third and Forty-fifth streets, the male prostitutes line up like whores in Hamburg—baby-faced youngsters and broad-belted, black-booted toughs, any type the trade demands. Around the corner in the alley-like darkness of Forty-third Street, homosexual exhibitionists skip between Broadway and Eighth Avenue, shouting affectionate female curses at each other. On Forty-second Street, beneath brilliant white marquees touting movies called *Orgy at Lil's Place, The Dirty Girls* and *Rape*, flow streams of degenerates of all varieties. And everywhere, up and down the pre-

cinct, are the junkies, the pill addicts and the pushers.

George Barrett's precinct is small—384 acres,
15.8 miles of streets—and you can walk it end to
end in twenty minutes. But into its seventy square
blocks are packed Rockefeller Center, Radio City,
the theater district, the diamond center and Times
Square. In it every month are reported fifteen robberies, twenty felonious assaults, twenty burglaries,
320 larcenies, two rapes, and more acts of prostitution, perversion and extortion than anyone has ever
tried to count.

Looking south into the chaos of his precinct, Barrett says, "This is a fast track, and if you can't stay in
the ball game you get farmed out. If you're a little-
old-lady detective, you end up in a little-old-lady
precinct. Over twenty thousand guys in uniform
want to be detectives, because they want the title
'Detective,' and they think they'd like this job—
'Broadway Detective,' very glamorous."

Barrett works in a "block" of four men. They take
turns "catching squeals," recording and investigating complaints. This evening two of his partners are
back in the station house typing out reports and
answering phones, while Barrett, who types fast
and would rather be on the street, patrols with the
fourth partner. Barrett says that he feels "ambitious," but he wants to be particularly selective tonight about making an arrest because his "swing"
(days off) begins tomorrow. If he makes an arrest
tonight he will have to spend tomorrow in court on
his own time, extending his workday to more than
twenty straight hours. So he is going to be selective.

But there are ways to discourage crime without going to court.

Barrett has walked less than a block when he and his partner stop next to a parking lot and stand casually continuing their conversation about the New York Giants. Neither has mentioned it to the other, but both have spotted a tall thin man who started into the empty attendant's shack in the parking lot, then quickly backed out when he saw the attendant looking at him from the lot. Now the thin man walks past them, and they resume their stroll, watching him. He moves fast, looking in cars as he hurries by them. He is down to Forty-seventh and Broadway when he stops short at a car, peers in and opens the door. He reaches into the car and comes out with a toy camera which he shakes, listens to and tosses into a trash can.

"That's petty larceny, no matter what the thing's worth," Barrett says, "but let's see what develops."

The man eyes sidewalk merchandise, goes in a drugstore and cases the counters. Finally he is coming out of a clothing store with his hands full of ties and Barrett grabs him.

"Hey, man, what you doin' to me, why you grabbin' me, I'm gonna pay for them, I was gonna pay."

Barrett and his partner take the man back into the store and find the manager, who says he is being robbed blind and will definitely go to court as a complainant. The thief is making a fuss, playing to a crowd of shoppers.

"I'll pay for the ties, man. Let me go home and I'll be good. I promise, man. I'll be good. I wouldn't lie to you."

"You wouldn't lie," Barrett says. "No, you wouldn't lie. What about the toy camera?"

"What toy camera?"

"The one you took out of the car."

"What car?"

Barrett and his partner take the man to the station house and up the antique spiral staircase to the squad room. The five-story brick building—often condemned but never vacated—has been there since the Civil War. Its scarred walls are flaking off their millionth coat of paint, and the thick wooden floors creak with the burdens of a century. They walk past a small wooden bench for waiting complainants through a waist-high, steel swinging gate with a broken latch. Barrett tells the prisoner to sit down and he settles into a broken wooden chair tied together with twine. The five desks are scarred and ancient, one of them steadied with a quarter-inch stack of arrest cards under a short leg. Wastebaskets overflow onto the tobacco-brown floor, littered with discarded forms, cigarette butts, rubber bands and pins that serve for paper clips. Light comes from four ceiling lamps—the broken globe on one has been replaced with a piece of bent cardboard. The green walls are covered with framed pictures of the FBI's ten most wanted criminals, and smaller shots of teen-age boys and girls who have run away from home to seek the glamour of Times Square (some go home after the first taste, others end up as drug addicts or prostitutes).

A wire cage the size of a large closet contains four prisoners in one corner of the room. Three are addicts arrested for boosting cars and one is a female impersonator loudly demanding to be separated from "such riffraff." A blind boy is explaining to a detective at a desk how someone walked up to him on Seventh Avenue, grabbed the wallet out of his pocket and ran. At another desk a man, his wife and her sister are reporting a burglary, all of them talking at once.

A detective questions a twenty-five-year-old A&R man arrested for attacking a passer-by with a knife on Forty-eighth Street. "What's your name?" he asks.

"Who, me?" The prisoner is a pro at countering interrogation.

"Yeah, you. What's your name?"

"My name?"

"Your name. What's your name?"

"My name's Sonny."

"What's your last name?"

"My last name?"

"Look! What's your name—all of it?"

"Sonny Davis."

"Where do you live?"

"Where do I live?"

It goes on like that, and Barrett looks disgusted. He does not interfere, but he would not have put up with it. He is a good interrogator and he knows that you do not get anywhere with a prisoner until you break down the barrier between his world and yours. You are neatly dressed, relaxed, secure, educated and a cop. He is shabby, nervous, defiant and a prisoner. There is no communication until by a soft word, a tough word, a cigarette, a slap in the

face—depending on the individual—the gap is
bridged and real talk begins.

Not long ago a junkie prostitute and her boyfriend were arrested for robbing and beating to
death an old man in a cheap West Side hotel. "They
brought her in," Barrett says, "and people started
questioning her. Everyone was talking to her like a
lady and she was loving it and they were getting
nowhere. I looked at her sheet and saw whore, and I
decided it was time someone talked to her like a
whore. So I took her into the C.O.'s office and I
turned out the lights—people find it easier to tell
you things in the dark—and I said to her, 'Look,
you're nothing but a cheap junkie whore and I
know that and you know it, so let's just talk to each
other that way, okay?' A few minutes later she was
crying on my shoulder and clutching my hands and
telling me how she went through the old man's
pockets while her boyfriend played the anvil chorus
on his head with a fire-hose nozzle."

Screams—long, piercing female screams—rise
from downstairs. Scuffling sounds on the stairs, and
then a tall, attractive blond prostitute arrives with
two plainclothesmen. Tears and mascara flow down
her cheeks. "I want to see the captain! You can't
lock me up! I didn't do anything! I want to call my
lawyer!"

The plainclothesman who arrested her is short,
fat, bald and looks like anything but a cop. Her eyes
flash with the fury of a prostitute whose ability to
spot a cop has just been proved defective. The
plainclothesman quietly hunts around for the necessary forms and she keeps screaming. "I knew you

were a cop! I didn't say nothing to you! You can't bust me!"

A detective fingerprinting the A&R man suddenly turns from the fingerprint table and yells, "Shut up, will you? We all know how tough it is these days for a whore to make a good honest living and how all your civil rights are being violated and all that, but just shut the hell up!"

Surprised by the outburst, she quiets down and sits in a corner muttering through her tears.

A patrolman walks in with a sharply dressed young lawyer who is slightly tipsy. The lawyer and a friend, also drunk, had been creating a disturbance on Broadway, and when the cop told them to move, the lawyer informed his friend that he would "take care of this," then offered $25 to the cop "to get lost." Afraid that the lawyer might later claim that he had succeeded with the bribe, the cop arrested him for attempting it.

"I want to call my lawyer," the lawyer said, and was given a phone. He dialed a number and waited for the answer. "Hello, Charlie? This is Sam. You sitting down, Charlie? Charlie, I've been pinched. Charlie . . . Charlie . . . Charlie, don't make jokes."

The lawyer was put in the cage with the others. In a moment a detective he had not seen before walked in and another detective began asking where he had been. Taking the first detective for a suspect, the lawyer shouted from the cage, "Don't answer that! You don't have to answer any questions! You want a lawyer? I'll represent you!"

The detective looked at him, incredulous. *"You'll*

represent *me?* Buddy, *you* are the one in the cage.
Me, I'm going home."

"That's too bad, really too bad," Barrett said, discussing the lawyer's case. "I mean he was just a little
drunk, showing off to his friend, and now he has to
go down to court and really feel humiliated in front
of the judge and the other attorneys. Not much will
happen to him, but it's a shame it ever got this far. It
never would have if the cop hadn't suspected he
might pull a fast one on him. He did break a law
offering the cop money, and the cop had to protect
himself."

Barrett was typing up records on his thief when a
distinguished-looking middle-aged man appeared
in the doorway. Barrett looked up and stopped typing, but did not take his fingers from the keys. "Yes,"
he said, "may I help you?"

The man came in and sat in a chair by the desk.
He said he had been walking on Forty-seventh
Street when he felt for his wallet and it was missing.
It had had $250 in it. His car was in a garage and he
needed $5.00 to get it out. He was a vice president
of a business in New Jersey, where he lived, and was
very careful to be polite and agreeable.

Barrett listened to the man without a word.
When he was through Barrett sat back and said,
"You just told me what happened. Now, listen,
okay? Because I'm going to tell you what really happened. You thought you were going to get something from the Gypsy, right? From the shop there
on Forty-seventh between Broadway and Eighth
Avenue. You had a couple of drinks and she looked

good and she hustled you into the place and picked your pocket, right?"

The man looked startled and confused, trying to decide if he should lie.

"Look," Barrett said, "you're a big boy now. You thought you were going to get laid, and what you really got was fucked. So be a man and go over to the phone there and make a reverse call to New Jersey and ask your wife or a friend to come and get you. And don't tell me cute little stories about losing your wallet, you understand? Because I wasn't born yesterday either." He paused. "If you want me to go over and try to get your money back, I'll do that."

The man stood up and offered his hand to Barrett. "Thank you," he said. "You're a good man, a really good man."

Barrett stared at the typewriter, and did not shake hands.

The man went back down the stairs.

Barrett sat there looking at the keys, not typing. Finally he said, "All he wants is five bucks to get home. He never thought of taking a tube for thirty cents. He comes in here with a phony story like that and he expects me to give him $5.00."

A patrolman came up from downstairs and said the man was still there and that he said he had changed his mind and would like Barrett to go over to the Gypsy shop and try to get his money back.

Barrett went with him and on the way the man said, "You are really very nice. May I ask, sir, what school you went to? I went to Dartmouth."

"That's fine," Barrett said. "I went to P.S. 12."

They got to the shop and Barrett banged on the

door, but the lights were out and no one answered. "When they make a good score, they move to another shop," Barrett said. "If you want to come tomorrow, I'll come back with you and see what I can do."

"No thanks," the man said. "Come back yourself and if you get the money give it away." He walked off.

"He couldn't care less about locking up someone who just beat him for $250," Barrett said. "All he cares about is $5.00 to get his car."

Barrett went back and finished the paper work and fingerprinting on his prisoner. He was not about to spend a day off to take a petty thief to court, so he found another detective who had to go to court anyway and asked him to take this prisoner too. The court appearance would only be to set bail and there would be no sworn testimony, but nevertheless the detective would be violating procedure to take in someone else's prisoner. He had never done this before, argued, and finally agreed reluctantly. Leaving the station house to continue patrol, Barrett's partner asked what the problem had been. "Nothing," Barrett said, "he just lost his virginity tonight, that's all. He'll be a good cop."

Back on patrol at 2 A.M., they walk from Broadway's bright lights into a cave of darkness on West Forty-third Street. The back of a theater, a flat brick wall with iron fire escapes hanging on it, rises high on the left. On the right a dim glow of light comes from the loading platforms of the New York *Times* pressroom. A few pressmen, wearing hats folded from newspapers, stand by the platforms

watching an argument across the street. Two homosexuals are shouting at each other and four others
are watching. All are wearing wigs, long earrings,
false eyelashes and makeup. Barrett stops beside
the watching pressmen and listens to the argument.
His partner keeps going and says, "Come on,
George, you know you're not going to make an arrest, so why look?"

Suddenly one of the homosexuals, a Negro,
knocks the other into the street and jumps on top,
hitting him. Barrett starts toward them, and a pressman says, "Look out, he has a knife." Barrett grabs
the Negro by the shirt, yanks him off the victim and
slams him up against the theater wall. The man's
wig goes flying into the gutter.

The one who was on the bottom gets up, a cut
under his left eye. The others are walking away,
trying to get out of sight before Barrett notices
them. Barrett yells for them to come back and he
collects them all under a fire escape. The man who
had been on top is still against the wall, and Barrett
ignores him. The others are all talking at once.

"Quiet!" Barrett orders. "No one talks unless I ask
something. Because I won this little show, right? So
we play this ball game my way."

He writes their names and addresses in a note-
book and then asks the one who was beaten if he
wants to prefer charges.

"No, I just want to leave it where it's at."

Barrett then asks each the same questions and
gets from each the same answers:

"Are you male?"

"Yes."

"Are you a homosexual?"

"Yes."

"Are you a female impersonator?"

"No."

They have said no to the last because impersonating a female is a crime, but so long as they do not actually wear female clothes they cannot be arrested.

The man who had been on top walks over to the gutter and retrieves his wig.

"Hey, germ!" Barrett yells at him. "Come here!"

The man adjusts the wig on his head as Barrett asks him his name and address. The man gives the same answers to the same questions.

"Now," Barrett says, indicating everyone except the attacker, "all you germs walk up this street to Broadway and get lost. Don't come back." They take off.

Then he starts walking the other way, toward Eighth Avenue, with the last one.

"Now listen to me, germ," he says as they walk. "A lot of people saw this little thing and I'd be a lot better off if I locked you up. But I'm not going to."

"Man, don't lock me up. I didn't do nothin'. That bitch called me a nigger, and I'm not gonna take that from her or anyone else."

"Yeah. Well, I'm a member of the NAACP myself, but I don't go around trying to put knives in people. And you're not listening to me. I'm not going to lock you up. I'm going to walk you around the corner to the subway and you're going to run down into that hole and get out of here and if you ever come back I'm going to drill you right between the eyes, you understand that? You get that? And do you know how unhappy that's going to make me? That's going to make me so unhappy I'm going to go out and eat a big steak dinner and then go home and sleep for ten hours. So get in that hole and get out of here."

The man disappears down into the subway.

Later, in a Times Square bar, Barrett felt he should explain what he had done. "I have nothing against homosexuals," he said. "They're sick, and I understand that, but that doesn't mean they have a right to go around trying to kill each other. I mean, no one said it was open season on fags this week. A lot of detectives wouldn't have done anything about that, especially since the guy was a Negro. They would have been afraid to get involved. Afraid of ending up in front of a grand jury. I got their names and addresses and admissions that they are homosexuals and that no one wants to prefer charges. So tomorrow when one of those guys from the *Times* calls up headquarters and wants to know how come some detective was manhandling a fine upstanding citizen, I'll be prepared to explain myself. But most cops would have been afraid to do that in front of all those witnesses, so they would have either walked away or just stood there and watched a homicide. So I roughed someone up—all right, but at least he won't do life for murder, and the guy he was on top of isn't dead.

"Lawyers spend weeks preparing a case, a judge spends weeks considering it, but I've got to make a decision in a second. Does he have a knife? Does he have a gun? Should I hit him? How hard? If I don't hit him hard enough he can kill me. If I hit him too

hard I'm brutal. I don't move unless I know I'm
right, but when I do move I'm prepared to move all
the way. Most cops today just stand there running
the whole legal case over in their minds, and meanwhile someone's being stabbed to death. That's why
I like working with Sam Huff [a nickname for an
enormous detective named Bob Kenney, one of
Barrett's partners]. Because if you're standing outside a door with Sam and there's a real bad guy
inside and you say, 'Okay, Sam, let's go,' he's going
to hit that door and go right through it, whereas
most guys would start reciting sections of the penal
code to you. They know there's a bad guy in there,
but they want to try the case out in the hall before
they go in. I like to collar the guy before he kills
someone, and then let them try the case in court."

The bar he was in was filled with hoods, and for
that, Barrett knew, he could get in trouble too.
"Some cops see you talking to known felons and
they figure there's a romance going on or something. They say, 'What're you talking to him for? He
a friend of yours or something?' But then they'll call
you up on a homicide and say, 'Gee, George, do you
think you could talk to that guy about this or that?'
When something big breaks they come to me because I know who the actors are."

A young, short, very heavy man stopped to talk to
Barrett. Barrett shook hands and asked how much
time the man thought he was going to get.

"I don't know, George. Maybe a year. It looks like
maybe a year. But I don't want to do no time at all.
It looks tough."

He left and Barrett said, "He's a real bad guy. For

$1,000 he'd take a contract to hit you in the head. My only claim to fame with him and these other animals in here is they know I wouldn't hand them a wrong one. But I lock up enough of them every year so they know Barrett's around. I'll tell you, I really *like* locking these bastards up. People—even cops—say to me, 'George, why are you so cynical, why are you so mean?' Well, I've got guys up there doing twenty to life wishing they could cut my heart out, and I sleep like a baby. I don't feel bad about them at all. Because I think of the victims. I went for a long time on a case once, and somewhere near the end of it, the D.A. says to me, 'George, what's the name of the victim, the deceased?' Everyone was so deep into litigation that no one could remember the name of the victim. Whenever I start to feel sorry for these animals I think of the victims, and I'm all right again. But most of the cops today don't think of the victims or the bad guys or anything. I don't say all cops are like that, but a lot of them are. They just don't want to get involved. 'Don't get involved,' they figure, 'don't get involved.' "

Barrett has been involved since he was twelve years old. He was living with his family in Brooklyn, and he got a brutal taste of what crime can mean. His father, a newspaper pressman, was on his way home from church when he was robbed, beaten and left for dead in a doorway. He lay there for two hours before a neighbor found him and called a doctor. Barrett remembers that the beating was so severe that "when the doctor arrived I had to help him press on my father's stomach to keep everything in place."

A year later young Barrett was walking behind his two brothers when he heard two thugs planning to attack them. "I slipped into a doorway," he says, "and grabbed a couple of empty milk bottles. Then when the two guys started to go up on my brothers, I stepped in and tattooed them into the ground with the bottles. I did what had to be done. And ever since, that's been the story of my life. I do what had to be done."

Barrett began his climb into the detectives' ranks on a December night in 1954, the only time he has ever shot to kill. He was a patrolman then, off duty, on his way to visit an aunt. He heard calls for help and saw a cab driver struggling with three male passengers. Barrett approached the cab, saw a gun in the hand of one of them and opened fire. The bullet missed, and the passengers piled out. Barrett hit one in the mouth with his gun, sheering off the man's teeth. The other two ran. Barrett rode with the prisoner in the cab to the station house. "I had him on the back floor of the cab with my gun in his mouth," Barrett says, "and he decided to tell me who his friends were."

All three admitted to twenty-two other stickups and burglaries—one had shot a man just the night before—and were convicted. Barrett won a promotion to detective.

A ring mark on a murdered man's finger produced Barrett's next promotion three years later. A twenty-year-old ex-con named Henry Dusablon, working with a twenty-eight-year-old friend, robbed and murdered six shopkeepers in five days, four of them in one day. One of the dead men ran a novelty store in the Sixteenth Precinct. Investigating that killing, Barrett noticed the ring mark, assumed that the ring had been stolen by the killers, and from the dead man's wife obtained a description of it. Hoping the killers would try to sell the ring, Barrett and other detectives went to work on pawnshops. They finally found the ring, pawned by Dusablon under his real name. The pawnbroker said Dusablon had known the exact weight of the stone, indicating he had already had it appraised somewhere else. The detectives canvassed other shops and finally came up with a clerk who said a man answering Dusablon's description had tried to sell him the ring. The clerk had asked him to return later and Dusablon had remarked that he was staying in a hotel nearby on West Forty-eighth Street. The detectives checked the hotels, found him, and in 1963 Dusablon and his accomplice were convicted of murder. Barrett was jumped to detective second grade.

The kind of detective Barrett accuses of wanting to play it safe and shun involvement can easily do so. The city itself has inadvertently conspired to keep the detective off the streets, to urge him into inactivity. He must spend hours every day typing out forests of forms regarding not only serious crimes but such relatively petty and alien matters as lost key chains and fountain pens, clearly unsolvable petty thefts and the chronic, crank complaints of almost anyone who wants to walk up the twenty-three steps to the squad room. If he makes a significant arrest, the number of reports multiplies. He must fill out forms on everything from the prisoner's aliases to detailed descriptions of his hair, eyes, nose, mouth, chin, ears, eyebrows, build and speech ("Check one: gruff, soft, refined, coarse, accented, effeminate, high-pitched, lisping, stuttering, rapid speaker, slow speaker, mute, tongue-tied"). A juvenile drug addict arrested under anything but the most ordinary circumstances precipitates a flurry of twenty-two forms and reports, all typed out by the arresting officer. A detective who could make ten or twenty vice or narcotics arrests in one night actually makes only one or two because he knows it will take him the rest of his time to finish the paper work. And when the detective is not filling in forms and answering phones, he performs other nonpolice functions, such as fingerprinting applicants for government jobs and credentials. Many detectives feel like clerks. "We may not be fighting crime," says Barrett, "but we're sure recording it."

When the detective is not typing, he is in court. Though many large cities require the arresting officer's presence in court only when his testimony is needed, New York demands him there whenever the defendant appears. Criminals and their lawyers, knowing this, sometimes delay cases repeatedly, waiting for the one morning the detective does not show up to move for dismissal on the grounds that he is not there and cannot testify. For every arrest made, the detective spends hours, often days, in court, much of it on his own time.

When the paper work and the court appearances are out of the way, the detective is permitted to be a detective—almost. He goes out on a case with the very certain knowledge that for being too much of a cop he can wreck his career. He knows that he may have to decide between risking his life or his job, and it is this knowledge that pressures him not to be a cop.

This urge to play it safe, not to get involved, not to enforce the law has had a long, gradual genesis. In recent years Supreme Court decisions concerning search, seizure of evidence, arrest and prisoner interrogation have created an atmosphere of confusion and uncertainty among the police. Not sure what they can legally do, the police have frequently responded by doing nothing. This state of mind worries and angers Barrett. "Today," he says, "the police are running scared. Over the years the pressure groups have been chipping away at us, chipping away, until before long we'll just be a bunch of lamplighters, a bunch of guys marching up and down with broom handles, and the streets will be full of hoods. Just keep marching, keep marching, that's the idea, and if a body falls in front of you, step over it. These cops are just marchers. A bad guy commits a crime today, and he practically tells the cops what to do. He knows no one wants to get involved."

A cop who does want to get involved can have trouble with his own colleagues. Early one morning when Barrett was in the station house, a young off-duty patrolman in civilian clothes came in with a prisoner. The patrolman told Barrett he had just left the station house and was on his way home when the prisoner, a large man about twenty-five, stopped him on Eighth Avenue and demanded money. The patrolman told him no, and the man threatened him. The patrolman then found a uniformed cop, identified himself and suggested that the cop keep an eye on the man who had accosted him. The off-duty patrolman then continued on his way home, but the man approached him again, angry now for having been reported. The man pulled a knife and said, "I'll fix you."

"And then," the off-duty patrolman told Barrett, "this man I had talked to who is in uniform, who is *supposed* to be a cop, sort of ambles up and wants to know what the matter is. He does nothing. Nothing. This guy is standing there with a knife on me, and the cop becomes a spectator. He says to me, 'What do you want me to do?' I think he's crazy or something. Then he says, 'Do you want the collar?' Like he's not going to do anything just because he doesn't want to get involved, because he's *scared* to get involved. So I say, 'You're damned right I'll take the collar.' And then he disarms the guy and I bring him in."

He handed Barrett the knife.

"Then," the patrolman continued, growing more and more frustrated and angry as he relived the story, "then I get to the station house and the lieutenant down there wants to know what I'm doing. He wants to know if the guy actually *hurt* anyone or not. He knows I put my resignation papers in last week and that I'm leaving soon and so he says to me, 'Look, you're leaving anyway, so why bother about it?' Here this guy has just tried to knife someone—

just tried to knife *me*—and this guy, a lieutenant, is telling me not to bother."

He turned from Barrett to another man in the room, whom he took to be a detective, and said, "They give you a shield and they tell you you're a cop and you figure you're supposed to uphold law and order and all that, and then they put you out on the street and castrate you. They make you feel like if you do your job, you're an idiot. Don't get involved everyone says. What is this? Can you just tell me that? What is this?"

He turned and looked at his assailant, and his rage exploded. "Look me in the eye, you son of a bitch," he shouted. The man looked up, and the cop swung at him. The prisoner ducked, and the cop swung again. He was much smaller than the prisoner and not much of a fighter. But he managed to land a couple of punches, which the prisoner accepted without apparent fear and without striking back. Two hours later the prisoner was sitting quietly waiting to be locked up for the night, and the cop was back from a neighborhood hospital with a sling on his arm, which he had wrenched in his fury of missed punches.

A few nights later Barrett was patrolling in a taxicab (lawbreakers easily spot unmarked squad cars) when he saw five uniformed patrolmen and two plainclothesmen trying to get three prisoners into patrol cars for the ride to the station house. One of the prisoners, a female impersonator, carried a sharp-pointed umbrella. Barrett told the patrolmen to get the umbrella. He said it three times and finally a cop obeyed. Driving away in the cab again,

Barrett was dismayed. "He could have run someone
through with that thing. They didn't want to get it
away from him because they were afraid someone
in the crowd would think they were manhandling
him. But we're still allowed to disarm them. It's not
that bad, yet."

Later Barrett was telling a friend about something he had seen a few nights earlier. "A woman
OD'd on Broadway and there's a guy there who is
built like a cigarette machine and he has six cops at
bay, just standing listening to him swear at them.
There's a crowd and the cops are afraid to do anything, even question him, because he's yelling
about brutality and swearing at them and the crowd
is watching and he feels like a great man because
everyone's seeing him abuse those six cops who are
afraid to go near him. I didn't want to jump into the
middle and act like a big hero or something, so I
stepped into a doorway and told one of the cops to
bring him in to me. Just for openers, I was going to
hit him in the stomach. And then what happened
after that would depend on what kind of ball game
he wanted to get into. But the cop says, 'No,
George, I can't get him in here. He's too nasty.' So I
told another cop to go out and bring him in. He
went into the street and then he came back and said
he couldn't get the guy, that he was too mean, that
they had to let him go. So I asked the cop what he
was going to say if this woman died of the overdose.
That guy was the last person to be with her. Maybe
he gave her the OD. Maybe he killed her. And the
cops didn't even know his name. They wouldn't
even talk to him. And I can tell you that now that

he's told six cops where to go in public and got away with it, I feel sorry for the next lone cop who sees him making a disturbance and tries to stop him. The cop'll get killed. That was a real bad guy. And the important thing is that those cops weren't afraid of *him*—they were big enough to eat him up—they were afraid of the crowd, of someone who might accuse them of brutality and get them kicked off the force."

He had grown intense, impassioned, and thought he recognized in his listener a lack of total attention. "These are not *words* I am using to you," he pleaded suddenly. "This is *important.*"

"Bad guys" are always important to George Barrett. He uses the phrase often, and means by it a person who pursues brutal crimes as a way of life. He means armed robbers, killers, professional extortionists—not check forgers and petty thieves. He talks about bad guys with the solemn intensity of a man whose whole soul and being is focused on the pinpoint of a single idea. He does not question who he is, where he is going, what he should do. His mission is the extermination of bad guys. He says, "I am forty-five years old, a cop for twenty years, and I am still a real cops-and-robbers guy."

Barrett can detect bad guys as quickly and certainly as they can detect him. He has no more trouble pinpointing a veteran armed robber than a doctor has spotting a smallpox victim. He treats a petty thief who has been arrested for shoplifting as nothing more or less than a petty thief. But let the thief reveal an inclination toward violence, and Barrett can respond violently. His body moves with a pow-

erful, controlled force that in an instant can be released into calculated, thought-through violence.
For two hours one night he stalked a Murphy man.
Ordinarily he does not bother with petty criminals,
but he knows that often a Murphy man unsuccessful
at conning money from a victim resorts to assault,
usually with a knife. Finally, when he had observed
enough to make a case in court, he arrested the man
and put him in the back seat of the squad car. He sat
next to him. The man was wearing a trench coat
and Barrett asked what he had in his pockets. The
man said, "Nothing." Barrett asked again, and the
man, looking defiant and arrogant, again replied,
"Nothing." Barrett asked once more, got the same
answer, then plunged his left hand into the trench
coat's right-hand pocket. He came out with a
switchblade knife. In an instant, Barrett's right
hand flashed up and struck the man across the
mouth.

"Nothing!" Barrett said, his face twisted in contempt. "You had nothing. What were you going to
do with this? Cut me? Cut me, germ?"

The man wiped his mouth. The arrogance and
defiance were gone. "No, man, I didn't even know
it was there. I don't cut people, man. I may be a
Murphy man, but I don't cut people."

A few nights later Barrett was patrolling with
another man in a taxicab when he spotted a Murphy
man waiting on a corner for a mark. Barrett parked
the cab, and the two of them walked back past the
Murphy man.

"Hey, mister," he said to Barrett, "you want some
girls?"

Barrett played dumb, and the Murphy man fell
into step beside him and began to explain the mar-
vels of the imaginary brothel he worked for. It had
scores of girls of all nationalities, it had a bar, a
restaurant, a floor show. The three of them walked
and talked, and the man continued with his pitch
until he realized their stroll was taking him closer
and closer to the precinct station house. He stopped
talking and so did Barrett. They walked in silence
for several minutes, and then the Murphy man said
hesitantly, "I sure do hope I haven't made an error
with you gentlemen."

Barrett put handcuffs on him and took him in. He
asked him if he had any arrests for assault. The man
said no. Barrett checked his record with headquarters and found he was telling the truth. If he had
had a record for assault, Barrett would have booked
him and gone to court. Because he did not, Barrett
let him go and avoided wasting time in court just to
lock up a con man. But before he let him go he
warned him not to come back to the precinct. He
looked at him hard, and the man seemed impressed. "I use my eyes more than my jack," Barrett
said later. "I look at a bad guy with my nasty eyes
and I deliver the message. Even my wife says I have
mean eyes. The other day someone told my son *he*
had mean eyes. Here I am with perfect teeth, and
he has to inherit these nasty eyes."

If Barrett hates the bad guys, he grieves for the
good. He walks through the west side of the precinct, among the crowded apartment houses, and
he points to the heavy wire screens and bars covering the back windows over the alleys and empty

lots. "Look at that," he says. "They have to make prisons for themselves to keep the germs out. They have to hide themselves behind bars."

It is Sunday and he walks over to a playground where some West Side men, mostly young Irish stevedores, are playing softball. He watches for a while, talks to them and promises to meet them after the game in their clubhouse. Three hours later he walks over to a first-floor room with a small backyard in an apartment house and they are all there. They welcome him with shouts and mugs of beer drawn from a keg behind a bar. In the backyard—a weed and dirt rectangle half the size of a tennis court—they are barbecuing steaks and drinking beer and listening to the second baseman play an electric guitar. Brownstone apartments rise five stories high at the yard's back and front, and at the sides stand twenty-foot stone walls topped with broken glass and barbed wire.

"This is the end of the old West Side," Barrett says sadly. "They've been backed up into a stockade and this is the end of it. They stand out here drinking beer and singing and telling war stories about the old days, but these walls and the barbed wire tell you it's all over. The streets belong to the germs."

Another detective is there. He and Barrett talk and then someone asks what they think is the single most important quality in a detective. Barrett answers easily. "He has to be able to move with people, to move with anyone. He has to talk to a Fifth Avenue businessman and communicate with him, and then go over and talk to some guy who's maybe a janitor or something like that and communicate with him. He has to be able to move with anyone."

He talks to one of the older men, a stevedore boss with bright, sparkling Santa Claus eyes. The man is not entirely untarnished. He has had his connection with the underworld, and Barrett asks him, "What do you hear from Tony?"

"Tony? Nothing. I haven't heard anything about him."

"Oh, yeah? I heard he died."

"Yeah? Oh, that's right. That's right. Yeah, he died."

"When did he die?"

"Oh, I don't know. Maybe yesterday. Yeah, maybe yesterday."

They all laugh and Barrett laughs too, not really having expected an answer.

It gets dark and they leave the yard for the little clubhouse room with the bar in it. They are almost all stevedores and they talk about the docks and sing old Irish songs. They ask for a song from Barrett, who is not Irish, and in his thick husky voice he sings them one:

> *Sure me name it is McGuire*
> *And I'll quickly tell to you*
> *Of the pretty girl I admire*
> *Name of Kitty Donohue*

He finishes singing of Kitty Donohue, and they cheer, toast him in beer and demand an encore. He pulls his head down on his neck, cocks it, puts his hands in front of him at the waist, thumbs up, and

does an impression in dialect of a Mafia hoodlum.
They laugh. Not just because he is a cop, but because they know he understands them, because he
can move with them.

Many of the people Barrett knows and moves
with in the precinct are disillusioned about the law.
They have lost faith in cops and in the courts. They
see men on the streets around them who have been
convicted of murders and assaults, and they cannot
take seriously what they consider the duty of cops
and courts—to separate criminals from society. And
so sometimes when they are in trouble they go to a
cop they believe in for help—not for an arrest, but
for real help.

An old Yugoslav man who owned a bar on the
West Side asked Barrett to come see him. For years
the bar had catered to a small but steady clientele of
neighborhood Yugoslavs. But lately West Side
toughs had started taking over the place. They sat in
it and used the pay phone for taking bets on horse
races and were turning it into a bookie joint. His old
customers had stopped coming in. When he complained, the toughs threatened him. He was terrified of losing his bar license because of the bookmaking. He told Barrett he knew that if the men
were arrested they would be out of jail in no time
and beat him up and ruin his bar.

"So one of my partners and I took the guys—and
they were real bad guys, old-time West Side hoodlums—over to a quiet little place by the docks and
we put the bull on them. We told them what the
score was, and we used a little muscle to get the
message home. And then the next day one of them

goes over to the old man's bar and asks him how much he paid to get me to put the bull on him, and that made me mad because no one buys my muscle. So I got him and we went back over to the docks, and now everything's taken care of and he calls me Mr. Barrett."

In some crimes an arrest does so little good that neither Barrett nor the victim even gives it a thought. He is walking up Sixth Avenue and a junkie girl comes toward him. Hurrying after her is a man in a butcher's apron. Barrett stops to watch. The man grabs the girl, reaches into her purse and pulls out two cellophane-wrapped packages of bacon she had stolen from his store to sell for drugs. He takes them back to his store, without a word, as casually as if he had just borrowed a match. Barrett does not make an arrest.

"The butcher doesn't want to be a complainant," he says. "There could have been a uniformed man standing right there and he wouldn't have called him. He gets beat all the time by shoplifters. He knows what kind of a bargain basement that court is down there. She'd be back on the street before his shop closed for the night. He figures he got his bacon back, so he's a winner."

Another day Barrett had been checking on a case in a Sixteenth Precinct hospital when he ran into another detective. The other man had two drug addicts with him he had arrested for possessing barbiturates, and he had brought them to the hospital to withdraw from their stupor. Late that same night Barrett was in Times Square and telephoned the squad to check in. As he spoke, the same two drug

addicts who had been in the hospital walked past
him. In less than ten hours they had been arrested,
taken to a hospital, treated, returned to the station
house, fingerprinted, booked, taken to court, released and found their way back to Times Square.
Barrett was talking on the phone to the detective
who had arrested them. He was still typing up the
arrest records.

Some time ago Barrett visited Nevada to pick up
a prisoner, and since then he has been telling
friends—maybe joking, maybe not—that what he
really wants in life is to be sheriff of some quiet
western county where people are not yet so callous
to crime. He can remember when he was a teen-
ager in Brooklyn, "and the cops always seemed to
be the best, the straightest kids around. But now a
man comes on the force just because it's a job, because instead of being a carpenter or a plumber or
something he figures he'll do twenty easy years, not
bothering, just stepping over the bodies, and then
relax with a pension. Or maybe he's a kid who's
intelligent but never really got street wise—who
thinks a criminal is someone with shifty eyes and a
hat brim pulled down over his face—and he wants
to spend hours thinking over every move, while
meantime the body's getting cold. And if you do get
a really savvy, bright, ambitious guy, after a period
of collaring everyone who's wrong, he's going to
find that he's living in court and the germs are the
ones on the street. So he'll start getting more selective, just grabbing the really bad guys and forgetting about the others. He finds out that with the
courts down there, the bad guys are getting more

and more right every day, and it's him—the cop—
who is wrong."

So Barrett thinks about America's less sophisticated areas "where people still know the difference
between the cops and the robbers." He is in a motel
talking to the security man when a report comes in
that a guest has been burglarized. Barrett and the
security man go to the room. Someone has entered
the room while the guest, a Wyoming businessman,
and his wife and little boy were out sightseeing. The
burglar took exactly $2.17.

Barrett and the house detective leave the room
and as they walk to the elevator the house man says
disgustedly, "What about that? A crummy $2.17
and he wants to make a big federal case out of it."

"No, no, you're wrong," Barrett says. "He's from
Wyoming and someone was in *his* room. That's
what's got him mad. And I subscribe to that completely. We're beginning to take this stuff for
granted. 'Someone in my room? Oh, okay.' Like it
was the standard thing. Well, it shouldn't be the
standard thing. I'm with the man from Wyoming.
He's one of the good guys—and there aren't too
many of us left."

TWO

THE COURTROOM HAS A SINK ON THE WALL, A bathroom mirror, peeling paint and in fact resembles less a courtroom than a public toilet. Trials here are secret—lawyers may attend, but not the public, and newsmen enter only by permission. The defendants are children. As young as seven, they come accused of everything from rape and murder to simple truancy and staying out too late. The secrecy, it is said, protects these children. But it also protects a system which—fully exposed, scrutinized and properly dealt with—could not, one hopes, survive an instant.

In a waiting hall outside the courtroom, long brown benches and the brown tile floor are littered with the shrapnel of exploded families—crying children, distressed and tired parents, small clusters of sorrow sitting for hours to await their minute with the judge. A boy of ten races between the benches, laughing, yelling, trying to play tag with a young Legal Aid attorney. The boy is dirty as only a street kid can be dirty. He is wearing torn sneakers, black pants, ragged green sweater and, on top of long tangled hair, a beret tipped slightly over one eye.

He has survived the streets and subways and clearly finds nothing here worthy of alarm.

A uniformed officer emerges from the courtroom and calls a name. "Torres!"

The boy stops playing and runs quickly up to the officer. Two Puerto Rican adults rise wearily from a bench and pass with the boy into the courtroom.

Half of all major crimes in the United States are committed by people under eighteen. The war against crime has become necessarily a war against children. This year 44,000 children will flood through New York City Family Court, where thirty-nine judges struggle to find homes and treatment that frequently do not exist. In this single squalid courtroom on Manhattan's East Side, thirty cases will be heard today. Some of the accused will be sent home, some to mental hospitals, some to state training schools, some back to the streets. Few if any will receive the care and treatment they require. The judge is a woman, sixty-nine-year-old Justine Wise Polier, who in thirty-six years on the bench has heard more children's cases than any other jurist in the nation. She knows better than anyone what this system does for and to children.

Tall, slender, gray-haired, Judge Polier sits at a desk across from a large paper calendar Scotch-taped to the wall. She is flanked by a court stenographer and a probation officer. She has open before her a thick folder of reports, studies and other documents concerning the Torres boy. His name is Manuel, and she remembers him from earlier appearances. Though he looks ten, he is in fact fourteen. He has three brothers and sisters in a children's

home, another in a state training school, another in
a mental hospital. A psychologist wrote that Manuel
is "good-looking, bright, pleasant, alert, perceptive,
cooperative, has many internal strengths and controls, is reaching out for support, starved for affec-
tion and recognition." A school report said "he
makes a great effort, is thought well of by his teachers, attendance is regular." A social worker found
the family's neighborhood "saturated with drug addicts . . . many robberies . . . living conditions
far below standard. . . . Difficult to see how the
boy can survive in this environment."

His parents brought him to court for running
away. Manuel said he runs away from home because
his father gets drunk, beats him up and attacks his
mother. He said his father once chased his mother
out of the apartment with a gun. Last time in court
the parents said Manuel had bitten their dog on the
ear and pushed its nose into a light socket. The
father said, in front of Manuel, that he wanted to get
rid of the boy. Judge Polier asked if it would not be
better to get rid of the dog. The father replied that
that was impossible because the dog protected
them from drug addicts.

After an earlier trip to court Manuel was taken
from his home and placed temporarily in a children's jail called Juvenile Center. A social worker
who saw him there reported that "he was scared
and afraid that the other children would do bad
things to him." Moved to a children's home, he ran
away, claiming later that a guidance counselor "always wanted to watch us get undressed."

When a psychologist asked Manuel what he

wanted to do in life, the boy answered, "Be a policeman so I can get rid of the drug pushers." Manuel said he had had a dream in which a man killed his mother and raped his sister. Manuel was a policeman and caught the man and took him to the gas chamber.

Today Manuel says he wants to leave his parents and live in a foster home. The parents tell the judge they want that too. But at the moment no foster homes are available. Neither is there a place at a children's home. Judge Polier studies the files, studies the boy, studies the parents—and tries to think of what to do. There is no solution. She may return the boy to his home, where he is not wanted and does not want to go, and from which he will certainly run away, or she can send him to Juvenile Center, to jail. Between the hazards of ghetto streets and jail, she picks jail.

Manuel is sitting between his mother and a Legal Aid lawyer, elbows on the table, back straight, biting his thumbnail, beret on the table in front of him. The judge explains that the court will try to find a place for him where he can live and go to school, but meanwhile he will have to go to Juvenile Center. When he hears "Juvenile Center," his face contorts in anger and he grabs his beret. A court officer leads him to the door. Manuel shouts back, "I'm going to run away."

The judge shakes her head and puts the case down for next week, with instructions to the probation department to seek placement.

Judge Polier came to the bench strong, but not tough, and has managed to remain so. When she

was twenty-one she took an $18-a-week job in a
New Jersey cotton mill to investigate labor conditions. She was discovered, fired and threatened
with arrest. She went to Yale Law School and in
1935 became the first woman in New York to hold a
judicial post higher than magistrate. Female judges
were so unheard of that when the first man to
emerge from her courtroom was asked how it had
gone, he replied, "Well, the judge wasn't there—
but his wife treated me just fine."

Despite her sex, age and judicial dignity, Judge
Polier is not afraid of ghetto language, often insists
on verbatim four-letter testimony, and coolly em-
ploys the words herself where necessary. With children she tries to be dignified, but gentle and reas-
suring, low-key, not too aloof. She does not wear
robes ("There is nothing about a black robe that
encourages a child to talk to me like a human being"). But thirty-six years of judicial authority have
given her a glance that does more than robes or a
gavel to command respect. Confronted by a teen-
age mugger in a deserted courthouse stairwell, she
gave him her stern, reproving look, and he backed
off. "I was just going to give you some money," he
said. "Do you need some money? I thought maybe
you needed some money for lunch." Then he ran.

A woman of enormous energy, she works twelve-
hour days, often skips lunch, sprints for taxis, goes
coatless in near freezing weather and emerges from
court after a forty-case day fresher and more lively
than youthful court officers. Asked how she could
have endured thirty-six years of witnessing day by
day the tragedies of children, she answers, "I tell

myself each time that I am trying to do the best that can be done for this one child in front of me now. And then, starting after court, I try to do what I can for the others like him." She works what she calls a "second day," beginning after court and extending often far into the night. She has created, chaired or served on scores of boards, committees and foundations working to broaden services to troubled children and their families. She is married to an attorney and has two sons (both attorneys) and a daughter.

"I have been very lucky," she says. "I have had love from my parents, love from my husband, love from my children. When you've always had love, it's easy to love. There's a tremendous amount of sanctimoniousness in us when we expect terribly troubled people to survive problems in their lives that we probably couldn't survive in our own. We expect a young woman who has never had an instant of security in her life, who never knew her parents, who was brought up in neglect and violence, totally without love—we expect this woman to be a sustaining, loving mother in a drug-ridden, crime-ridden ghetto, and wisely and successfully to raise her child to be a whole human being. We make irrational demands on people, demands utterly unrelated to the ones we make on ourselves. The people in power are so alienated from the powerless. It's very hard to live in two worlds and really feel both. The troubled people you see in court often get only token feeling, token giving, token caring. Over and over you see parents weary and plagued, children who have grown walls and masks to defend themselves."

The judge's day goes on and on, child after child, folder after folder. "The child comes in as a piece of paper," Judge Polier says, "and you look through the probation reports, psychiatric reports, psychological reports, the petition, searching for this child, to find some glimmer of who this child *is.*"

Often it makes very little difference who the child is. After all the studies have been made—and few could wish them more voluminous or thorough —it develops that the treatment recommended is unavailable. In folder after folder, Judge Polier encounters severely disturbed children and the desperate demands of doctors that intensive treatment begin immediately. Rarely if ever is such treatment provided. Not infrequently the frantic prediction of a psychiatrist that the alternative to immediate, intensive treatment is murder or suicide ends up bloodily fulfilled.

Like most American cities, New York pays hugely —up to $24,000 a year—for the care of a child in a private institution. But these homes and hospitals insist on admitting only those children whom they can best serve. Judge Polier claims that these restrictive admission policies are maintained to protect the institutions' track records. "They want the children it's easy to help, the ones they know they can help. And what happens to the others?"

The others include children who are disruptive and difficult to treat—those with histories of assault, suicide attempts, drug use, absconding, those with low IQs and those who simply happen not to fall

within the institutions' racial or religious prefer-
ences. In New York City, it happens that a black
Protestant with an IQ below 70 *or* a history of assault, suicide attempts, drug use or absconding is
not merely denied treatment. He is denied admission even to a state training school (which demands
IQs over 69) and ends up in a children's detention
center, endlessly awaiting placement in a state
"school" for the retarded.

Even state mental hospitals—their budgets cut,
staff reduced—often turn away psychotic children,
certified schizophrenics with histories of attempted
homicide or suicide. One such child is Sandra Rogers, a fifteen-year-old black girl with a schizophrenic mother. Investigators sent to her home reported "no beds . . . mattresses on floor . . .
broken refrigerator . . . no hot water . . . garbage strewn about." The mother, who had five illegitimate children by three different men, was
chronically alcoholic. She attacked Sandra with a
knife, saying she hated the girl because she reminded her of Sandra's father. Sandra ran away
from home, and was later hospitalized for an overdose of drugs. She told a psychiatrist she had halluci-
nations, saw spiritual figures surrounded by clouds
and often heard voices calling her name.

"Sometimes they are mean to me," she said.
"Sometimes they tell me to do things I don't want to
do." She said that sometimes she walks along the
street in a daze and heads into the oncoming traffic.
"She knows she is doing this but can't stop herself,"
the doctor reported.

A psychiatrist who examined her after the drug

overdose diagnosed her as schizophrenic. "My recommendation," he wrote, "is urgently for pro-
longed hospitalization because Sandra is truly in
danger of killing herself if she is not contained. It is
patently absurd to leave this child in an open setting
where she is free to destroy herself."

She was sent to Bellevue Hospital for a one-
month study. The diagnosis was "schizophrenia,
childhood type, chronic." A psychiatrist reported
that "since she has a tendency to follow what the
voices tell her to do—such as taking an overdose of
pills, or walking in front of a car—she could be a
danger to herself or others." Another Bellevue doctor wrote, "It was strongly felt that this young girl
was in need of long-term psychiatric hospitalization
in a state institution."

So she was dispatched to a state children's psychiatric hospital. But after an examination of only one
hour, she was rejected and returned to Bellevue.
Bellevue in turn packed her back to the court, with
this apology: "Because Sandra's evaluation at [the
state hospital]revealed no severe pathology, the patient was returned to Bellevue. We have exhausted
every other possible avenue of approach in seeking
placement for Sandra, to no avail, and have no other
recourse than to return her to court for final disposi-
tion. Our facilities do not permit our keeping her
here any longer."

The night before Sandra will appear in court,
Judge Polier and her husband are having dinner in
an Italian restaurant. "The way these children are
knocked around like pawns, like inanimate objects,
is absolutely indecent," she says. "That child is com-

ing into court tomorrow and she's going to stand there and I have the choice of returning her to the community where she'll kill herself, or remanding her to Juvenile Center. The state hospital looked at her for *one hour,* ignored a one-month Bellevue study and just turned her away."

Her husband tries to calm her. "You didn't turn her away, they did," he says.

"But she comes back to court. The child is on *my* doorstep. What do I do with this psychotic, suicidal child?"

"You can't take all the problems on your shoulders."

"But I'm the one who has to remand her."

"That's not your problem. You aren't doing it, they are. Don't take all these problems on yourself. What are you trying to do, save the universe?"

"Yes."

The next day Judge Polier faces Sandra Rogers in court—and orders her returned temporarily to Bellevue while attempts are made to force her admission to a state hospital.

Not everyone who comes to Judge Polier's court is poor. Late one morning a young man and woman, both well dressed, enter silently with their lawyers. The lawyers are wearing identical gray suits, white shirts, dark ties, and when they sit down before the judge and spread their notes, they produce identical gold pens. The dispute is over visiting rights to the divorced couple's young son. One lawyer outlines a complex schedule both sides have agreed upon. The father may take the child from the home at certain hours on certain days. He may also take him on other specified days, but only to sporting events. Phone calls may be made on certain days at certain times. In the event of rain on the second Tuesday of May at 2 P.M. . . . In the event of illness on a Monday, a phone call may be made between 6 P.M. and 9 P.M. unless . . .

It goes on and on, the parents sitting passive and tight-lipped in mutual hatred, the lawyers coldly gold-penciling entries in their files.

Finally the judge stops it. "Gentlemen, this is a *child*. What you are reciting sounds like a railroad timetable. *Please.*"

The lawyers begin a detailed analysis of the father's income. A quarrel erupts over the addition of a set of figures. It's too much for Judge Polier. "I am sorry," she says impatiently. "I will not permit you to take the court's time to add up numbers. I have children waiting, emergency cases. Add the figures outside and I will call the case later."

She takes a five-minute recess and walks into the chaos of the waiting hall. A woman is stretched out on the floor in an epileptic fit. Someone has put a white vinyl handbag under her head, and court officers are holding her legs down and trying to keep her from biting her tongue. Children, including her young son, stand watching. Adults fearful of losing their places on the benches ignore the commotion and stick with their newspapers.

Judge Polier steps into a small, closet-sized office with desk, chair and telephone. A young Legal Aid lawyer follows her in. "She's been here with her son since nine-thirty," he says. "She's epileptic and she just—"

Polier turns on him. "Well, can't they put the *child* someplace where he doesn't have to watch?"

The lawyer shrugs. "He knows his mother's epileptic and she's had attacks before, so it isn't anything new to him."

Judge Polier sits down, shaking her head. Joan Strumer, a probation officer, comes in. "Your honor, can you sign a warrant? Helen says she's going to be killed, and—" Helen is another probation officer. This morning Richard Holland, a fifteen-year-old escapee from a Bellevue psychiatric ward, called her and said he had a gun and was going to kill her.

When Richard was eleven, he was caught mugging another boy in a Harlem subway station. A psychiatrist found no evidence of neurosis or psychosis, but nevertheless suggested therapy. None was given. Now, after many more robberies, many violent escapes—and no treatment—the diagnosis is paranoid schizophrenia. Richard is regarded as homicidal and extremely dangerous.

"Helen is scared to death," Joan Strumer says. "I called the youth squad and they said they'd stake out his house if they can get warrants."

"Talk to the intake judge," Polier says.

Judge Polier goes back to court and hears more cases. A ten-year-old heroin addict is ordered into a treatment program. He is furious. "Why do I have to go in a program? I can stop by myself when I want to."

A sixteen-year-old addict, who has given birth to an addicted child, refuses to attend a drug program.

Her mother, who has given up on her and says so, is beside her.

"I know you are going to send me to Juvenile Center anyway," the girl shouts at the judge, "so it don't make no difference what I say. My mother don't want me and I don't want her."

The judge mentions a drug program.

"I don't want no program. I ain't got no habit."

The judge orders her sent to Juvenile Center while reports are prepared.

"I'll kill myself!" she screams. "And I ain't gonna talk to no psychiatrist neither. Next time I'm here I'll be in a coffin."

Two teen-age boys have broken into a blind woman's house, beaten her, robbed her and taken even her Braille wristwatch. The judge sets a trial date.

It is lunchtime.

Every day Judge Polier sees neglected infants, homicidal teenagers and all the stages of maturing violence between. Often she must attend helplessly at the early opening of wounds in which, she knows, hatred, madness and murder may take seed and fester. Not in the chaos of the squalid courtroom, but in the silent, subdued solemnity of her private chambers she talks to the parents, and takes the children in her arms. She meets the social workers, probation officers, police, doctors, lawyers, other judges—and grieves at the brutality of a system that studies, considers, suggests, reports, but rarely heals. She has in her chambers a six-year-old girl, raised in love, who has never done anything more disturbing or criminal than temporarily refusing to eat her spinach. But now destruction threatens, and the law is on its side.

When Martha Jackson was thirteen, she was raped by her brother. She gave birth to a daughter, surrendered her to a placement agency and was herself sent to a state training school. Now, five years later, Martha Jackson wants the girl back. Martha Jackson is mentally ill, unemployed, an alcoholic and lives on welfare in a small, shabbily furnished ghetto apartment with a six-month-old illegitimate son. Three days after birth, her daughter was placed with carefully selected, middle-class foster parents, and now at the age of six still lives with them and two older children. They want to adopt her. She wants to be adopted by them. But the law may prevent this.

The case is before Judge Polier, who must decide not only if it is in the girl's best interests to stay with her foster parents, and to be adopted by them, but if the natural mother is herself unfit to care for the child. The law is very strong in this respect. The mother's alcoholism, instability and unemployment, the condition of her home and neighborhood —none of these is necessarily proof of unfitness. Nor are the findings and recommendations of doctors, social workers and probation officers. A psychiatrist said the mother "appeared incapable of providing adequate child care because of her own confusion, poor judgment and lack of energy, motivation and resources." A probation officer said the foster parents "appear to be well adjusted, stable, religious persons with noble ideals. Their sincere efforts appear to reflect in the well-adjusted appearance of

the children. Their hopes are to raise the children
to be useful citizens. These plans include a college
education." The report concluded, "Returning the
child to her natural mother may indeed disturb,
shock and profoundly disrupt her positive orientation to life."

Judge Polier is concerned that a ruling to permit
adoption of the girl over the protests of her natural
mother will be reversed in an appellate court. It has
happened before. She has met the natural mother,
and now wants to make a personal assessment of the
girl and her foster parents. She asks the adoption
agency to have them visit her in her chambers at
9:30 in the morning.

They arrive early. Judge Polier leaves the girl in a
waiting room and takes the parents inside. She sits
behind a large desk, and they settle nervously into
chairs across from her. They are dressed as if for
church.

"I think you've done a wonderful job giving this
girl a start," the judge says warmly. "I can realize
from your faces how deeply you feel about the
child. But in a guardianship proceeding like this the
law is very strict. The question is whether or not the
mother is unfit to raise her. I hope someday we have
a better law, but this is the one we have now. I know
it means so much to you, because you are her parents in truth."

Both parents nod.

"How long have you had Susan?" the judge asks,
knowing the answer but trying to draw the parents
out.

"Since she was five days old," the mother says,

sitting up so straight her back does not touch the chair.

"What have you told her about her mother?"

"We've told her that when she was born her mother had some problems and she couldn't keep her, but that we are her foster parents and we want to adopt her if we can."

"What does she call you?"

"Mommy."

"And Daddy," the father adds quickly.

The judge talks with them a few more minutes and then asks them to wait outside while she sees the girl.

The girl comes in shyly, wearing a dark skirt and white blouse. She stands in front of the judge's desk, quiet but not frightened. The judge smiles at her. "I've just been talking to your parents. They're lovely people."

The girl smiles.

"I know you think so, too."

"Yes, Ma'am."

She asks her about her school, how she likes her teachers, what she does after school, then she lowers her voice a tone, becomes just slightly more serious and says, "Susan, I'd like to ask you something that's hard, but I'd like you to be very honest with me. I know you haven't seen much of your mother. When you do see her, do you have a good time?"

"Yes." She is hesitant.

"What do you do?"

"Go to the movies. And to the park."

"Would you like to go live with her?"

"I don't think I'd like to stay with her."

"Come here, dear," the judge says, and the girl walks around the desk to the judge's chair, moving up closely against her shoulder.

"When you talk to your mother, what do you talk about?"

"I say I want to stay with my other mother."

"What does she say?"

"Nothing."

"When you're with her, do you get any fun or happiness from her?"

"Not much."

"You like your parents?"

"Yes."

"If you stayed with your parents, would you like to keep seeing your mother?"

"No."

"You'd like to make it so they're your home?" The judge nods in the direction of the waiting room.

"Yes." Susan raises her hand and rests it on the arm of the judge's chair. The judge touches the lapel of the girl's blouse and says, "I don't want you to worry about this, because we're going to work it out." The girl smiles and the judge takes her face in her hands. "I'm delighted that you're doing so well and that you have parents who love you so much."

The girl nods. The judge walks out with her and sees them all to the elevator. Back in her chambers, she turns to a visitor who has observed the interview. Her large eyes fire a look of anger and distress. "It's scary, isn't it? That child may have to go back to her natural mother." She lights a cigarette and walks to the window. "Our courts still deal with

these problems as though the rights of the mother
are more important than what's best for the child.
They seem too often to assume that *every* woman
who bears a child is capable of giving that child love.
Unfortunately, that's just not true. I must remove
this little girl from this preadoptive home, the only
home she has ever known, unless I find that the
mother is unfit. Here are these people bringing out
everything in this child, and I'm asked to put her
back with a mother who is disturbed, alcoholic, who
has been in and out of institutions, who—" She
stops, looks down to the street and draws on the
cigarette. "And none of these things, by itself,
necessarily makes her unfit. The courts have so
held."

"What does?" she is asked.

"That's a good question. Every case is different."

Judge Polier eventually ruled in favor of the foster parents. The natural mother is appealing.

"Do you want him placed in an institution and
put out of your home?" Judge Polier is in court
questioning a middle-aged man dressed in leather
jacket, cap and a pencil behind his ear.

"I'll just have to let him go back where I got him,"
says the man, stern and unshakable. He is talking
about his six-year-old grandson. The boy's mother is
an alcoholic. Several months ago her neighbors
heard screams, went in the apartment and found
her hitting the boy's head on the floor and trying to
choke him. He was naked except for a cotton shirt,
and was spitting blood. The mother then took him

out to the street and told him to leave and not to
come back.

The boy was taken from the mother, who has
since disappeared, and placed with an agency who
located his grandfather and step-grandmother, described in a probation report as "warm, open people, with genuine interest in the boy." They agreed
to care for the boy "until grown, if need be."

It was not long, however, before the grandparents called the court to complain that the boy was
hard to control and had broken one of their children's bicycles. They wanted him to behave, and
they wanted to be paid for keeping him.

Now, while the boy sits alone outside in the waiting hall, Judge Polier asks the grandfather what he
thinks about keeping the boy.

He is annoyed. He says he works nights, seven
nights a week, and should be home sleeping. "My
wife is the one who takes care of the children. When
I get home I go to bed and the door is closed. When
I get up it's eleven o'clock and I'm gone. This boy, if
he comes in and bothers me, out he go. All my
responsibility—I just make sure my wife gets
money for the family."

The judge says she wants to talk to the child
alone. She goes out to the small office by the waiting
hall and someone brings the boy in. She smiles at
him and says hello and asks him to come around
behind the desk and stand next to her. She puts an
arm gently around his shoulders. A probation report described him as "reserved and serious as if too
mature for his age, but it is not difficult to make him

smile; a pleasant personality." He moves in against the judge's arm and smiles shyly.

"I want to ask you something," the judge says. "And I want you just to tell me what you think." She asks if he is happy with his grandparents. He smiles and nods. "Are they nice to you?" He nods. "Is there anyone else you would like to see?" He shakes his head. "Just them?" He nods.

She returns to court. She explains to the grandfather that because he is related to the boy he cannot receive regular foster-care payments. He can, however, receive a lesser amount from welfare. Will that be enough?"

"No. Fifteen or twenty dollars is not enough."

"Well," says the judge, "since he loves you and wants to be with you and has no one else, are you willing to keep him?"

"No."

The man is solid-faced and adamant. "He'll just have to go—go back where we got him."

"It's going to be very hard on him. You know that?"

He shrugs. "It'll just have to be that way."

"Well, are you willing to take him just until we can try to refer him for adoption?"

He bends. "Okay. I'll take him till you get yourself straight."

Judge Polier has lunch with a friend who has spent the morning in her court. "At least he was honest," she says of the grandfather. "He certainly had no pretensions of fatherhood." She thinks a moment. "When I put my arm around the boy, I could feel him react. He wants to be loved." The boy is black, Protestant and already six years old. "He'll be difficult for adoption," she says.

The friend asks if she has seen an improvement over the years in the way troubled children are treated.

"It's getting worse," she says. "The delinquents and predelinquents today appear more disturbed than they used to be. I think it's because of the breakdown in the old basic controls, the conventional respect for one's parents, teacher, minister. There's so little help from any caring adult for these children. They don't get it in the schools, in the church or at home. Problems aren't spotted until something happens, until there's an assault or a theft or an overdose. And that's awfully late."

She stops talking and looks down into her plate. Her friend asks if it all makes her angry. She looks up. "I don't think angry is the word for me. It's not my way of functioning. I get *very* determined, and 'How do I break through this. . . .' But I'll tell you when I really do get angry. When I sense in someone, 'Well, it's part of the system. What are you breaking your neck for?' I get angry when I see a greater concern for the system than for what it's supposed to be doing. The system fails to reach out and serve the people it was created to serve. And it makes you terribly distressed and angry when you see this in terms of a child—a child like that boy today whose grandfather doesn't want him and who will be so difficult for adoption. A child—a human being—reaches out for love. And gets hit. And he reaches out again, and gets hit again. And he keeps reaching out, and every time he's denied. And then finally, defensively, he stops reaching. And in no longer looking for love, he loses the ability to love, and the ability to feel. The capacity to feel for another person is cut off, and he can destroy other people without reaction. And then you get rapes and robberies and murder. Take this little boy— he's tried to reach out to be loved. He's made a desperate effort. And he's been turned off. How long can you expect a child to keep reaching?"

THREE

TWO MICE RUN UP THE CELL'S BARS TO A SMALL table welded to the wall. They circle briefly around a roll of toilet paper, lick at the hardened remains of coffee spilled from a prisoner's cup, then scamper back down and drink from a puddle covering the black concrete floor.

The cell is number six on the Lower-A section of the eighth floor of the Tombs—Manhattan's jail. These are very special cells. For if one were to look at crime and violence in America, and seek the centroid, the tiny ultimate point through which one could thrust a pin and say "Nowhere worse than here," he would very likely be directed first to New York, then to Harlem, then to the Tombs, and finally here, to Section 8-Lower-A. There are only twelve cells on this tier, but nowhere else in the nation could one find a dozen men more vicious, violent or filled with rage. Most of these prisoners are insane, have been declared so by psychiatrists, have been to mental hospitals. But the hospitals are full, and the men have come back to 8-Lower-A.

The prisoners here are under a twenty-four-hour-a-day watch. Their records read: "Lock in. Feed in.

Do Not Double." They are alone, they never go out, and they are looked in on once every half hour. But a strip of sheet—folded, wetted, knotted into a noose—can kill a man in less than thirty minutes.

It is 11 P.M. Light overflowing from the cells on Lower-A gets as far as steel tables and benches bolted to the floor of the "flat," a high open area in front of the cells that serves as a day room for prisoners from neighboring sections. Above the tables to the steel ceiling, beyond them to the bars and tile walls, the light dissolves quickly into gloom. The floor is dark. But it is not quiet.

"Hey! You got a fire here! The whole A side! You got a fire, man! You got a fuckin' *fire!*" The prisoner's voice dies out, and the smell of smoke quickly fills the cells.

A guard hurries up, keys jangling. A fire extinguisher squirts. The prisoner yells, "Hey, man, crack the gate!" More squirting. Bits of ash and smoke float through the section. The guard walks back.

On the left of the cell with the fire, a prisoner pounds on his table, using it for a bongo drum. The noise and vibrations shake the section. Someone yells, "Knock it off!"

"Motherfucker!" the man yells back, and pounds louder and faster.

A black guard walks past the cells. A prisoner calls to him, asks him to carry a pack of cigarettes to another prisoner in the section. He does.

Prisoners are singing in another section, far off in the darkness. It ends and the prisoners there whistle and applaud.

A prisoner on the other side of the bongo man is pacing in his cell. His body casts an enormous throbbing shadow on the wall outside the bars.

The black guard walks by again. A prisoner yells, "Hey! What's goin' on, house nigger!" The guard keeps walking.

The bongo player stops pounding. Now he's practicing whistles—loud, piercing, fingers-in-the-mouth whistles that echo like bird cries.

A prisoner yells, "Hey, Jackson!"

A voice: "Yeah?"

"You were right about the help. I'm gonna get him. Then I'll have another homicide on me."

"Well, they're cheaper by the dozen. I been thinkin' about the Man, myself."

The Man includes all the guards, three of whom at this moment are in semidarkness on "the bridge," a central area connecting the floor's four sections. The only light on the bridge comes from a bulb over the guard's desk, and from the twelve cell lights in Lower-A. Tonight the floor's 122 cells hold 192 prisoners—twenty-seven of them charged with homicide, thirty with assault, most of the rest with armed robbery and other crimes of violence. Keys connecting the bridge with the Tombs' elevators have been removed to the main floor. Guards and prisoners are locked up together. Any riot on the floor will be contained.

It's midnight now, and the guards move ghostlike through the darkness, quietly mopping up water that has flooded from the cell of the bongo player. The address blank on his floor card is marked "No Home." He is serving thirty days for petty larceny, but his real crime is insanity. He has overflowed his toilet into a lake created by arranging folded blankets on the cell floor. When the lake is filled to his satisfaction, he removes the blankets, swabs the water out of the cell and starts over. The water has flooded most of the section and run out onto the bridge.

A phone rings, and the sound echoes through the quiet darkness of the tiers. Somewhere a man cries for help. Two guards hurry to his cell.

At 5 A.M. the guards turn on the lights and a radio. The prisoners awaken to the morning news, blasting from speakers in the four sections, ricocheting off steel cells, cement floors, tile walls. *"A nineteen-year-old Negro has been shot by police in Chattanooga. . . . Two men arrested in the lobby of the Daily News Building have been held in $100,000 bail in connection with the murder of two police officers in Harlem Friday. Police said both men were carrying loaded guns. . . ."*

The two accused cop killers are here, in separate cells just a few yards from the bongo player.

The radio screams rock music from WLIB. It goes off for a second while a guard reads the names of men going to court. Prisoners are getting up, screaming and yelling. A squat, very fat black prisoner in a dirty T-shirt walks by handing out spoons. In a minute he's back with paper plates and bowls. Each man gets four slices of bread, jelly, hot cereal, a hard-boiled egg and a dark liquid meant to be coffee.

On the bridge, prisoners are dragging garbage cans.

The fat man in the T-shirt comes by again with a swab. The bongo man swears at him, screaming, wailing as if tortured. "You motherfucker! Pussy!" T-shirt takes as much as he can, then picks up his bucket, gives it a swing and half-empties it into the bongo man's cell. Desperate screams. "Off*icer!* . . . Off*icer!* . . . Off*icer!* . . ." T-shirt rears back with the bucket and gives him what's left right in the face. "Offic—" His cries break off with a gurgle.

A guard comes. "He threw water on me, Officer! For no reason, for *nothin'*. No reason at all. I'm gonna tell the captain about this!"

The guard leaves. The bongo man yells and swears at T-shirt. "Pussy! Motherfucker!"

The music goes off. Over the speakers a whistle blows. "On the count! On the count! Stand for the count!"

Bongo man is still screaming, shaking the bars. T-shirt walks by with empty trays. "Open my gate! I'm gonna fight your ass, your ass, your ass . . ." The words fade lower and lower, until finally they are inaudible beneath the radio and the yelling and the banging of steel gates and crashing of garbage cans.

Smoke pours from the bongo man's cell. A guard rushes by with the fire extinguisher, squirts it into the cell. T-shirt fills two buckets with water, climbs up on a table like a pitcher on the mound and fires a deluge into the cell. The bongo player sounds as if he's drowning. T-shirt goes up on a catwalk to open a window near the ceiling and let the smoke out. Water swirls around the bongo man's cell. Bits of ash float along with the current.

From the PA system: "On the lockout! On the lockout!"

All over the floor, mechanical locking devices bang and clang and cell doors slide open. Hundreds of prisoners explode onto the flats, surround the tables, stomp and swear and shout. The noise expands and swells until it will burst the steel and tile walls.

Outside bongo man's cell, prisoners from other sections wander idly. The radio goes off and a TV set comes on full volume.

The men mingling on the flat are, for the most part, killers. Some have impressive credentials known nation-wide. The two accused cop slayers are in the crowd. So is James Sullivan, the first man in history to escape from Attica State Prison. By way of celebration, he walked into a bar, said, "This is a stickup" and blew the head off a customer to prove he wasn't kidding. Now he's here.

Lunch. Chili beans, gravy, rice, shredded cabbage, applesauce, tea. Someone has scratched a heart on the table in the bongo man's cell.

A young guard tiptoes through the water outside the cell and glances in. "Haven't you had enough water?" The bongo man yells an obscenity.

A maintenance man arrives, looks into the cell, then disappears and shuts off the water. The guard walks by again. "No more play toy now," he says. The bongo man swears.

T-shirt collects the lunch leftovers. He throws spoons and bowls into a garbage can, and food scraps into a pillow case. He reaches down with a bowl, scoops up some water and tosses it in at the bongo player. Then he picks up another prisoner's cup, notices tea in the bottom and tosses that in too.

Two prisoners are yelling, arguing about which one's cell last had a murder or suicide.

A guard's voice over the PA system: "Richard Williams, where do you lock?"

Have they lost someone?

And then: "José Martinez. Upper-B-6. Pack up. Bail."

A prisoner screams: "Give me my motherfuckin' money back! Give me my motherfuckin' wallet! Give me my motherfuckin' *gun!*"

Then another voice: "God help us all!"

On the bridge, a guard fills in his count slip: five razors, ten keys, 240 spoons, 196 men. He looks up at the other two officers and smiles. His shift is over. He is going home. "Well, gentlemen," he says, "today no one died."

FOUR

WHEN MANHATTAN WAS WOODS AND MEADOW-
land, the prison was a pond. Early Dutch settlers
called it Kalchhook, Shell Point, after oyster shells
heaped on its shores by Indians from a nearby village. For more than a century New Yorkers skated
on the pond in winter and boated there in summer,
picnicking on the grassy, tree-shaded hills around it.
In 1789 someone suggested they make a park by
the pond. Someone else said it was too far north.
Who would come? By 1838 the Indians were gone,
their village was the intersection of Broadway and
Canal Street, and the pond had been drained and
filled with dirt. Near its center a dark, squat bully of
a building stood slowly oozing down into the mud,
as if determined by its weight to keep the pond
from pushing back to the surface.

The building was the Tombs, Manhattan's jail, so
called because it was designed to resemble an en-
graving of an Egyptian tomb on the cover of a book
published by a Hoboken, New Jersey, man who had
been to Egypt. The first prisoners were a prostitute
named Catherine Hagerman and two men caught
leering at females.

After fifty years New York tore down the jail and built a larger one, which continued to settle slowly into the muddy remains of the old pond. New Yorkers still called it the Tombs, but they were happier with the new building because its yard became the scene of many public hangings. The executioner was "Little Joe" Atkinson, a friendly carpenter from Brooklyn who came to build the gallows and stayed on to use it. In July 1860 he hanged Albert Hicks, a pirate. It was a big day for Little Joe, and for many other New Yorkers, too. Hicks, a federal prisoner, had to be executed on federal property, which meant a boat trip to Bedloe Island (now the site of the Statue of Liberty). It was a warm summer and the entire city prepared for the event. People with boats laid in food and drink and invited friends. Huge barges with bright-colored awnings sold cold beer and soda pop. Little Joe, Pirate Hicks, the sheriff, forty deputies and fifteen hundred invited guests cruised out into the harbor in the steamer *Red Jacket*. So fine was the day, so festive the mood, that someone suggested a short side trip upriver to take a look at the steamship *Great Eastern*. They asked the pirate if he minded. Hicks, unopposed to delays of any duration, made no complaint.

Two hours later, back downriver, Little Joe hanged Pirate Hicks. Ten thousand New Yorkers watched.

In those days the presumption of innocence was taken seriously. For men awaiting trial, the Tombs was a hotel—you got what you could pay for. You had to pay to get a blanket or a bed. Five cents to a tier captain bought a piece of meat. Much more to the right politician could get you—as it did some prisoners—a carpeted cell, damask curtains, antique furniture, walnut toilet stand, whiskey, oysters, quail, champagne, Havana cigars, fresh flowers, women, poker games (with the warden sitting in when invited) and nights out at the theater accompanied by two guards who doubled as servants.

That jail was torn down, too, and when the third and present Tombs opened in 1941, enormous cement-filled caissons thrusting 140 feet down through mud and muck fastened the building solidly to bedrock.

So much for the pond.

And so much, some say, for the city of New York. Today the pond is gone, the woods and meadowland are a plate-glass jungle, and men who work in New York's jails worry more about their safety than about grafting an extra buck. The jails today, like the city itself, are in a constant state of incipient riot. Rage and violence within stone and steel walls bubble just below the level of critical mass, held there desperately by guards and administrators who know that someday soon the level may rise and the riot explode—as it has before—into the streets and newspapers. "I have a husband in this jail called overcrowding," said Tombs Acting Warden Albert Glick. "And his wife is idleness, and when they get together and copulate their children are called sodomy, assault, murder, suicide and riot. Is there going to be another riot? Of *course* there's going to be another riot."

Tension in the Tombs is felt, and feared, most

acutely by the guards, who know that when the riot
comes, they will be the hostages. Or if not hostages,
then—perhaps as bad—they will be the men with
tear gas, helmets and riot sticks who step off elevators onto a floor of 240 men driven to the edge of
madness by a fury fermenting for months and years.
In the last Tombs riots, prisoners took twenty-six
hostages and, armed with no more than bare hands
and rage, ripped up iron table legs bolted to the
floor, smashed through steel locking devices, tore
holes in foot-thick walls of brick and concrete.

As with many other combatants in the crumbling
arena of criminal justice, jail guards feel they are
made to wage a poorly funded war that they, and
society, can't possibly win. And they are reluctant
gladiators in the first place. They are not, despite
their public image, head-beating sadists spoiling for
a brawl. Most are family men who became jail
guards for the security of civil service. Their greatest ambition is to survive to retirement.

"If you're a prison guard," says Captain Dominick
Ghezzi, who has been one for sixteen years, "the
public thinks you're a goon. You're a guy who's not
too bright, and you like to hit people over the head.
Well, no one wants a riot, no one wants violence, no
one wants to get hurt. A lot of people don't understand that the correction officers at the Tombs, the
officers at probably just about every jail in the country, are men trying to do their jobs like everyone
else. I'm not a violent guy. I really wish that this job
could always just be 'please' and 'thank you.' It'd be
a beautiful eight hours."

Ghezzi has spent more time in the Tombs than

most of the prisoners. For years he has stared at the same bars, sweated in the same heat, eaten the same food, smelled the same smells, shouted above the same noise. The Tombs is for transients, for men serving short sentences or awaiting trial (some wait up to two years), and it is to a state penitentiary as a butt-littered bus station is to a luxury hotel. There are no neat rows of uniformed prisoners who live in single cells with radios, bookcases and pet goldfish; who play baseball in the yard, watch evening movies, go to school and to jobs in the machine shop. Most Tombs prisoners live dirty and ragged two in a cell, released three times a day into cramped lockout cages. Before the riots, many cells held three men, the weakest sleeping on the floor crawled over by mice. Many of the men live in their shorts, or wrapped in sheets or blankets, saving for court the clothes they had on when arrested. Many are mad—flooding cells, setting fire to mattresses, crying out to tormentors no one else can see. Suicide attempts are frequent. Riots, tension and overcrowding have all but eliminated recreation. Each day progresses monotonously with the blowing of whistles and ringing of bells: lock out, eat, lock in . . . lock out, eat, lock in . . . lock out, eat, lock in. Even guards held hostage in riots support the demands of prisoners.

Dom Ghezzi knows that rehabilitation in a jail like the Tombs is impossible. Guards with an eager desire to help the prisoners—and there are many—discover quickly that the most help they are able to render a prisoner is to try to keep him in control, to prevent assaults and suicides. When every minor luxury of life is removed, and existence is whittled to the most minute essentials, those essentials acquire enormous proportions. Men will kill themselves, their cellmate or a guard in a fury ignited by a piece of butter, a blanket, a bar of soap. "If an inmate has a problem," says Ghezzi, "if he wants to make a phone call, or see a doctor, or get a free stamp, I can help him out. And then I feel I've eliminated a problem. But I can't really help him. Because what he really wants is out, and I can't give him that."

Ghezzi is a slightly overweight Italian with a round face and a slow, engaging smile that helps convince prisoners he would really like to help. The smile is a weapon in the Tombs, and Ghezzi uses it. As a captain, he is a troubleshooter, a last resort for harried guards without the time, nerve or knowhow to cope with special crises. His job is to solve with a smile, with a willing ear, with words firm or gentle the problems that, untended, would soon need settling with tear gas and riot sticks. Such problems abound in the Tombs, and every day produces scores of confrontations.

Ghezzi has just arrived on duty when a phone call reports that a prisoner named Rizzo refuses to come out of his cell. Construction work is beginning on Rizzo's floor, and the prisoners have all been moved. All but Rizzo. He has been a problem since he came into the Tombs four months ago. In the receiving room, he refused to undress for a shower and medical examination, and swore at the guards. "At least he was democratic," said one. "The black guards were nigger motherfuckers, the Italians were guinea motherfuckers and the Irish were Irish motherfuckers. He didn't leave out anyone."

Ghezzi has seen Rizzo several times, and each time has talked amiably with him and handed over a cigarette. "Rizzo is a guy I'm trying to develop," Ghezzi says. "Some inmates, you do little things for them, give them a cigarette, and you never know. If there's a riot in his section, he's going to be in the middle of it. Some guys are the type who'd incite a riot, and then turn right around and give you all the names."

Riding up in the elevator to Rizzo's floor, Ghezzi smiles slowly, a thin reserved smile that barely curves his lips, and says, "Now we'll see how much good the cigarettes did."

A guard unlocks the gate onto the bridge, a central area joining the floor's four tiers, and says, "He's not coming out, Captain. He's a nut. He got all packed up to leave, and then he got up on the bunk and he says he's not coming out."

Ghezzi walks back to Rizzo's cell. The floor is empty and silent. Of the 120 cells, only this one is occupied. Rizzo is in his court clothes, lying on the top bunk with his hands clasped behind his neck. He smiles at Ghezzi, and Ghezzi smiles back. "Look, Rizzo," he says, "you're gonna make me look bad. You can't stay here. They're doing construction work here."

Rizzo sits up, and surrenders. "Okay, Captain. But it's just for you. It's still all bullshit. I'll move for you, but it don't change nothin'. It's still all crap." He jumps down from the bunk and starts gathering his things. The walls are covered with pinup pictures, stuck there with globs of toothpaste.

"Take any of your pictures if you want them," Ghezzi says.

"I'll just take this one," Rizzo says. "I'll leave the rest for some degenerate bastard to steal."

At the elevator Ghezzi looks at Rizzo's full name, typed on the prisoner's floor card, a record that moves with him to his new location.

"What's this 'Carl'?" he says.

"It's not Carl," Rizzo says quietly. "It's really Carlo."

"Yeah," says Ghezzi smiling. "I got stuck with Dominick. That's almost as bad as Salvatore." He hands Rizzo a cigarette.

It's a busy morning, and wherever Ghezzi goes, emergencies track him down by phone. In a special fourth-floor section reserved for effeminate homosexuals, a man is unconscious on the floor of his cell. Ghezzi has him carried down to the doctor. A prisoner on seven insists that his neighbor be moved because "he keeps jumping into the walls all night and I can't sleep." Ghezzi says he'll see what he can do. A man on five says he's going to set his cell on fire "and make a lot of trouble" unless he gets a single cell. Ghezzi calms him ("Everyone wants a private room, but we don't have them") and the man agrees to behave until a psychiatrist can see him tomorrow. On four a man throws up his lunch tray and nearly sets off a riot by yelling that he found a rat tail in his potatoes. The cook is called, says it's not a rat tail but a growth from the eye of a potato. The prisoner agrees that it could be a potato growth.

Then it's the wall jumper again. He's tearing his cell apart. Ghezzi calls the receiving room, where officers processing new prisoners can be borrowed for emergencies. "I'm coming by," he says. "Pass me through a set of cuffs and give me two officers."

When he gets to the elevator, the men are waiting with helmets and sticks.

"He's been tearing up his mattress," a floor guard tells Ghezzi. "And he climbs up on the top bunk and I have to keep chasing him off because I'm afraid he'll take a swan dive into the floor."

"Wait here," Ghezzi tells the helmeted officers. "I'll just talk to him."

The prisoner's cell is covered with pieces of mattress. He is wedged into an eight-inch-wide gap between the bunk and the cell door, mumbling to himself and trembling. He looks terrified. When he sees Ghezzi, he pushes farther into the gap, trying desperately to move the bunk, or the wall, or the cell door, to cower farther and farther into the hole.

Ghezzi slides the door open and speaks gently. "How're you feeling? You okay? We're going to help you. I'm not going to hurt you." The man squeezes in tighter. "That's all right," says Ghezzi. "No one's going to hurt you." He reaches in a hand and takes the man's arm. The man relaxes. "I'm just going to take you to the doctor. It's okay. It'll be okay."

Ghezzi pulls the man out of the cell and, supporting him by the arm, leads him down to the clinic.

The doctor sees Ghezzi coming. "Oh, there you are, Captain. I've just had a case that I will leave in

your hands. An inmate caught his penis in his zipper
and demanded penicillin, which I refused to give
him. He is very displeased. I told him frankly that
the best treatment for his condition would be pre-
ventative. He has only one of those, and would be
well advised to keep it out of zippers."

Ghezzi grins, hands over his patient and starts to
leave. Another doctor somewhere in the jail has
called and asked to have his stethoscope brought to
him. Ghezzi takes it. "All I need now," he says, "is a
night stick and a cross and I'm ready for anything."

On the fifth floor Ghezzi is collecting interview
slips, on which prisoners communicate to the deputy warden their requests and complaints, when an
officer gestures toward a prisoner on the bridge and
says, "That's gonna be trouble."

The prisoner is twenty-two, thin, delicate, with
shoulder-length hair, black leather boots, black
leather pants and a white silk shirt. He smiles politely at Ghezzi and tosses his hair back. "He came
in last night," the officer says, "but he wouldn't admit he was a homosexual."

Ghezzi has a problem. If he leaves the man here,
he will almost certainly be assaulted. But if he
moves him to a special section for passive homosexuals, the man might claim he was forced to go there
against his will. "Look," Ghezzi says in his most
diplomatic tone, "we have a section on another
floor where the people aren't as rough as they are
here." The man smiles sweetly. Other prisoners
walking by blow him kisses and yell, "Homo!
Homo!"

"On the fourth floor," Ghezzi says, "the inmates

are more, ah, mild-mannered, like yourself, and maybe you'd be better off there."

"Yes, I am a bit frightened here."

"Well, nothing personal, you understand, but are you a homosexual?"

The man admits that he is and writes out a statement. Ghezzi waits while he collects his things—magazines and a long, black, orange-lined cape—and takes him down to four.

From four Ghezzi goes back upstairs to attend a prisoner found lying unconscious by a toilet bowl. The man's name is Henry Williams. He has revived when Ghezzi gets there, but refuses to speak. "How're you feeling?" Ghezzi asks. The man stares. Ghezzi takes him to the clinic, and then, with no immediate emergencies at hand, he goes to lunch.

Guards are not allowed to leave the jail to eat. Nor, lest they be accused of selling food to prisoners, are they permitted to bring their lunch in with them. They eat in a cafeteria that serves the same food the prisoners get. Ghezzi, because he's a captain, has lunch in a special dining room that offers steak as well as the regular jail menu. He takes a chair, and another captain says, "So what was it? A rat tail or not."

Ghezzi laughs. "Frankly, I have to say that to me it looked like a rat tail." The other captain pushes his potatoes away.

The food is served by inmates, and no guard ever forgets it. "This is Captain Henderson's plate," a waiter says, and Captain Henderson says, "That's okay. I'll take another one. I'd just as soon not have a plate with my name on it."

There's a visitor at the table today, and the captains are explaining their apprehension. "They can take hostages any time they want," one says. "With organization, they can take the whole house anytime they want. Three officers on a floor? With two hundred and forty inmates? Are you kidding?" He nods toward the kitchen. "One of them can come out of there with a butcher knife, and that's that."

Ghezzi is halfway through his lunch when a phone rings. Before it's even answered, he has his hat on. Two prisoners on five are slugging it out in their cell. A locked cell doesn't provide much running room for the loser.

On the bridge a Puerto Rican stands covered with blood. Ghezzi moves past him with a floor guard to the cell, where a large black man is slowly pulling on his pants. Except for scratches on his face, he is unmarked. Magazine pictures stuck to the walls are splattered with blood, and blood is smeared on the floor and bunk sheets.

"I don't want no trouble with no one," the black prisoner tells Ghezzi. "But he been botherin' me and botherin' me and I just can't take no more. I know he got problems. I got my problems. But I don't bother no one else, not the policemens, not the inmates. You ask anyone on the block. But he take his blanket and start beatin' it on the wall, and I tell him, 'Hey man, you're gettin' my clothes dirty. I gotta go to court in them clothes.' And he tells me, 'Fuck you.' And he grab me. And I just had enough."

Ghezzi takes the Puerto Rican down to the clinic, where the doctor looks at a deep cut over his eye and orders him sent to Bellevue. Ghezzi is leading the prisoner past a holding pen where the black is waiting his turn with the doctor. Suddenly the Puerto Rican lunges for the pen, screaming and sobbing, thrusting his hands through the bars at the black. The black, accepting the challenge, grabs for the Puerto Rican. Ghezzi throws his arms around the Puerto Rican, drags him away from the bars and with the help of another officer puts him in a cell.

With blood on his shirt, Ghezzi goes to an office and starts making out an "injury to inmate" report, detailing what happened and what action was taken. Outside the office, a guard's wife is explaining to an assistant deputy warden that her husband has just had a nervous breakdown and won't be in to work for a while. Behind her, two detectives from the Fifth Squad quietly inform the tour commander of an anonymous tip that there's a bomb in the building.

"How's it going?" another captain asks Ghezzi. Ghezzi looks up from the report, smiles and says, "This is the worst day I've had since yesterday."

Dominick Ghezzi's youth saw moments when he himself stood in danger of doing time in the Tombs. Raised in tough South Brooklyn, he quit high school at sixteen and found himself initiated into a youth gang called the South Brooklyn Boys. "You know, peg pants, guys talking about how they mugged someone the night before, and getting into fights— not fist fights, iron pipes. I figured the hell with this, I could go to jail with these guys."

Instead, he went into the Marines. He got out when he was twenty, worked on a construction gang, then as a longshoreman and finally took the test for correction officer. "One day I got a notice to report, and I raised my right hand and the next day I'm in jail in my blue serge suit with a shield hanging from my lapel."

Today he's forty-two, married, has two sons and makes $14,000 a year. When he reflects on his background—the South Brooklyn streets, high school dropout, immigrant parents (his father was a construction laborer)—he feels he's lucky to be where he is. But he doesn't want his sons to follow him. "I can retire in another three and a half years, but I won't. I want my sons to go to college. I'd never let them be correction officers. Not that there's anything wrong with it, but you sentence yourself to jail for twenty years. I go home to sleep and I see my family, but for forty hours a week I'm locked up, surrounded by bars. The Tombs is a very depressing place. It's worse than a hospital. At least in a hospital something pleasant might happen once in a while, like maybe the X rays come back and it's good news. But nothing nice ever happens to anyone in the Tombs."

As Ghezzi talks, he sits sipping beer in a bar called Maruffi's on a narrow street behind the Tombs. It's one of New York's last true saloons, with every third round on the house and a big black book recording loans to customers. The bar is filled with neighborhood workingmen, cops, court personnel, and there is a low tolerance for whatever radical forces are at large in the city of New York. A bumper sticker stuck in the mirror says, "If you don't like cops, next time you're in trouble, call a hippie."

Ghezzi talks now of his surprise at the number of repeaters in the Tombs. "If I ever had to do time in the Tombs," he says, "whatever I'd done to get in there, I'd never do again—*ever*. I don't even like walking into one of those cells. Even when you know the gate's open, you can feel the walls closing in. And to hear that gate slam shut behind you must be the most horrible feeling in the world. Especially at 3 A.M., and an officer with a flashlight puts you in and shuts the gate and walks away, and you're standing there in the dark with your arms full of blankets wondering who's in there, who's that lying there. And you stand there for ten minutes trying to figure out where the hell you are."

Most of the Tombs's prisoners, like most of its guards, are black. Feelings of black solidarity run high on both sides of the bars, and there are disputes about where loyalties should lie. One black officer who wears a black liberation pin in his lapel ignores the insults of militant black prisoners who demand he remove it. Another black officer is at the bar now next to Ghezzi, and someone asks him how he feels when a black prisoner calls him brother. "How do I feel? I say, 'Hey, man, don't call me brother. I ain't your brother. I have got one brother and one half brother, and three sisters and one half sister. That's all. You ain't my brother.' "

Ghezzi and some other officers in the bar drift into a discussion of their public image, a sensitive subject. "I was sitting with my wife watching something on TV about a suicide in the Tombs," Ghezzi says, "and they were implying that it had really been done by a guard. And my wife said, 'The guards don't really do that, do they?' I looked at her. Here's a woman I've been living with for sixteen years, and she asks me that."

He thinks for a minute over his beer, and then his face broadens in a grin. "You know what I really like to do when I'm not working? I like to go to the beach. I like to lie there and look across the sand and the water way out to the horizon. I just lie there for hours. And from me all the way out to the horizon, as far as I can see, there's not a single set of bars."

About twice a week Dom Ghezzi is relieved of his crises-calming chores as a "house captain" and does eight hours locked in a hot, airless, cell-sized cubicle loaded with alarms, telephones and log books. Tucked away in a corner near the Tombs's main entrance, the glass-enclosed control room is the jail's communications center, crossroads for every problem from leaky faucet to full-scale riot. As Ghezzi sits sweating at the desk (the sidewalk temperature is eighty-five degrees, and the control room blower is out of order), he has around him on the floor two locked steel boxes filled with tear-gas canisters, an emergency resuscitator and a doctor's bag (rushed by an officer to a prisoner's cell, it saves the doctor the time of going by the clinic for his own). Keys hang on a panel to Ghezzi's right, one of them bearing a bright red tag marked "Riot Box— Middle Gate." Any floor phone kept off its hook without a connection for more than thirty seconds rings an alarm and flashes the floor number in the control room. Riot sticks, helmets and gas masks, kept in a locked box in the central "Middle Gate" area, are picked up by guards responding from the receiving room and clerical offices.

Newly installed floor telephones for prisoners also go through a control-room console, and Ghezzi now picks up the receiver and punches a button. A woman is talking. "I'll try to make the first visit, honey. I don't know, but I'll try." She doesn't sound very enthusiastic. Ghezzi shrugs and cuts in on another line. "I pray for you," a woman is saying. "I pray for all of you." Then the prisoner: "Thanks, Mom. Okay, Mom."

A phone on the desk rings and Ghezzi picks it up. "Right. Okay. I'll call the clinic." He hangs up, dials a number. "Captain Ghezzi. I just had a call from seven. He's got a guy with a bad asthma attack. . . . Okay."

As he talks, another phone rings. He picks it up. "The water? Off? Right. Lower-A-Five. . . . Okay." He dials a number. "The water won't go on in Seven Lower-A-Five. . . . Okay."

Five phones are on the desk, and they rarely stop ringing. All day Ghezzi is lifting them up and putting them down, answering and dialing. A captain walks by outside and Ghezzi unlocks the door and waves him in. "The officer on ten just called," Ghezzi says. "He found an interview slip on his desk. The guy says if he's on ten much longer he won't be around. Maybe he's thinking of hanging himself."

"I'll talk to him," the captain says.

Ghezzi glances through his window at the main entrance and sees a young girl coming in accompanied by a photographer and a man with a clipboard.

The Tombs is examined and investigated almost
continuously. Ghezzi shrugs. "Everything stops
here except the Fourth Avenue local." A city councilman is also in the building, and he stops at the
control room. Ghezzi leans forward in his chair to
let him get at the inmate phone console. When the
councilman leaves, Ghezzi leans back again and
rubs his eyes. His shirt is dark with sweat. Two
phones are ringing. He says, "Where were they
when we had three in a cell?"

The next day Ghezzi is in the clinic with a nearly
incoherent prisoner who says his cell is full of spiders. "I paid my rent for a week," the man says,
"and there's spiders all around." He tells the doctor
he has steam inside his head and can hear it escaping through his right ear. The doctor is selecting
pills for another patient. As he does so, he asks,
"How big are the spiders?"

The man holds his hands a foot apart.

"That big? How many are there?"

"Twenty-five or thirty."

"What are their names?"

"I don't know. I can see them, but I can't touch
them. They're eating inside my head. Right here. I
can feel them in here eating my head."

The doctor hands him a cup of paraldehyde, an
alcohol substitute used to relieve the DTs. The man
downs it, chokes and clutches his mouth.

"It's not a vintage year," the doctor says dryly,
and examines the man's eye, which is red and half-
closed. He asks the prisoner the month, which he
gets wrong, and to count backward from ten, a
chore that leaves him confused and helpless. The

doctor examines him further, and then says to Ghezzi, "He's been around jails and hospitals so much he's become a paraldehyde addict as well as an alcoholic and a psychotic." He glances at the man's medical card. "He went to Bellevue and Bellevue returned him. It's grotesque. Grotesque."

Another doctor passing through the clinic notices the patient's eye. "Does he have a vision impairment?" he asks.

"Quite the contrary," says the first doctor, sighing. "He sees excessively. He sees a range of flora and fauna that would astound you."

Ghezzi is no longer listening. His attention has been drawn to a prisoner sitting on a bench outside the clinic. He is Henry Williams, the man found unconscious by the toilet bowl. Motionless except for trembling lips, Williams is staring blankly at blood flowing from two three-inch slashes across his left forearm. An officer who brought him to the clinic gets a paper towel and lays it over the cuts. In a minute Williams removes the towel and again stares down at the wounds and the blood.

The officer tells Ghezzi that Williams was spotted sitting in his cell with blood trickling down his hand. He gives Ghezzi a fragment of a razor blade found in the cell. Ghezzi looks at it. "I wonder where the other three quarters of that damn thing are."

The doctor opens a cabinet, gets a syringe and material for sutures and prepares to stitch up the cuts. "I'll send him to Bellevue, and he'll be back by tonight," he says quietly as he works, more to himself than to Ghezzi or the patient. "So why am I sending him to Bellevue? God knows. It's wild. Just wild."

The doctor lays Williams' arm across a table and makes an injection under the cuts. Williams watches without reaction. "I ain't comin' back here," he announces now, the first words he has spoken. "I ain't comin' back here never. *Never.* People don't live here. They just exist. I wouldn't even work here."

Ghezzi nods sympathetically.

"I'll get her ass," Williams continues. "If she comes to court, I'll hang her right there." He looks at the doctor. "I could kill you if I hit you in the throat. I'll get her ass."

Williams looks at Ghezzi. "I'm sorry this had to happen on your watch, Captain. If I'd talked to you I probably wouldn't have done it. I found the blade two nights ago, but I didn't do it then. I talked to you, and I didn't do it."

Ghezzi is filling in a report and now has to ask a question he knows will sound stupid. "I've got to ask you, Henry, for the report here, why'd you do it?" Williams is silent. "I mean, because you were depressed, or what?"

"I wouldn't do it now," Williams says. "It was a waste of time. Now I'd cut my throat. I got tired of jail, tired of the cell, tired of the bars. I hear voices. I know there's no one there talking to me, but I hear the voices. Did anything ever happen to you where you knew it couldn't be happening, but it was happening?"

The doctor is finishing with the stitches.

"What's going to happen?" Williams asks him.

"I'm going to finish closing this up."

"And then?"

"We'll send you to Bellevue."

"And then?"

"They'll try to help you."

"And then?"

Indeed.

Two spoons are missing after the evening meal on the tenth floor, and a slender black captain named Frank Bealer goes up to help the officers look for them. Ten is a particularly bad floor, housing not only the punitive segregation cells, but also a few prisoners thought to have been ringleaders in earlier riots. These are among the most dangerous men in the jail, a totally different kind of prisoner from the junkies, madmen and professional criminals. They are militant would-be revolutionaries, highly eager to precipitate a riot for its own sake. Two missing spoons are no trivial matter. A spoon with the bowl broken off, the stub scraped into a point, the handle wrapped with a piece of sheet, produces a knife. And in a jail like the Tombs, a knife is nine tenths of the way to a killing.

Bealer and an officer start their search in "the bing," the segregation cells. Each man steps out, is frisked and waits for the officer to search his cell. Bealer skips one man, a patrolman accused of homicide who is in segregation for his own protection. Then he gets to a prisoner sitting defiantly in his shorts on the top bunk. It's Rizzo, the rebellious inmate Ghezzi has been trying to cultivate with friendly talk and cigarettes. But Ghezzi is off today, and the problem now is Bealer's.

Bealer tells Rizzo to come out. Rizzo stares back furiously and does not answer.

"Come on out," Bealer says.

"Why?"

"Just come out. We have to search your cell."

"Why should I? I don't have nothin' in here."

"Come out."

Rizzo stays put. It is 6:45. Normally, prisoners on the floor would have been released from their cells into a barred "lockout" area at 6:30. Angry at the delay, they now begin to kick the bars and cell walls. The kicking is rhythmic and deafening.

"Come out," Bealer yells above the noise, giving Rizzo a long steady blast of a very determined glare.

He comes out.

Bealer moves on to the next cell. The noise of the kicking is now suffocating. The steel walls tremble with the pulsing roar. When it seems that the floor can no longer contain the explosions of steady, throbbing pounding, the sound suddenly grows louder still. Between the kicks and banging, the prisoners are screaming, "Kill! Kill! Kill! Kill!"

The spoons are finally found—one in a pantry area, the other in the cell of a man indicted for rioting and taking hostages—and the prisoners are released from their cells. Two hours later, when it is time to lock back in, the seventy-five men in one tier refuse. A few among them move steadily through the group, encouraging the others not to lock in, pleading, arguing, threatening. Bealer confronts the prisoners through the bars. "You have five minutes to lock in," he says. They swear at him.

Bealer goes to the bridge phone and calls the tour commander downstairs. "They're not going to lock in," he says. "I think we're going to need a little force."

In two minutes an elevator arrives with ten men in helmets, riot sticks and gas masks. They move in by the bars. Another elevator comes up with ten more guards.

Prisoners and officers now confront each other through the bars.

"You have five minutes to lock in," Bealer says again. After that, gas will go in and then the guards and the riot sticks.

The prisoners shout and swear and move sullenly into their cells, angry animals subdued by the chair and the whip. One of them passes by the bars near a guard and for an instant their eyes meet. The prisoner spits into the guard's face. The guard stands there stunned, saliva dripping down his cheek, his eyes locked with the eyes of the man who spat on him. Neither man moves, neither speaks. As if suddenly struck dumb by some horrible vision, they face each other—enraged, helpless and imprisoned.

FIVE

THE BODY IS THAT OF A MIDDLE-AGED WHITE MAN, five feet nine inches tall, scale weight not yet determined. There is a heavy rope ligature looped around the neck. The wrists are tied together with an intricate series of turns of a yellow woven plastic cord which also encircles the abdomen. [*In the New York City morgue, the chief medical examiner stands over the body of a man found floating in shallow water at a Queens County beach in the summer of 1964. As he examines the body, he dictates his findings to a stenographer.*] There is also a rope around the abdomen tied with several knots, and this yellow cord passes through it. The rope projecting from the abdominal ligature is a heavy triple-stranded one, and to one end of this was tied two concrete blocks, which are also tied together with similar heavy rope and yellow cord and chain. . . .

I identified him in the morgue. Identified him! I couldn't *even* identify him. It was just like a skeleton with some stuff on it. [*Willie Rupoli, a bookie, talks about his brother Ernie, who had been a Mafia gun-*

*man and professional killer before his body was
found on the beach.*] I told them, "To tell you it's my
brother, I can't. Not the way he looks. Not what
you're showing me." When I saw him he had the
cinder blocks on him. And the rope around. That's
an awful thing. That's what I can't see, why they
had to do it like that. It's not even a clean knock-off.
It's, I don't know, savages. Shot him, stabbed him, I
can't understand it. To kill him, that's one thing. But
not like that. Not only me, but even the others in
the underworld, his own friends, they can't figure it.
If you live by the gun, you die by the gun. But do it
right. Wait outside his home or something and hit
him when he comes out, but not like they did it. If
you want to get rid of him, hit him clean. Like get
him in a car, hit him and throw him out of the car.
What's all this here rigamajig? I don't know if they
saw television, or what.

. . . The iron chain, fairly heavy, is at present
rusted and covered with sand, as is the body. This
chain is also attached to the ankles. There is a considerable amount of mud and sand, still moist, on
the body and in the clothes, and also some broken
mollusk shells. . . .

He was brought up by his mother to be another Al
Capone. He'd come home and give his mother
money, and she knew it had to be from something
bad, and that pleased her. Because she was always
after him to be another Al Capone. [*Harold Fox, a
retired detective, knew the dead man well and calls
him by his underworld nickname, "The Hawk."*] I

said to him, "Hawk, you come from good people, how'd you ever get mixed up in this?" And he said his mother, she told him he could be another Al Capone. The Capones had lots of money. He'd come back here from Chicago, and he had lots of money. The mother knew people he gave money to, and he'd say how he left Brooklyn and became a big shot in Chicago. She figured if Al Capone could do it, why couldn't her son do it?

Ernie had dreams, you know, that someday he was gonna be the head of the Mafia. And I says, "You couldn't! You can't tell *me* what to do. How're you going to tell anyone *else* what to do?" That was my answer. [*Eleanor Rupolo, the dead man's common-law wife for the six and a half years before his murder, talks to friends.*] And he'd say to me, "You don't know what you're talking about. If it wasn't for me, they'd kill you." Because like I hated his friends. They were ready to shoot me on sight any time they ever saw me because I couldn't stand any one of them. I told Ernie, "The only reason they hang around is because you're a good-time Charlie, and if you weren't buying them drinks and dinner and everything else, you wouldn't even see them. They haven't got two dimes to rub together so they're kissing your ass. Roy Roy and Butch and all those other bastards."

Ernie used to tell me, "But they're my friends. They'd lay down their lives for me."

And I said, "The only thing they'd do for you is kill you."

* * *

So I couldn't even identify my brother. I explained to them that for me to make a positive identification would be hard, that there was a doubt, because what I saw was—well, you couldn't tell if it was a human being or what. So I gave them information about a mesh in his stomach, that he had an operation for a hernia and there was a mesh screen in his stomach. And I told them, you'll find a bullet in him because he's been walking around with a bullet in him for years and years, and they could never take a chance of trying to take that bullet out.

And I identified the shoes he wore, and the pants. I can't miss them, those were my pants. That day he was wearing my clothes. The zipper was broken on his pants. He was in my store, a real hot muggy day. He went to the bathroom and he must have pulled the zipper and he came out and he says, "I broke the zipper, now how can I walk around?"

And I says, "Sit down, my wife'll be here in a minute. She'll fix it. Or take a pair of my pants, a pair of my slacks." And I says, "Don't worry about it." Because every time he had a fight with his wife, Eleanor, and he needed to sleep someplace he used to ring my bell three and four in the morning, and he'd say, "I want to sleep here."

And I'd say, "Go ahead, brother." Because he wouldn't go to no other brother, but he'd come to me. Then when he made up he'd go back. So a lot of times, he'd be wearing my socks or my shoes.

That day he's there in my store, and he's got Roy Roy with him, and he says to Roy Roy, "I gotta go to my brother's house and change my pants." And Roy

Roy drove him to my house, with me following in
the Caddy. They come upstairs and I gave him a
pair of slacks and a sports shirt. He was broke so I
gave him $20 out of my register in the store. "Here,
put this in your pocket." And then when he got
found in the river, he had $50 on him.

So when they were leaving, Roy Roy invited me
to come with them for a drink at the Coco Poodle,
and I say no I was too tired and that I'd have to
make it some other night.

That's when he left with Roy Roy, and I never saw
him again. That's the last I saw my brother. I don't
see him. I don't see the kid no more.

. . . There is evidence of an old hernia operation
with the presence of a small fragment of recogniz-
able tantalum mesh and some black silk sutures.
There is a pair of trousers, extensively torn, with a
leather belt now pulled down to the left knee and
leg. The zipper is partly open. On removing the
shoes and socks, the epidermis of the feet, which is
macerated, comes away with the socks. . . .

When I was about ten, in school in Brooklyn, I
liked the teacher, I was her pet, and I schemed up
something that I could annoy her, to make her pay
attention more to me. [*Some years before his murder, the Hawk sat with Detective Fox and talked
into a tape recorder about his past crimes.*] And
what I did scheme was I looked up her name in the
phone book and I started to call her up at night. I
called her up night after night, and every time a
different story about what had happened to a pupil

in school, where he got run over or he's sick. And she would get grief over it and say, "Who is this calling?" Well, I never told her who was calling, but one day the call was traced and I was caught in the phone booth by two detectives, and they took me to the station house where they made me face the teacher. And she was shocked to know it was me. I couldn't face her. I was ashamed. I was brought to court, she had signed a complaint, and I was given six weeks in the New York Catholic Protectory in the Bronx.

And then I went back to school and the teacher told me that she was sorry she had signed the complaint, that she didn't know then it was gonna be me. And I said I was sorry for what I did, I was punished for it and that's all.

And I stood in school awhile and then when I was twelve I had in mind to get out of school. I schemed for my birth certificate to be forged. I erased my date of birth, I made myself fifteen years old and I brought it to the school, brought it to the Board of Health, and the school fell for it, and I got my working papers and got out of school. I got out of school and I started what I always wanted to do, a career of crime.

I started by burglarizing. We called it the bucket racket, myself and one other boy about eighteen. What we used to do is ring a bell and if a woman came out we'd have a car outside and we'd say, "Can we have a bucket of water? The car's steaming." And if nobody answered the bell, we'd break in. We'd ransack the house, go for the bedrooms, jewelry, money. The jewelry, we'd get rid of it, take

it to a pawnshop or sell it to people out on the street
that we knew. I was twelve. We did about seventy-
five or a hundred burglaries. Then I was arrested,
me and this other fella. Then I was thirteen, but I
told them I was sixteen and they believed me. I got
a suspended sentence of three years.

So I kept on burglarizing. There were three of us
now. I was arrested again, coming out of a home. We
were all shot at by detectives, caught red-handed. I
was sentenced to one day and three years in the
New York City reformatory. I was still thirteen. I did
ten months. Then I went out and this time I went on
with crime, but no burglaries. I did robberies with
three other fellas, older than me. I bought a gun off
another hoodlum. I was fourteen.

One day we were given chase by two cops in a
radio car. While they were chasing us, we threw the
guns out of the car. They got up to us, stopped us,
searched us and took us in. I was held for violation of
parole and went back for another eight months.

Then I went back to the neighborhood. I was out
a couple of weeks, and I got a letter from my
brother, that he was in trouble, to go and see him at
Raymond Street jail. He was in trouble for robbery.
He asked me to help him out, to go to New York
[Manhattan] and get in touch with these fellas that
he associated with, to join them, to join their outfit,
to help my brother, join them in what they were
doing, committing robberies. I went to New York, I
joined them and any robbery we did I put my share
on the side for my brother, to help him with his
lawyer. So what happened was that my brother re-

ceived five to ten years in state prison and I was shot, which I almost died.

When I used to go out with these fellas, one of the fellas was taking a share out for a girl he was living with at this apartment. There were four of us. He wanted to put the girl in for a share. And he did put her in a few times. So I had an argument with him. I told him I wouldn't take it from him. I called him names. So I was going on and on and he told me to shut up, "or I'll shoot you right in the head." And I told him, foolishly, that he hadn't got the guts enough to shoot me in the head.

Well, the first thing you knew, I was shot. As I'm falling down, the girl started screaming. The two other fellas scrambled out and this fella told the girl, "Let's throw him out the window." So she hollered, "No," and that's all I could remember.

So I hated Ernie's friends. I told him all they'd do was hurt him. Like when his eye was shot out. His version to me about how he lost his eye, they were in a hotel, and he was with some people, and somebody was bothering somebody else's girl, and he told the guy not to bother her. And the guy says to him, "Shut up. Mind your own business or I'll let you have it." And Ernie says, "You punk, I wouldn't care what you did." And the guy turned around and he opened a drawer and he took a .45 out and shot him. And he falls over the table, and the last thing he remembered the radio was playing "My Blue Heaven" and they said, "Let's throw him out of the window." Ernie told me, "I wasn't even dead and I hear these guys saying, 'Let's throw him out the window.' They didn't kill me by shooting me so they're gonna throw me out the window."

After my brother lost his eye, and his face was disfigured, he didn't care for his life any more. That's what really turned the kid. When he looked at himself in the mirror—and before he was a real good-looking kid—he just went berserk. He went berserk. And the smart guys who was coming up, they knew that this kid is going to be, a good kid for us to use. In other words, that's what I call it, to use him, so we'll put him on the payroll, and give him this, and make him stop this here stealing or anything like that, and he became under their wing. Because when he had both his eyes he was doing a lot of robberies, and that's how he got the name "The Hawk." He never missed anything. He had eyes like a hawk. So they made him stop the stealing and they gave him contracts. And that's all he did after that. He was just a hit man, since he was sixteen.

Examination of the head discloses considerable maceration and separation and loss of the skin of the nose, with fracture of the nasal bones. The right eyeball is absent, and the socket is scarred. . . .

Ernie used to call me "My Heaven." He'd call me on the phone, "What are you doing, My Heaven?"
"Nothing."
"All right," he'd say, and he'd call and call. He'd leave to go to Brooklyn and he'd call up from the

station, he'd call up when he reached the bar he was at, he'd call up at least ten times a day.

On Sundays he'd be home and he'd baby-sit and I'd go antique hunting all day with my niece. You know, we'd go driving around. He would give me the world if he had it. If he went to the *moon,* he'd come back and say "What are you doing?" I would throw him out and say, "This is it, this is the end!" I would move away from him, right? And two days later, there he'd be. I would move, I would disgrace him, embarrass him. He'd be having dinner with people and I'd walk in, "Give me money and get out of my life!" You know—insult him, degrade him. And he would always be there.

. . . When the scalp is examined there are two entrance bullet wounds found on the right posterior parietal region. More posteriorly there is a third bullet perforation, and exit wound. The brain tissue, which is liquefied and pultaceous and green in color, oozes through this large exit wound, and during the manipulation of the head a tarnished, 380 metal-jacketed bullet emerged from this hole with liquefied brain. . . .

I was shot right in the eye. When I gain consciousness in the hospital I seen this fella that shot me and a girl brought in front of me with a squad of detectives, and they told me, "Here's the fella that shot you. We know he did it, now tell us yourself."

I said, "I don't know him and I don't know the girl. Leave me alone." I didn't want to get revenge on him that way. I figured if I recuperate, I'll take care of him myself.

So when I got out I look for him, but I couldn't catch up with him, and later every time I was out of jail, he was in jail. Every time I was in jail he was out.

After a while I had an opportunity to meet one of the two fellas that was in the room and ran out and left me when I was shot. And they was supposed to be friends of mine. I never forgot that. I met him in a hangout, playing dice. I got alongside of him, and I started gambling against him. He told me, he says, "Don't bet the way you're betting. It's foolish. I'm going to take your money."

I says, "There's no friendship in gambling. If you take my money, you take it." Which he did.

So when I lost my money, I went downstairs from the hangout. I went down in the cellar where I used to have guns hid down there. I took one gun, went back to the hangout where the dice game was and I stuck up the game. I told the fellas in there that it's not meant for them, that it's meant for that fella in the corner. Well, they were satisfied to hear that. So I asked him, I said, "I want all your money and make sure you produce it." Well, at first he didn't give it to me, he says no. I says, "I'll count three. If you don't give it to me by three I'm going to shoot you in the leg, and the second shot you ain't gonna feel it."

So I count three, and he didn't produce his money, so I shot him between the legs. But I didn't hit his legs, I grazed them. When I did that, he took his money out of his pocket, put it with the money he had in his hands and he gave it to me and he pleaded with me, "Don't shoot me, don't shoot me no more." And that was that. I went downstairs, put the gun away and went across the street in the poolroom and stood around.

People used to tell me, "Eleanor, I don't know how you get away with it. I've seen that guy *kill* people for less than that, the way you talk to him." And I'd say, "Why that son of a bitch couldn't fight his way out of a paper bag." Because this was the way he treated *me*, but he could *terrify* anyone else. And I could never believe that he could terrify anybody else, because I'd walk in and give him a smack and that would be the end of it. I mean scenes like that were commonplace. We'd fight, I'd kick him out and then he'd call with stories, you know, and I used to feel sorry for him and I'd say, "All right, come on home," and I'd go and I'd get him wherever he was and bring him back home.

After I stuck up the guy in the dice game, I joined this outlaw outfit, fellas that were against the racketeers, that knew that the big shots and racketeers had everything sewed up, that would take money off different people. So we figured we'd take it off them, off the racketeers. We'd stick them up.

We got called on the carpet many a time. We were warned by the top men. They'd tell us to lay off what we were doing. But we'd deny it, and we always told them, "You don't know what you're talking about." Because we all—five of us—used masks, and they weren't so sure it was us. We felt very bitter towards them, because anything you tried to do, they would come over and say, "That's *my* spot.

This is *my* store. Don't touch *that* fella. Don't touch *this* bookmaker." You couldn't do nothin'.

My brother was a hit man for them. And they were afraid of him. They figured if they were gonna hit *him*, they'd better do a good job. You know, that's the reputation the kid had. That's why the kid kept walking around. And then the kid was good. I mean the only time he went bad was goin' to people he shouldn't of gone to, grabbin' people by the throat, takin' money off them. Like he walked in behind a bar, Dino's Bar, and he asked for money and got refused. He went behind the bar, he took the money out of the register, gave everybody drinks. That's the type of guy he was. "If you don't wanna give me no money, I'll take it."

In the later years he was not a thief, he'd just grab you for your money. In other words, he didn't go out on stickups, he didn't go out on burglaries, he just, "I'll get my money, I'll walk into this guy and I'll get my money." He'd go to a bookmaker, put a pistol to his head. "I want a thousand." He'd go into a shy, he knew the guy was shying, that he had money, and "I want $5,000." That's the type of kid he was, "I want $5,000 or you don't operate." So he'd bring a couple of hoods with him, and he'd make sure he got the $5,000. So he always got the money.

But he knew it couldn't go on like that forever. He knew he was gonna get hit sooner or later. He used to tell me when he got drunk. He'd say, "You know, Willie, I'm living on borrowed time. How

much more do you think I can go around takin'
people, takin' people, takin' people?"

. . . There is also a bullet perforation with
macerated edges on the anterior surface of the
neck. This bullet is a 380 deformed missile and
drops out of a segment of the spinal canal. . . .

It sounds ridiculous, but it really was like this,
back and forth, six, seven times a year Ernie'd move
in and out. One time I put all his clothes down the
incinerator. I said, "I quit, I don't care if you walk
around with your ass hanging out. Don't come
back."

And he would come back. His brother Willie said
one time, "Eleanor, if he knew that you were going
to hit him over the head with an ax when he walked
through that door, he'd walk through the door anyway, as long as it was *you* hit him over the head with
the ax."

One time he's not living with me again and runs
into some guy who says he had a couple of drinks
with me. And now he comes home, he's going to
murder me! This is it. He's killing me now. And a
friend came home with him. So his friend told me
later they had gone into the kitchen, he got a big
kitchen knife and he was gonna cut me up to rib-
bons.

So anyway I went to bed. You know, like he's
telling me he's going to kill me, he's going to murder me, and I says, "Oh yeah? Go frig you, too." And
I'm getting undressed and I'm going to bed because

he's telling me this all the time. So I'm lying in bed and I'm going to sleep. I'm *tired*, right?

I hear something going on outside, but I don't know what. I don't even care. I'm just going to sleep. But he comes in and says he's gonna give me a beating. For some reason he forgot about the knife. He picks up the coffee table and he comes *charging* into the bedroom and—CRASH!

I says, "Now you've had it." I says, "I've been waiting *five years* for you to put a finger on me. That's *it*."

I pick up the phone next to the bed, dial operator. "I'M GETTING MURDERED!" I scream at the operator. So I get connected with the police, the Sixty-sixth Precinct. I say, "THIS SON OF A BITCH IS KILLING ME!" I says, "HURRY UP!" I says, "I'LL BE DEAD BEFORE YOU GET HERE!"

Now they come charging over, up the fire escape and everything else, and now they've got him, right? And I says, "I don't care *what* you do." I says, "*Look* at this, look what he did to my leg, look at this." I says, "He's gonna *die* for this. That did it. Get him out. I don't care where he goes, just get him out of here."

They took him down in the elevator and off he went. They let him go. So Ernie took it on the lam for a couple of days. And now I have him. He hit me, right? And, oh, how the presents start coming, and, oh, I really had it made then. He came with hundred dollar bills. "Honey, buy yourself something." *Nothing* was too good for me.

* * *

. . . The entrance of the bullet which popped out of the scalp is the mouth. The bullet penetrating the mouth grazes the tongue and produces a rather deep furrow. . . .

So we were very bitter about the big shots and we kept on taking money from them, and this went on several months.

Then I got a contract by an organization to kill two fellas, two hoodlums [*Willie Gallo and Ferdinand "the Shadow" Boccia*]. And there was another fella with me in on the contract. It was well planned. Nothing could go wrong. There was plenty of time and plenty of money involved. I had one of the fellas that was going to die most of the time, sometimes I had the two of them. And lots of times they were lucky, that they missed by inches. Something would go wrong. You know how that is.

Well, the time finally came that everything was clear. I had one of the fellas [*Willie Gallo*] that was gonna die with me, and the other fella that was gonna do the killing with me. We gave this fella dinner, we drank, a woman—in other words we gave him a good time. When the party was all over we knew what we were gonna do. We walked out, we drove to a certain block, I took a gun out of my pocket, I put it to this fella's head and I keep firing and it don't go off.

So the fella told me, "What are you doin'?" I says, "Well, I'm only kidding you."

"Kidding!" he says.

"That's all I was doin'," I told him. Well, he was a

little drunk, he thought that probably I was kidding. He says, "The way you're marked? You carrying a gun with you? Put it away."

I was going to ask to go and put the gun away anyway, and I'd be right back, but not really to put it away, to put some oil on the gun. Which I did. And I tried out the gun, and it went off. And I went back to where my partner and him were waiting for me, and I says, "Okay, I put the gun away." I told him, "Let's go a few blocks. We're going to meet a certain party." He okayed it. He says all right. He was wobbling a little bit from the liquor.

So when we got to this certain spot, I let it go off. So between I and my partner, we gave him seven shots. We thought he was dead. The only thing he said was, "Oh, Mom," and that's all. We figured we left him for dead.

Well, we went to sleep for a couple of hours and the next day we went down to see this organization where they were at. Well, they didn't like the idea, that the fella had lived. They knew the other thing was taken care of, the other fella [*Boccia*] was killed, a few hours before this one was shot. Well, they did a little yelling because it was done wrong, but we just listened.

Then they sent us to some of their people in another state. We were there awhile, and my friend that was with me was afraid. He figured that we didn't do it right, that we were gonna get killed in that state. I told him, "No, they wouldn't kill us. What do you think that for?" Well, the next day I was taken to a doctor, to be operated on for my eye, to get a glass eye put in. And after the operation, which didn't work anyway, I went back to where we were hiding, and that night my friend told me, "I'm sorry, I have to leave you alone." He says, "I'm going home, back to the neighborhood." He says, "I don't trust these people."

I says, "Wait till I get better. I'll come with you. Don't leave me this way." What really had got him scared is when we were alone in the hideout he happened to open a closet and he seen machine guns, shotguns and pistols layin' around like nothin', and that made him scared.

So he really did what I didn't expect him to do. He really left me alone, so if there was anybody to be killed there, I would have been killed alone. So I was there after that two weeks. All I did was ate, drank and had a good time up in the hideout. And then I was sent back to New York. I was given information that the fella I shot talked on me and my partner, told everything he knew, that we shot him. And that he's living yet, that he's still in the Kings County Hospital, still in serious condition. They told me that they'll take care of it, to come back, that they'll take care of things.

But before I went to New York, I went to Brooklyn. And when I got there I met a fella, the same fella that was in the room when I got shot. The same fella that I shot in the dice game.

He came over to me, he shook hands with me and he says, "I'm sorry for what happened, let's be friends." I said, "It's all right with me." He says, "Where are you going now?" I says, "I'm going to New York." He was the only person that knew I was going to New York, beside the organization. Well, I

took the train and I went to New York. I got off at
Canal Street. When I got upstairs, it was no coinci-
dence, there was a squad of detectives waiting for
me, just turning the corner. And they grabbed me
and threw me right in the car.

I was brought in front of the man I shot in Kings
County Hospital. He identified me. The detectives
told me he had made a deathbed statement and
"You're just lucky he's living yet. We don't know if
he'll still live."

He wanted to talk to me. He asked me, "Why did
you shoot me?" I told him, I said, "Why did you talk
on me?" He said, "But that ain't the question I'm
asking." I says, "What's the difference what I shot
you for? You could of got revenge later on, instead
of talking, saying that I shot you." Now the reason
for that was this, that he was no lily himself. He was
a gunman himself. He held a gun in his hand many
times.

Ernie would get up in the morning—I never got
up one day in six and a half years before twelve
o'clock—Ernie would get up in the morning, shut
the bedroom door, change the baby, wash the baby,
get Ellen's lunch, then he'd get Ellen's breakfast
ready, do everything, wash the floors, clean the
house, make my coffee and knock on the door.

"It's twelve o'clock, honey. Do you want to get
up?" He'd come in, stroke my hair and say, "Do you
want to get up?"

And I'd get up and I'd drag myself to the kitchen
table, and I'd say, "Ohhhhhh, I'm so tired." Because
I would be up all night waiting for him to come

home. He never really told me too much about what he was doing. I mean he wouldn't tell me anything to make me nervous or worried or anything like that. He'd come home, he'd say, "There was trouble tonight" or this happened or that happened, and I'd listen with one ear.

This guy that was a gunman himself, that was supposed to be a tough guy, well, he says that he's not going to identify me in court. But he lied. He did identify me in magistrate court, and I was held for the grand jury.

While I was waiting trial in Raymond Street jail, I had a lawyer, hired by the organization. He came over to see me in jail, and he told me not to worry about nothin', that everything would be fixed up, just to take it easy. Well, I was there about two months. And then I was brought to trial, and before my trial started the judge talked to me in his chambers with my lawyer and with my partner and he told me, "If I was you, I wouldn't gamble on this case. If you take a plea of assault in the second unarmed, I will give you two and a half to five years."

Well, I just listened and then my lawyer grabbed me on the side, and he says, "Don't take no plea. Everything is fixed up. You're going out this afternoon."

So I told the judge, "No, your honor. I want to stand trial. I'm innocent." Well, he says to me, he says, "Once that trial starts there's nobody gonna stop it. Remember that."

Well, he kept his word. The trial started, the man

I shot got on the stand and he *buried* me. He told the truth, and how I shot him and everything. So I was found guilty of assault in the first degree. I was found guilty in five minutes by the jury. The judge gave me and my partner ten to twenty years in state prison.

So I was sent to state prison, and the same baloney used to go on. We used to get word not to worry, that when a different governor comes in we'll be out. All that, you know. Years go by and by and you still live on hope. And live on their baloney stories that they give you.

And many a night I would stay up, and think what really went on and how foolish I was. Sometimes I would look in the mirror and look at myself, that that was part of my crime career, by looking in the mirror and seeing the way I was. I seen that I was a different person. And plenty of times I used to spit at the mirror. I used to hate myself.

Ernie knew, he knew. I'd say he knew it for about six months, that he was gonna get killed. I didn't believe him. Would you believe it if somebody just came out and told you, "Honey, they're gonna kill me?"

He wouldn't get in the car with me for six months before he got killed. He was always with these bums Jerry and Roy Roy, and he'd always get some jerk to drive him around. And I'd say, "Hey, what's the matter with this guy? I've been driving him around for years and now all of a sudden he'll never get in the car with me any more."

And Willie, my brother-in-law, said to me, "He

never gets in the car with you because he's afraid they're going to kill him and they're going to kill you, too, if you're with him. So he won't drive with you."

And here's another funny thing. Ernie had a lot of papers that this woman was holding, and he always told me, "They'll never do anything to me because I've got these papers that this woman is holding in her safe." He goes there about, I'd say, two weeks before he gets killed to get this stuff from her, and now all of a sudden all this stuff she's holding for Ernie like for about seven or eight years is gone. And two weeks later, so was Ernie.

. . . An old bullet is found just to the left of the midline, encapsulated in fibrous tissue. There are six bullet tracks in all. . . .

I did eight years and six months of the sentence, and I went home. Everything was strange. I hung around awhile, felt around awhile. They contacted me and they told me things had been tough, that they had been double-crossed. Well, I couldn't get so fresh with them. I was alone, and just out. A lot of things happen while you're away so long. I just yessed them, and they told me things are tough, that I've got to be careful now that I'm on parole.

Well, one day I got myself into another swindle. This fella here, he was double-crossing everybody, double-crossing his own organization. He would give tips to certain card games, and get in with these people and then he would turn on them and rob them.

And he was trying to set me up, and a couple of other fellas, and I turned around and I went to certain people and I told them about it and they said the next time he comes in just hit him right in the head. If he comes in with another proposition.

Well, it just happens that one night he pulls his brand-new car in front of my place, sits me down and tells me he's got a good thing. Well, I was waiting for him to come. I says, "All right, what's the good thing?" And he explained it to me. He says, "We'll make a good buck on it." Well, I turned around, I says excuse me a minute. And I went in back of my store, put a gun in my pocket and came out and just kept talking to him. And I says, "Well, okay. We do it."

And in the meantime there was a fella come in I knew, drunk like a pig. Well, I had an idea to get in the guy's car with the drunken fella. I told the guy, I says, "Look, let's get this drunken fella out of here. We'll take him home. We'll talk in the car." He says all right.

Well, when we get outside, the drunken fella gets in the center. And I get by the door. So I'm directing him where to go. "Go up this block, turn right, turn left." Well, when we get to a certain spot, the car is going slow, and I says, "Take it easy here."

So I take out the gun, and I told him in Italian, I says, "I'm sorry this is gonna happen. It was gonna be either you or me."

Well, he started hollerin' and sayin', "Please, what are you doin' to me?" I says, "Well, I'm gonna shoot you right in the head."

So the car was going slow. He couldn't even step

on the motor almost, his legs were shakin'. Instead he turns the wheel on the sidewalk a little. And I shot him twice, right in the face.

And the drunken fella is what saved the guy's life. When I fired the two shots, this drunken fella opened the door and run like a rabbit. He's hollerin', "Don't shoot at me! Don't shoot at me!" So that threw me off. And I had to go back and shoot the guy two more times.

And then I took a handkerchief out of my pocket, took all the fingerprints I could off, closed the door and went back to my business.

Well, it wasn't long. The next day I was arrested. The man was dying. He identified me in the hospital, told them everything what I did. And here's another fella that's supposed to be a tough guy, a big racketeer, a man that was known as a killer in the mob. He couldn't meet his maker either.

So I did seven years more. It was another one of the cases where everything is "fixed up." And it was all a lot of hooey.

You know how other people, they lie in bed and tell each other how much they love each other? Well, Ernie used to lie there and tell me all these murder stories. This guy he shot. And it was his *friend,* he told me. And he said the guy was good-looking. He said, "Honey," he said, "he was the best-looking guy. He was *really* a good-looking guy." And he says, "He was my best friend."

So they call Ernie down—Vito, I guess—and they say he's gotta hit this big shot.

"But he's my best friend."

"Hey, it's you or him. Get rid of him."

So now they're out, and they're wining. And he tells me, "We're out having a good time, big dinner, drinking and everything else, and who comes along but this guy Kip." He couldn't get rid of this fellow Kip. And Kip is drunk out of his mind. So Ernie tells me, "I can't get rid of Kip, and I don't know what I'm gonna do." He says, "I can't go home. I gotta kill this guy."

I said, "How could you *do* such a thing?" So he said, well, what happened, they're in a car, they're all drunk out of their minds, right? Kip is in the front seat, but he had passed out, he was so drunk. And Ernie tells me, he says, "We drive up this block, and I take out the piece and I empty the gun at the guy." He says Kip wakes up—he sobered up in a minute—and says to Ernie, "Ernie, what did you *do?*"

"Shut up!" Ernie says. "Don't say a word." And they take the guy and they threw the guy out of the car. And Kip is petrified, so Ernie drove him home, and he went in and Ernie went home.

He tells me the guy didn't die. I say, "Didn't die! With all those bullets in him?"

"Yeah," he says. "He *crawled* all the way to Sixtieth Street, to the bar," he says. "And he *lasted* till seven in the morning. And I don't know if it was the milkman, or the guy came to open the bar, but he sees him laying right in the door. The guy *crawled* all the way there."

Now they pick up Ernie, and the guy says Ernie did it. They take Ernie to the hospital. Ernie tells me, "I run to the bed, I get down on my knees," and he tells the guy, "Who did this to you? I'll get him if it's the last thing I do." And the guy says, "*You* did it!"

Ernie told me, "I almost came down with a heart attack." Ernie says to the guy, "What's the matter with you? I'm your friend. I wouldn't do such a thing."

And Ernie's telling me the whole scene. How he raced into the hospital room, he's kneeling next to the bed and he's telling the guy, "Who did this to you?" And he's the one who did it, right?

And then there was the other one my brother muffed. Where he shot the guy, that there big shot, what's his name? That's when my brother blew his top against the whole organization, because the big shot opened up on him. So they picked my brother up at home and went to the hospital and the big shot fingered him from his bed, and the kid says to him, "I'm your friend. I didn't hurt you." And they locked the kid up.

So then what happened, the big shot's own brother went to see him, and he says, "Look, what are you going to do? You gonna rat?" And the big shot says, "What, are you crazy? No, I'm gonna change my story."

So all the big shots sit down. They went to my mother's house, and they told my mother, "Look, don't worry. He will be saved. He'll walk out of the courtroom. The guy's taking the stand and he's just gonna say he had it in for the kid, that's why he said he did it."

So now my brother's wife, my mother, my father,

they went up to the court. So this guy takes the stand. Now, the night before they had all met at my mother's house, all the big shots, Genovese's men, and all of them says, "Don't worry about it. The kid'll walk out."

So, now this is a big boss, and he takes the stand, and the first thing he says, "That's the hired killer."

So that's why my brother blew his top on the organization.

THE HAWK POINTS CLAW AT GENOVESE

The Hawk, a one-eyed perpetually sneering trigger man, leaned from the witness box in Kings County Court today, pointed his finger at Vito Genovese, Manhattan racketeer, and identified him as one of the men who hired him to help murder "The Shadow" Boccia in September, 1934.

Genovese shifted slightly in his chair and stared at the Hawk, who wears a patch of adhesive tape over his right eye socket, yanked at the knot in his tie and unbuttoned the collar of his shirt.

"What was your occupation at that time?" Judge Samuel S. Leibowitz asked the Hawk.

"I was a gambler," he replied.

"And a killer?" queried the judge.

"Oh, sure," the Hawk declared.

The Hawk, questioned by Julius A. Helfand, Assistant District Attorney, revealed that he met Genovese in a Brooklyn restaurant in March, 1934.

There he was introduced to Genovese by Michael Mirandi, who described Genovese as the *"don vin*

done," which in the Italian underworld lingo means "the big man—the great man."
—*World-Telegram,* June 7, 1946

. . . In addition to the bullet tracks, there are multiple stab wounds, seven on the anterior surface of the chest and four on the right. . . .

That Friday, the last time I ever saw him, he was in the kitchen, leaning up against the refrigerator, and he tells me, "Honey, they're gonna kill your daddy."

He wasn't living home then, but he was coming home every day. You know, all that same garbage, back and forth. And I says, "Oh, another crazy story to get back in the house." I says, "Don't worry." I says, "If they kill you, I'll make sure that whoever did it goes to jail." He says, "Yeah. Don't say that," and on and on.

Now, the next day, Saturday, he's supposed to bring me money. So he calls on Saturday morning, and he's in a bar on Fort Hamilton Parkway somewhere and he tells me about a fire. He says, "I almost died last night in a fire. Two guys came to the door and I wouldn't let them in and they were screaming and I was cursing." He says, "Your daddy was out in the street in his underwear." He was telling me all what was going on.

I says, "Ernie, why do you think up these fantastic tales? Anything to get back in the house." Then he says, "I'm meeting the guys. I'm gonna have the money for you." And I says, "All right."

Now it's Sunday and he's calling, and the last time

he calls is Sunday night because I'm moving and they shut the phone off Sunday night. He calls Sunday night and, "I'll be there, I'll be there with the money," and on and on. Now I don't hear from him Monday, right? Because I have no phone, and he obviously didn't get the money because he didn't come. Tuesday I don't hear from him. Wednesday morning I move. Now I figured, "Oh, this dope is gonna show up." By Thursday when he doesn't show up, I call my sister. "Did you hear from Ernie?" She says, "No." I says, "Gee, that's funny. I was so sure he was coming with the money." So Thursday passes by. Now Friday comes and I says, "Something happened." This has never happened in six and a half years, because this man *never* stayed away a week no matter *what* happened.

All right. Now it's Friday, I don't see him. What's going on? I haven't heard from him since Sunday. By this time he would have had my sister on the cross—"Where is she, what's going on?" So now I start calling. And calling. And calling. Calling Roy Roy's mother. "He went away, he went away for a few days," she says.

"He went away for a few days? What do you mean he went away for a few days? Where did he go?" Roy Roy's mother says, "I don't know. He's coming home, he's coming home, he's coming home."

I called everybody. Everybody Ernie ever knew, I have on the phone. Nobody saw him. Now I call Frances back, Roy Roy's mother. I says, "Look, I'm telling you now," I says, "you better get Roy Roy to the phone. I'm telling you Ernie is *dead*."

* * *

. . . Of the seven stab wounds on the left anterior surface of the chest, four penetrate backward at various points, cutting through the costal cartilages and also through the interspaces. . . .

SINGING 'HAWK' NEAR LIBERTY

Ernest (the Hawk) Rupolo, killer-for-hire of the gangster decade '30s, was on his way to liberty from Dannemora Prison yesterday in proceedings before Judge Samuel Leibowitz. This was in accordance with a 1946 promise made by the Brooklyn District Attorney's office in return for his evidence against his alleged underworld paymaster, Vito Genovese, of Murder, Inc. fame.

All concerned in the release, including "the Hawk" himself, agreed he is now marked for murder himself and cannot expect to survive long. He had been serving a nine-to-20-year sentence.

With the promised aid of Brooklyn authorities and the expected collaboration of State Parole Board members, Rupolo will make a desperate effort to disappear completely.

—New York *Daily Mirror,* Sept. 24, 1949

So my brother blew his top on the organization. He exposed the big bosses. "I was hired killer for Genovese. I was hired killer for Mike Miranda. I was hired killer for this here." So he's supposed to get killed by this mob, because there is no forgiving.

According to the code of the greaseballs he was supposed to be killed.

But the kid *made* some of the bosses. Because they used him a lot when he was young, and they always depended on him to do the jobs that he was told to do. So they sat down on this—should he walk the streets or not? And they forgave him. They said, "Well, this kid did twelve years, solid years, for us." So for that he got a reprieve. In fact, Mike Miranda says to him, "Take care of yourself, kid. Don't worry about nothin'. If you need anything come to me."

That's why he ran wild the way he did. He didn't join the combination. He had to be a free-lancer. A guy like him, what he did, if it wasn't for the work he done for them so some became top bosses today —he wouldn't of lived two minutes.

They never tried to hit the kid. They were scared because, believe me, if someone went after him and he had an idea where it come from, he'd go right up to their doorstep, right to the boss. He didn't care who it was, he'd go right to the boss and wait on his doorstep to kill him. He wouldn't give them a second chance. That's the way the kid was. He didn't care for nothin'.

I don't think Genovese had a thing in the world to do with killing my husband. You see, Ernie knew Sonny [*John "Sonny" Franzese, a Long Island mobster*] from when they were kids. And he hated him. Because he said, "While I was doing sixteen years that bastard was out making money." Sonny never did a day, so Ernie figured Sonny was reaping the harvest while he was away doing time. They hated each other. They really, really did.

Now I think Ernie was stepping on Sonny's feet. Ernie couldn't make money in Brooklyn any more and he needed money and he figured he'd go out to Queens and start in in Queens in whatever Sonny was doing—bookmaking, muscling in on bars, whatever. And Sonny didn't want that.

What I think happened, I think Ernie was drinking all day, right? And now he's pretty—he's not with it any more. He's like in a fog. They go to Willie's house, Ernie and Willie and Roy Roy. My personal feeling is that Roy Roy had an appointment to meet somebody and that he stalled at Willie's house. And then Roy Roy told Ernie he'd drop him off somewhere, or something like that. And then he was killed on the way. Roy Roy met some people and they told Ernie they would drive him, and they killed him in the car.

. . . On the left lateral surface of the chest there are seven more stab wounds. These are up to six inches in depth. . . .

When they finally did hit my brother, Roy Roy had to be the one to set him up. He drove for him. He was the only one he'd of gone with. That's what they do. They take your best friend and he has to do what they say, even if he *is* your best friend. And they make him walk you into something, take you out, wine you and dine you and then walk you into it. Roy Roy had to be the one.

But the stab wounds. I don't know. That's what

I'm sick over. I seen this here before. Like Joe Jelly. They say, "Oh, they threw him in the river. They ripped his stomach and threw him in the river so he won't come up."

That's the only way I can see it. Like that's why they slit a guy's belly. They figure the water won't bring him up. This is just one chance in a million that my brother did come up. Because people who've been hit in the last ten or twelve years, their bodies were never found. Nobody knew, just rumors, talking, "He must be in the river somewhere." Because if a body is either buried or in the river, they figure it wouldn't come up and you won't see it no more.

"I'm telling you Ernie is *dead!*" I says to Frances.

"What makes you say that?" she yells.

"I *know* he's dead. I know he's dead, because if he wasn't dead he would have been breaking my door down by now."

"Don't say that!" she yells at me. "I'm lighting candles for you. He'll be all right," and this and that.

I says, "All right." So she gives me a time to call to get Roy Roy on the phone. And sure enough, I call and I get Roy Roy on the phone. So I says, "Roy Roy, where's Ernie?" He says, "He's on the lam in New Jersey." I says, "Don't give me that garbage. You're talking to *me!*" I says, "You *know* if he was on the lam in New Jersey, he's not going to New Jersey without me, if he had to take me there in chains." I says, "Just tell me where he is."

"What are you worried about?" he says. "You're always throwing him out anyway." And I says,

"That's none of your damned business. I live my life. I want to do what I want to do. But don't tell *me* this guy isn't going to call *me* for a week," I says, "because you *know* better than that."

So he says, "I don't know where he is." I says, "Roy Roy, you're the last one that saw him alive."

"DON'T SAY THAT!" He got hysterical when I said that. So I says, "I *am* saying it. And where is he?" He says, "I don't know, I don't know where he is." I says, "I'm going to call you up tomorrow morning and if you don't come up with Ernie by then I'm going to Brooklyn. And that's it. That's gonna be *it.*"

So I called back the next day, and Roy Roy's not around. And I went right to Willie's store, you know, the luncheonette. "Where's Ernie?"

Nobody saw him. So I says, "Willie, don't give me any of that garbage." I says, "Where is he?" He says, "I don't know. He moved out of his room. Roy Roy moved him out." And I says, "I don't want to hear that garbage! Who saw him and where did he go?"

"All I know is he left the house that night. My wife told him don't leave it's raining. He says, no, he had to go, he had to go."

I says, "All right." So then I see Ernie's jacket hanging in the store. "What's his jacket doing here?" So he says, "Oh," he says, "it was hot. He left his jacket here." I says, "Was he drunk?" He says, "No."

Now Ernie had reached the point where he couldn't drink any more. He'd have four drinks and he was stoned. I said, "Did he have his teeth in his mouth?" He says, "No." I says, "He was drunk. Where did he go?" He says, "I don't know. They dropped me off. Roy Roy said he was going to take him to the train." He says, "That's all I know." I says, "Okay. That's *all* you know?"

"Right."

"Willie, you don't know *anything* else?"

"No."

So I says I'm going right to the police station. Now by this time I'm crying. I says, "He's *dead*. I'm telling you he's *dead.*"

All right. I walked into the Sixty-sixth. I'm crying like a maniac by now, and I said, "Ernie's dead."

And the cops laughed at me. They said, "You're just looking for him because you want some money, right, Eleanor?" I says, "No, I'm telling you now, he's dead." Because I had called them a million times before. "Get that bum out of my house!" So now they figure I'm just looking for him. I says, "No, I'm serious." So they said they had to report it to Missing Persons. So I says, "But *look* for him. Look for him all over. Because I *know* he's dead. If he's not dead, they've got him tied up somewhere. I didn't hear from him for a week."

So they said all right. And I said, "I'll call you later."

From there, now, I go to his apartment on Berkeley Place. Now Willie told me he had moved out of Berkeley Place, that he's not there. But I look through the window and I see his jewelry box on the dresser.

Now I'm wild. I says, "Oh, my God," and I'm banging on doors and I'm kicking. I go up and I start ringing all the doorbells in the building. Who saw him? One guy was telling me about the fire, and I says, "Well, it was *true* about the fire."

But nobody saw him after that day. "We didn't see him. We didn't see him. We didn't see him."

And I'm calling. I call everybody and anybody. Nobody saw Ernie. I'm calling two or three times a day to the Sixty-sixth, to Missing Persons. I don't hear anything, and I'm bothering everybody.

Until the day that detective rang the doorbell. I opened the door, and his first words to me, he says, "You're right."

I said, "Where is he?" I figured they found him in some empty lot somewhere.

He says, "We have him in the 100th Precinct." I says, "I don't know where that is." He says, "Rockaway. Come with me."

And that was it.

. . . On the anterior abdominal wall there are six large incised stab wounds, all above the navel and from four to six inches in length.

Cause of death: Bullet wounds of head, brain, neck and spine. Multiple stab wounds of the chest, lungs, heart and abdomen.

Homicidal.

SIX

FROM LEGAL POPPY FIELDS IN TURKEY, BY CAMEL across the sands of Syria to the not-so-legal laboratories in Lebanon, then by ship to southern France for final refining and, courtesy of the Mafia, to New York's docks and airports—heroin comes to Harlem. And from Harlem the drug moves swiftly through the city of New York, as efficiently and regularly as milk from New Jersey or fish from Fulton Street. As it moves, the illicit stream swells into pools from which addicts in various parts of the city draw their daily needs. Addicts—and the police—are as aware of the selling locations as the housewife is of her neighborhood shopping center.

In the rush and confusion at Ninety-sixth Street and Broadway, addicts gather on the corner to meet the pushers and buy their drugs—ignored by crowds of New Yorkers on their way to work. On the southwest corner of Eighty-second Street and Columbus Avenue, two blocks from Manhattan's Museum of Natural History and the Central Park West apartments nearby, addicts spend thousands of dollars a day for heroin. In front of a drugstore at Forty-seventh Street and Broadway, within the chaotic glow of Times Square, unknowing tourists brush shoulder to shoulder with barbiturate addicts waiting stiff and zombie-like for their connections. It's the same just two blocks south, among the honky-tonk bars and night clubs, or down in Greenwich Village, where heroin and marijuana pass from hand to hand on the benches of Washington Square.

Of these hundreds of selling locations outside Harlem, one of the most typical is located at the corner of Seventy-first Street where Broadway pushes through Amsterdam Avenue on its diagonal slice across Manhattan. To subway riders who use the stop there, the intersection is Sherman Square. To the drug addicts it is "Needle Park."

John and Karen spend almost all their time in Needle Park. They have much in common with other big-city junkies. Karen is twenty-six, John, twenty-four. Both had broken the law before they started on heroin—she as a prostitute in the Midwest, he as a thief in New York. Karen is the first in her family to use illegal drugs, but John has two addicted brothers and a third died of an overdose.

Both John and Karen have used many drugs, but they prefer heroin to all the rest just as a gourmet prefers wine to beer. Both have been to jail (he ten times, she twice)—and have emerged each time to start their habits fresh.

John and Karen have been together—sleeping wherever they can find a place to lie down—for three years. They use the same last name, but never got around to formal marriage ("We did get a blood test once," says Karen). Karen's earnings as a prostitute also support John's habit, and he occasionally contributes a little money by breaking into parked cabs, in which drivers may have left coin changers.

Both John and Karen are at times all but overcome by revulsion for their habit and for the horrifying, unseen world it forces them into. "We are animals," says Karen. "We are all animals in a world no one knows."

Needle Park is peopled by a conglomeration of individuals who come from different backgrounds, have different ways of getting the money they need and who prefer different combinations of drugs. Simply by hanging around Needle Park for a while you can meet a whole spectrum of addiction: Irene, a slight, wispy Lesbian addicted to "goofballs," barbiturates. Goofballs usually produce a quiet drowsiness, but also at times a tense aggressiveness that can be frighteningly unpredictable. Irene's behavior when she is high on GBs, which is most of the time, has created such havoc in the neighborhood restaurants that they no longer let her in. So sometimes she stands outside on the sidewalk and tries to shout at her friends through the window. After a while, she laughs uproariously and goes running on down the street with another girl.

There is Billy, who never stays around for long because he is trying desperately to stay clean. He just finished three years in Leavenworth for smuggling drugs from Mexico. Now he has had enough and wants to be square. He is trying to get a job, "but how can you explain three years out of your life? And no one in his right mind is going to hire a junkie."

Hank is a regular habitué. He is on *bombitas*—

Spanish for "little bombs." In Harlem they cost a dollar. In Needle Park the price is $1.50 or $2.00. Hank has the customary symptoms of a bombita user. Because they are amphetamines, stimulants, he talks constantly, cannot sit still and his arms and face are covered with sores where he has picked at the skin, sometimes with the illusion that bugs are crawling underneath. And always, lurking in the shadows, haunting Needle Park, stands Mike, a tall, trench-coated black. Mike is a "take-off artist," and a man to keep away from. He supports his habit by robbing connections and almost anyone else in the junkie world who appears to have money.

When junkies meet, they talk incessantly about drugs. Which is better, heroin mixed with a bombita or with cocaine? Both cocaine and bombitas are stimulants, and either one combined with heroin, which is a depressant, produces a more pleasurable high than heroin alone. The mixture is called a "speedball." But cocaine is very expensive, so addicts agree that for the money, a bombita-and-heroin cannot be topped.

During one of these interminable conversations, someone said he had a friend who liked to shoot model airplane glue. No one else had heard of that. Sniffing glue, yes, but not shooting it. They had heard of people doing something to paregoric and shoe polish and then shooting it, but the high was reported to be no good. Heroin, of course, was the best. Heroin and a bombita. It gave the best high, completely relaxed, not a problem in the world.

But that's not really the best high, one addict said. Do you know what the best high *really* is? The voice was serious. Everyone turned and stayed very quiet to hear, maybe, of a new kind of high that was better than heroin, better than anything else. The best high—the voice was low and somber—is death. Silence. Man, that's outta sight, that's somethin' else. Yeah, no feelin' at all. Everyone agreed. The best high of all was death.

No square—the addict's word for anyone who does not use drugs—can imagine the strength of heroin's hold. The addict will beg for it, walk miles for it, wait hours for it, con for it, stay up days and nights on end to pursue it, steal from those he has loved for it, risk death for it.

The heroin addict is a very busy man. For those who would separate him from his heroin he has no use and no time. When he awakes in the morning he reaches instantly for his "works"—eyedropper, needle ("spike," he calls it) and bottle top ("cooker"). He dissolves heroin in water in the cooker and injects the mixture. This is his "wake-up," a morning shot to hold off the anxiety and sickness of withdrawal and get him "straight" enough to start the day. If his habit is costing him $20 a day, and that is not a large habit by any means, he must now start out to steal at least $100 worth of goods, knowing that a fence will give him only one fifth the true value of his loot. When he has stolen something, he must haggle with his fence over the price. The argument seems interminable to him, for it has now been hours since his wake-up and he is getting nervous again, his eyes are watering and he is beginning to feel like a man coming down with a bad case of flu.

Finally he gets the money and begins his search for a connection. Not just any connection, but a connection who deals in good quality stuff—"dynamite," not "garbage." Once the addict has bought his fix (has "copped" or "scored") he is faced with the risky business of getting it to his cooker and into his arm without getting caught and busted. When he has finally injected the heroin—he calls it "shooting up," "taking off," "getting off"—he may or may not go on a "nod"—his eyelids heavy, his mind wandering pleasantly—depending on how much heroin his body has become accustomed to and how much actual heroin was in the powder he injected.

He hopes that the shot will be at least strong enough to make him straight for a few hours. He can judge immediately the quality of the shot. If it is strong enough, he calms down, the flu feeling leaves and he instantly begins looking for money for the next shot.

The addict is haunted by anxieties, which only heroin can relieve. In the shaky families and oppressive environment of big-city slums, anxieties pile up fast—and it is in the teeming slums that heroin is handy. From friend to friend the drug spreads inexorably among the emotionally weak and unstable.

Junkies hang around Needle Park because it is surrounded by cheap hotels, needed by addict prostitutes; because three blocks away, a short walk for a sick junkie, are respectable neighborhoods good for burglary and "cracking shorts"—breaking into cars; and because, probably, a long time ago someone started selling dope there and the area just got to be known as a good place to score.

Today much of the heroin in Needle Park comes from a man who lives in a very nice apartment on a pleasant East Side street. He buys heroin in "pieces" (ounces), cuts it and bags it, and hands it over on consignment to a handful of pushers—junkies themselves—who sell it for him. The pushers do not really have to push. It's a seller's market with heroin, and junkies fight their way to any connection who has good stuff. The image of the sly pusher enticing nonusers into trying a free bag of heroin is pure myth.

The amount of payment the junkie pusher gets is the same anywhere in the city. Fifteen $3.00 bags are wrapped together with a rubber band (the package is called a half load). The pusher buys the package for $25, sells enough bags to recoup his investment and uses the rest himself. Often the junkie pusher will deal "nickel bags" at $5.00 each, as well as $3.00 "treys." These come in "bundles" similar to half loads, except that the package costs $75 and consists of twenty-five $5.00 bags. Sometimes a junkie pusher can get half loads or bundles on consignment. But if he decides to shoot up all the bags himself and beat the supplier for the money, his friends will soon be remarking that they haven't seen him around for a while. He usually keeps pushing until he is busted or until he gets scared and decides to stop pressing his luck with the police and returns to less serious crimes to finance his habit.

From time to time the addict may voluntarily interrupt his life on the street to enter a hospital.

His body has achieved such a high tolerance to heroin that he must shoot a huge number of bags—not just to get high, but to keep from getting sick. In the case of a prostitute, she may be getting so thin and sick-looking—so "strung out"—that she has been forced to reduce her price. In both cases the addict goes into a hospital to withdraw from the drug and get back to the point where just a bag or two will make him high.

The male junkie, when he isn't pushing, almost invariably turns to theft and burglary to support his habit. One of the most expert burglars among Needle Park junkies is John's brother, Bro. He is twenty-eight, with thick black hair and an intent, quiet face. He was first arrested—for purse snatching—when he was nine years old, and he mainlined his first heroin shot at thirteen. He has now done twenty "bits" in jail for a total of nine years, plus two years in the federal narcotics hospital at Lexington, Kentucky.

"I'm the best burglar on the West Side," he told me proudly one night. I was standing with him outside the door of a hotel room I had rented near Needle Park, fumbling in my pocket for the key. "Man, you don't need that," he said, and quickly slipped a celluloid card into the doorjamb. In an instant the door was open and Bro was in the room.

He has skill and daring—what junkies call "heart." "Burglary is my job," he explained soberly. "It's what I'm good at." In addition, he has an indispensable talent for talking his way out of tight spots. "You see," he said, "when I go into an apartment I jam the lock—stick some toothpicks in the keyhole and break them off—so if the people come back I can hear them trying to get their key in and can make it out the fire escape. But once in a while I get careless and don't jam the lock and then—well, like once this guy came back and got in the apartment and saw me.

"It was real tight, man. He was standing there with his wife and his little kid, and I grabbed the kid and said, 'Man, I don't want to do nothin' to the kid, but I'm a dope fiend and I'm real sick and I got to get out of here.' And I guess the guy thought I was really gonna hurt the kid or something—I mean, you couldn't blame him—and he let me go."

Bro is married, but his wife does not use drugs and so he spends as little time with her as he can get away with, preferring to stick with John and Karen and the other junkies. Often none of them has a hotel room and then they lounge around on the benches in Needle Park or in a nearby luncheonette, or just walk the streets. When Karen is working—and by that she means hustling, on the telephone with old customers when possible, on the street if necessary—she may end up with a room for the night and a little sleep.

That doesn't happen to John. If he cannot find a friend with a room, he walks around all night looking for cars to break into or for a place to lie down. Often he finds a public bathroom in one of the hotels around the park and sleeps there. Bro jokes about the time John actually moved into a fourth-floor bathroom in a hotel on Sherman Square. "I went looking for him there," Bro said, "and he even had laundry strung up in the place. A couple of more nights and the hotel would have put in a phone."

At one point John and Karen had a room in a tiny, seedy hotel sandwiched between more respectable hotels on West Seventy-second Street across from a row of high-rent apartment houses. The hotel did a fast business with prostitutes and junkies, possible because it had a night deskman who would send heroin to the room faster than you could get a ham on rye from room service at the Hilton. When a junkie has a hotel room, the word spreads fast. All his friends and their friends stream in and the place turns into a "shooting gallery."

I knocked on the door one night and John let me in. It was in the midst of a panic—a city-wide drug shortage—and the deskman was out of stuff. Heroin was so scarce addicts were kicking their habits in the street, and many had been forced to switch to barbiturates. The room was littered with the debris of addiction—bits of toilet paper and clothing that had been used to wipe blood from arms; glasses half filled with water tinted red from the cleaning of many needles; scraps of electric-light cord chopped up and separated into thin strands with which to unclog needles; charred metal bottle tops used for cookers. Everywhere on the floor—strewn so thick you could not see the carpet—were clothing, old comic books and cigarette butts. Sheets and blankets, cigarette holes burned in them by nodding addicts, had fallen from the bed and lay kicked into corners. Stuffing oozed from a waffle-sized burn in the mattress. The smell was of sweat and smoke and heroin.

Karen looked worse than I had ever seen her. Her eyes were widely dilated, partly from heroin withdrawal, partly from enormous doses of barbiturates. She had a $50 date with a "John" in New Jersey and Johnny and his friends were trying desperately to get her into shape for the trip. She was nearly unconscious. Two men held her up, and another whose name was Ronnie brushed her hair for her. "Come on, Karen," Ronnie pleaded, "you got to make that train. You got to get out there, baby. You can't miss this trick, Karen, you got to make it." She mumbled and slouched in her supporters' arms, and Ronnie kept brushing.

Johnny walked over to a corner of the room that was stacked high with cases of coffee and cellophane packages of women's hair curlers. He and a friend had spotted a truck unloading supplies onto a sidewalk in front of a grocery store. They had grabbed everything they could carry and ran with it in their arms to the hotel. Now they were going to try to sell the haul.

The men who had been holding up Karen sat her down on the bed. She fell back, anesthetized by the barbiturates. Someone knocked on the door and Johnny yelled at the men, "There's too much noise in here! Can't you guys shut up? That's probably the cops now. You make so much racket they could hear you inside the station house." He walked to the door and whispered, "Who is it?"

"It's the FBI." It was Bro's voice. Johnny opened the door. "Funny," he said as Bro slipped past him and sat down on the edge of the bed. He glanced at Karen and shook his head in mock distaste. He had a bag of heroin and dumped the powder into a bottle top. "Where'd you get that?" Johnny demanded.

Bro gave the name of a connection. "It's probably garbage." He produced a bombita, broke off the glass top and poured the fluid in with the heroin. Bro held a match under the cooker until the white powder dissolved. Then he put the tip of the needle —the same one Ronnie and Karen and the other men had used—into a pea-sized wad of cotton (used to filter out large impurities that might clog the needle) and drew up the liquid from the bottom of the cooker. Borrowing Ronnie's belt, he wrapped it around his arm, held the end in his teeth, stuck the needle into a vein and waited for the blood to start backing up into the eyedropper. Instead of shooting the fluid in immediately he squeezed in a few drops, let it back up into the eyedropper again, squeezed a little more, let it back up, squeezed in more, and continued the in-and-out process until the fluid in the dropper was dark red with blood.

The technique, known as "booting," is believed to prolong the drug's initial effect. He continued booting until there was so much blood in the dropper he was afraid it would coagulate and clog the needle. Then he shot it all in and withdrew the needle. Had the needle clogged, he would have dumped the mixture of blood and drugs back into the cooker, heated it until the blood dissolved and started over. Addicts call this "shooting gravy": "Because that's what it is—right? Cooked blood?"

Bro put the dropper and needle into a glass of water. "How is it?" one of the men asked. "Garbage," Bro said. "All I feel's the bombita."

Ronnie had Karen sitting up on the edge of the bed and was brushing her hair again, begging her to stay awake. But it was hopeless; she was too far gone to make her New Jersey date until the next afternoon.

The phone rang and Johnny talked on it for a minute and then announced he was leaving to sell some stolen coffee to a grocer. Around Needle Park it is not uncommon for addicts to steal from one grocer and sell to another, or to steal meat from a supermarket and sell it to a restaurant. "At one point," Johnny said, "Karen and I were robbing every candy store in the area, mostly for cigarettes. We told one candy-store guy that if he bought all our cigarettes, we'd leave him alone. We did quite a business for a while."

Johnny loaded three coffee cases into the elevator and I rode down with him. He put them out next to the desk in the lobby and we sat and talked while he waited for someone to pick them up.

Stringent search and seizure laws make it difficult for detectives to produce unshakable evidence against addicts and addict pushers. Merely being an addict is not a crime in New York; he must have drugs or a hypodermic needle in his possession. Many addicts—especially pushers—wear a rubber band on their wrists (a "dealer's band," some call it) which, if hooked properly around a deck of heroin, will send it flying if an approaching detective is spotted.

But when police are in a drug neighborhood they have no difficulty spotting addicts on the street. An experienced narcotics cop can with surprising reliability spot a user in a group of twenty people, state with authority what kind of drug he is on, approximately how long it has been since his last fix and whether or not he is at that moment "dirty," carrying drugs. Because heroin subdues appetite, the addict is almost always thin. He has a craving for sweets, and often carries a bottle of soda pop (although he may know that, to a detective, it is a badge of addiction). The backs of his hands are chronically puffed and swollen from shooting in the veins there.

The addict is habitually dirty, his clothes filthy and he stands slackly as if his body were without muscles. Waiting for a connection, he is nervous and intent, staring for minutes at a time in the direction from which he expects the pusher to come. Detectives know that when a group of addicts is standing around, talking, waiting, none of them is carrying heroin. But if you watch the group long enough suddenly it explodes, all the addicts walking off in different directions. The pusher has appeared and soon, one by one, they will make their roundabout way to him to cop.

Once the addict has drugs on him, he keeps moving. He is about to achieve the one thing for which he lives, and he is not slow about it. His shoulders are hunched, his head is down and he strikes out with what some detectives call a "leaving-the-set walk," as if he had just learned where a million dollars was hidden. When the heroin addict is high, his pupils are "pinned," constricted, and if the shot was sufficiently powerful and he goes on a nod, his head droops, eyelids heavy.

But though he appears terribly sleepy, he speaks coherently. His mind wanders, he daydreams, and everything he does, he does with maddening slowness. He can take thirty minutes to tie his shoelaces. But he always resists admitting that he is on a nod. He is very sleepy, he says, and if he stops talking in midsentence, he argues that he is not nodding, only trying to phrase the sentence properly. Once the addict has had his shot and is straight, he may become admirably, though briefly, industrious, suddenly deciding to shine his shoes, brush his coat, comb his hair—all the while scolding himself bitterly for having slipped so far.

Even the seasons conspire to identify addicts. In winter, waiting to cop, they alone stand around in the snow and slush, apparently aimlessly. In summer, they alone wear long sleeves (to cover their "tracks"—needle marks). Because heroin users almost always feel cold, they wear piles of sweaters, even in hot weather.

When male and female addicts gather together, in a hotel room or public bathroom, the narcotics detective knows better than to suspect sexual activity. Heroin depresses sexual desire—men may become impotent, women often do not menstruate. (If a woman gives birth while she is addicted to heroin the infant also will be physically addicted and must live the first three days withdrawing from the drug.) For most heroin addicts a sex crime would be impossible, and they are all contemptuous of stories about the "raging, dope-fiend, sex maniac."

Almost all heroin addicts are childishly immature: full of demands, empty of offerings. When they want something, they want it yesterday and they want it effortlessly. Nothing is their fault—their addiction, their degradation, their desperation. All are insecure, most dislike people, and—though the mechanics of obtaining and injecting drugs forces them into relationships with other people—most would prefer to be alone.

None can tolerate "changes." If the junkie goes looking for a connection and does not find him on the right corner at the right time, he grumbles about all the changes. Almost everything he is forced to do involves too many changes. He must go through changes to steal, to find a fence, to get a shot, to avoid police. He prefers simple, nonviolent crimes—theft, burglary, prostitution.

When they are off heroin, addicts tend to be morose and restless. On heroin, when they are straight, they are pleasant, gentle, likable. Psychiatrists who have studied them over long periods know that most of them are extremely narcissistic, that their intense preoccupation with heroin is a surface manifestation of a more profound emotional preoccupation with themselves.

In pursuit of the drug they can bring to bear extraordinary cunning, nerve and acting ability. But once they have the fix in hand and the problem shifts from how to get drugs to how to avoid arrest, these qualities vanish. An addict who is arrested because a detective discovered heroin hidden in his pants cuff may, once he is released, immediately buy a deck of heroin and hide it in his pants cuff.

Perhaps the dominant emotional characteristic of the addict is his enormous compulsion to abdicate all responsibility for his own life. He craves to be told what to do. If he is encouraged to go to a hospital by someone he trusts, he will go. But soon, when he finds the hospital not to his liking, he will leave, and then blame the failure not on himself but on the person who urged him to go. An addict will walk along a street openly displaying a container of drugs, all but asking to be arrested. If a detective does spot the drug and arrests him, the addict will blame it on bad luck. He thus purges himself of the responsibility of choosing between jail and abstinence or continued addiction on the street. He feels he has left the choice to fate.

Female addict prostitutes may, for the same reason, solicit men who are almost certainly detectives. One psychiatrist reported that when one of his addict patients saw another patient in an artificial lung, she became enraged and demanded the lung for herself, unconsciously demonstrating her wish to relinquish to the lung her ultimate responsibility —breathing.

After I had known John and Karen for a couple of months, I sat down with them individually and we talked of familiar events and ideas, and about some subjects that had never before been mentioned. Because most drug addicts, particularly those in big cities, live similar lives and display common symptoms, these tape-recorded conversations reveal much about the lives and personalities not only of John and Karen, but of the many thousands of other young people who suffer from drug addiction. Just as the paralytic's every step is twisted by his affliction, so every word an addict speaks is colored by

the symptoms of his disease—self-deception, imma-
turity, insecurity, guilt.

The morning the conversation with Karen occurred she was lying on a dirty, bare hotel mattress,
relaxing under the effects of a shot taken thirty minutes earlier. She had just discovered lice crawling
on her and had placed one of them on a table by the
bed. She stared at it while I connected the recorder.

"I can't stand these terrible things," she almost
shouted. "The filthy little things! Johnny must have
brought them home from jail. I put it on the table
there so I can see how tiny it is and then it doesn't
scare me so much."

"Karen, when did you first use illegal drugs?"

"I got this awful toothache and Johnny gave me a
shot, and it took the pain away, and it also took my
fear of drugs away. So I started doing it myself,
while Johnny'd be in the bedroom sleeping. I was
scared to death of Johnny catching me. And I had a
habit before I knew it. We were living right in the
same house and for a long time he didn't know I was
using it. I liked it. It made me very relaxed, very
high. I grooved with it. I dig junk. I won't kid anybody. I dig the high, the whole bit. I like the feeling.
I like the feeling of *not* feeling.

"What is it the Spanish say? *No siento nada*—I
feel nothing. That's just the way you get to feel—
nothing. *Nothing* fazes you. You could hear about
your mother dying an excruciating death and you
wouldn't even shed a tear. And I was still hooking
then—$100 dates, making maybe $2,200 a week.
Meanwhile Johnny was just sitting home doing
nothing. Shooting up, sleeping, watching TV, read-

ing comic books, having his buddies over, turning them on. He had a real ball."

"What do you think of other junkies, junkies in general?"

"They're pigs. I can't stand them."

"Why not?"

"I'm probably looking in a mirror and can't stand it. They're animals. We're all animals. We'll step on one another for a shot if there's no dope. I've seen it. I can't even trust Johnny. I had my wake-up shot three days ago right here on the table. When I got up, it was gone and Johnny was the only one that was straight that morning. Everyone was sick but Johnny. And I *know* Johnny didn't have a wake-up of his own.

"And I'm just as bad. I don't live from day to day or paycheck to paycheck. I live from fix to fix. Yesterday morning, as sick as I was, Johnny insisted that I go with this John. Johnny brought him up here and I turned the trick. I gave the money to Johnny, but I never saw any junk for it.

"I'm no different from any of the others. I'll beat somebody for their money just as fast as look at them. That's why I say we're animals. One time when I was sick myself, a girl came up here and she had $30. She said, 'Karen, can you cop?' I said, 'Yes.' I took the money and never came back. I didn't intend to come back from the very beginning. She waited ten hours for me, and I never came back."

"Karen, have you ever used a knife on anybody?"

"No. But I could, and I know how. I'm capable. And I'll cut anybody who threatens me. Like I said, that's what I mean about being an animal. Three years ago I couldn't have hurt a fly. But when you don't care about your own life—that much—then you know what you care about someone else's life. And when someone threatens the little bit of care you do have for your own life, then you know what you're going to do to them. If they're gonna hurt me, I could kill somebody and it wouldn't faze me. Just like Freddy—you know Freddy—said he ripped somebody's stomach wide open and when he found out his guts weren't falling out, he put his hand in and pulled them out. He made sure that guy died. And I could do the same thing."

"Has Johnny ever cut you?"

"Yes. He went crazy behind bombitas. He didn't cut me badly. I broke the blade of the knife off. But when you can't get stuff and you get sick, you get desperate. Like, let me tell you what you go through sometimes just trying to cop. When you cop, you don't know whether you're going to get it home. Let me tell you what goes on in your mind.

"All right, let's say it costs me $10 to get a fix—two nickel bags. Okay. Well, I have my $10. Now, if I can't locate a connection around Needle Park, what I have to do is go uptown. Last night I went up to 112th Street in Harlem, where the better junk is. Once I'm there, I walk with a knife opened, like this. That's the way you have to walk up there. They see a white in Harlem and they're ready to jump all over you. So you walk up there with a knife out—or like Julio did the other day. He carries a .45 right out in the open. Okay. I have my $10. I want to get two $5.00 bags. So I go and ask someone. 'Who's got the best stuff around here?' 'Chico has.' Okay. Chico has. Then someone says, 'Emmanuel has.' So I have to find out who's who and who has the better stuff. Emmanuel or Chico.

"Meanwhile you're walking on this street, you know darn well The Man [any cop] is watching you. You know it. You feel it. But you don't care because you're sick. So you're going to take that chance anyway. Now, you don't want to jeopardize the connection either. So all right, you're gonna cop off Chico. You walk by Chico and say 'I want two,' and keep walking. Then you turn around and you come back and you give him the money and at the same time you say you want two. Then you come back and he gives you the two.

"Now if Chico decides to beat you, Chico's just gonna turn around and walk away. And you're dead. Your $10 is gone with the wind. Or maybe you're gonna get the stuff home and find it's baking soda. The fellow you met steered you wrong because he's getting a piece of it. This doesn't often happen when it's not panic time.

"Now, after you cop, most of the time you have to walk home because you don't have that much money for a cab. Buses take too long, and you're standing on that corner with stuff on you. So all the time you're walking, you're praying too. You are saying to yourself, 'Is there a narco around that knows my face and is going to call me over just for the hell of it?' Which they do. Meanwhile, you've got stuff on you, and you're sick. You never know—you're never relaxed until you feel the stuff in you, and even then you know that within four hours you've got to get some more money, and get more stuff again. This is gonna go on and on. And you know that before you go to bed that night you not only have to have your bedtime fix but you have to have your wake-up. So that's $20 right there that you *must* have, you absolutely *must* have. And you have to cop before you go to bed because when you wake up you might be too sick to be able to go out and cop."

"Karen, I know you can think up a very glib story and with your acting ability deliver it to a doctor and get a prescription. Can you do this with other people as well?"

"I can do this with anyone. Anybody I want to do something for me, I can make them do it. Just by talking. I've been able to do that since I was a little girl, since I first told a lie to my father. My father was very strict. I had to think up reasons to get out of the house to do the things I wanted to do. So that was what I did. I started on my father. It worked on him, it worked on my mother, it worked on my teachers and it worked on everybody else. The only thing you really need is a sincere approach. If someone thinks you're sincere, they'll do anything in the world for you.

"If ever I was going to get a licking—not a licking, but a punishment, rather—that I didn't want, I used to cry and say, 'Gee, I'm sorry.' They felt so bad about my feeling sorry that they wouldn't do anything. I was a cute little girl—until they started telling me what to do and my father started to be a tyrant. My father started to use military tactics on me. Never hit me! But he messed my mind up. I had to sit on a straight-backed chair for three or four hours at a time with my hands folded without talking. Three years old. Or he made me stand at attention three or four hours till my back felt like it was breaking. I never cried to my father, or to my mother—she was an angel—but I cried to my aunts and uncles. I got what I wanted."

"Karen, have you ever been sorry that you went on the stuff three years ago?"

"I imagine that I've been sorry every day that I've had a habit."

"Why don't you kick and get clean and be square?"

"That's probably what will happen eventually."

"Why don't you do it now? Why didn't you do it a year ago?"

"Johnny didn't want to do it then."

"All right then, why don't you do it now?"

"I might, I just might do that. I don't want to start right into a job. I want to go on a vacation first somewhere. I want to go to Puerto Rico."

"How long ago did you have your last shot?"

"Half an hour ago."

"Do you ever look at a square girl on the street—"

"And envy her? Yes. Every day. Because she doesn't know what I know. I could never be a square like that. I was once, but once I took that shot, that shattered the whole bit—because then I knew. I knew what it was to be high. I knew what it was to groove with junk. Even the first habit that I kicked, which was the worst that I ever kicked, I kicked cold turkey of my own volition—and I still went back to junk. Right in this very hotel. I bought my first fix right here. Why? Oh, I don't know. I found some excuse or another to do it. I'll tell you right now. I wouldn't care if I died. I just hope it isn't painful, that's all."

"What do you think is going to become of you eventually, Karen?"

"I don't know. I'll probably die—early. It won't be from junk, but it'll be from something connected with junk. Hepatitis or something. I don't care any more. I really don't. Because there's nothing for me. I don't have any reason to quit using."

"Isn't it enough of a reason that you wouldn't be living the kind of life you live now?"

"That means nothing to me. I don't give a good damn."

The conversation with John was recorded in the same hotel room his brother Bro had entered so effortlessly with a celluloid card. John had just injected a bombita and began to talk long and easily about his addiction, his career as a pusher and his relationship with Karen.

"Johnny, how old were you the first time you used any drugs?"

"About thirteen. I smoked some pot. And I've seen drugs practically all my life. My brother was already hooked, not just starting but already hooked, at thirteen when he was still going to school. I was going with this girl, and like I used to walk the straight and narrow line. And then I think I had an argument with her, and instead of going drinking to get drunk, I went and bought a stick of pot. I was started. Ever since then, boy, I've been going real strong."

"How did you meet Karen?"

"My brother and his girl were living in Karen's apartment. And one day I went to visit them and my brother brought me into the bedroom and says, 'Karen, this is Johnny, the brother I was telling you about.' And like the first words out of her mouth made me turn like blood red. She said, 'Oh, yeah, but he's cuter than what you said he was.'

"Now I wasn't used to talk like that, because I'd been away at jail for three years and hadn't so much as kissed a girl. And I've always been kind of shy of girls when I first meet them. Usually when I first meet people I'm quiet. I sit and find out what kind of people they are before I even commit myself. So like right away when I blushed she thought it was cute. She started teasing me. So we got along right away.

"I wanted to get high. So I told my brother, I says, 'I want to get high.' So he says no. Now, Karen's listening to this—like she was *death* on drugs. She was *death*. Karen says, 'No, don't give him any.' So I said, 'The hell with you. I got money, I know where to score. I'll see you later.' So I started going out the door and my brother said, 'Look, Karen, one of my other brothers went with somebody else to get high and they left him, and he died. I don't want it to happen to Johnny.' So after she thought about it, she said, 'All right.'

"So I got high. I got high and then I left and when I was leaving I turned around to Karen and told her, 'Karen, I like you. You're real people.' Because like every hooker I've ever met—I'd never made it with a hooker before. Like, when you walk into the house and they first meet you, they start talking hundred dollar bills, five hundred dollar bills. I don't know, they're phonies. And she was regular people—like for real.

"And the second day I came downtown from the Bronx and I walk into this restaurant and they were sitting in the back. She had black slacks on and a black jacket and a black scarf. And I hadn't seen her before with any makeup on. It was raining out and I had an umbrella in my hand and I looked at my brother and I says, 'You told me she was pretty.' And like I could see that she was starting to get insulted, probably thinking like I was going to say she was ugly. But then I said, 'She's not pretty, she's beautiful.' And she didn't know how to act behind that.

"And neither did I after I said it. I was hung up for words. I started to turn red again. We went out and started running through the rain. We wound up in a drugstore and there was an iron Karen liked, a clothes iron, and they wanted $7.00 for it. So my brother said, 'Karen for a couple more dollars you could get a big steam iron.' She says, 'Yeah, but it's nice, I want it. I'm going to get it.' So I liked that. I went for the way she came on with it. So it stuck in my mind. I like people that if they want something, they'll get it. I'm like that myself. If I can't buy it, I'll steal it. If I can't steal it, I'll get it some way. Anyway, she bought the iron.

"So the next night I went over and my brother and his girl left and now my hand accidentally bumped against Karen's arm and her skin was *so* smooth, like I was fascinated by it. It was like silk. And then all these other people came over and Karen says, 'Everybody has to go, I'm going to sleep.' So I started to put my coat on. I figured she meant me too, and I was on parole anyway. I had to be home at certain times. And my brother says, 'Take your coat off. Karen says she wants you to stay.' And I says to my brother, 'I'm on parole. And if the parole officer comes over to the house, it's going to be all over.' So anyway, all he had to do was say it one more time. 'Karen wants you to stay.' That was it. I took my coat off. Ever since then, we've been together."

"She wasn't using drugs then?"

"No. And she was some beautiful girl. We used to go out for a walk and people used to look at her—twice. Boy, she was a doll. And then once we were in the bedroom, and we were lying down talking. And out of nowhere she says, 'Johnny, I'm on stuff.' I looked at her and says, 'What do you mean, you're on stuff?' She says, 'I've been using behind your back the past six months.' I don't know how I felt. But I felt so empty. Like I wanted to get up and bash her brains against the wall. And then I felt sorry for her.

"She's been using stuff ever since then. But even before she was using, she had this problem with her own mind—not sure whether she wanted to go with girls or boys. So like she was very unsure of herself, very insecure. And I started going with her and eventually, as the time went on, she found out, like she wasn't gay. And like she was always afraid, and then, I don't know, as time went on, she realized like she loved me. Like it was me and only me—first, last and always. Since then like everything was like real sweet.

"So anyway, she was hooking when I met her. So I didn't go for that at all, because I had never made it with a hooker before. So one night she had a date and she told me to come back later, in an hour or something like that. I came back later, I rang the bell and walked through the front door and was going to the apartment, and the door opened and she had the chain on it and she stuck her hand out. And I stopped dead right in the hallway. I don't know if I wanted to cry, run, kick the door in. I didn't know what to do, I was so hurt.

"Ever since that time, every time she'd go out with a trick, I'd get an attitude. Or if the trick would come over, I'd just be sulky, nasty with the trick. Even today I don't like her hustling. I'd rather have her stay home and I got to go out and steal. I don't think you or anybody else can understand the way I felt standing in the hallway—like, the only person I really loved in there with someone else. And like stopping me from coming in. Even today when we get to talking, like that always comes up. I never liked her to hook. Like a lot of times I tell her, 'Don't go out. Stop hooking. Get a job.'

"She's very timid in a lot of ways. She has to have me to lean on. With little problems she'd come to me. She'd cry in her sleep. She'd wake up crying. If somebody would wake her up too hard, she'd cry. It's hard to explain, I just never liked her to hook. She used to make like at least $1,500 a week, maybe more. Even with that money coming in—and most of it going on clothes and me, nothing but the best she used to get me—and even with that, I would have rather give that up than have her go out with other guys. Even today, like she's got two habits to support. I don't do anything. I don't contribute anything. Except another problem, another habit to support. And my love for her, that's all."

"Johnny, do you and Karen ever fight?"

"Do we fight? Boy! Like yesterday she woke up real sick. She had given somebody $25. She wanted to surprise me by coming home with the stuff instead of coming home and giving me the money and having me go out and get it. She wanted to surprise me by waking up and saying, 'Here, Johnny,' and I could just get off in bed. That's what she used to do—wake me up and have my fix ready, like breakfast in bed.

"Well, she gave the guy $25. He went uptown. This was nine o'clock in the morning. At nine at night we finally find out where he lives and we go up there and he says, 'Look, I don't know how to tell you, but I got beat.' Now that's twelve hours we're waiting for him. He could have called and we could have went out and got some money. We didn't get straight until about three o'clock this morning. And my last shot before that was close to maybe eighteen, twenty hours, something like that. It was a long time.

"When she woke up, she was very sick. She had a bombita and a $3.00 bag. And she started putting it on the cooker. I told her, 'Leave half of it in the cooker for me.' Now, we'd be lucky if *two* $3.00 bags would straighten either one of us out—the way stuff is out there now—never mind one, never mind *half* of one. She looked at me like I was crazy.

"She said, 'Johnny, it's only a $3.00 bag.' I says, 'I

know what it is, leave half of it for me.' She says, 'Johnny'—she started crying—'Johnny, I'm sick. Please let me do it and I'll go out and get some money fast. I'll turn a trick or something. I can get money faster if I'm straight,' which is true. I would probably have got straight in an hour.

"But I was like cold-blooded. I told her, 'I don't want to hear no stories. Leave half in the cooker, or I'm going to take it all.'

"It's not like me to do something like that. That's just vengeance, some kind of vengeance. I'm very spiteful. Like if I have an argument with somebody and they bite me on my big toe, you know eventually I'm going to get their big toe and bite it back. I don't like myself like that. It scares me. Maybe it wouldn't even bother me with someone else. But with her, who's supposed to mean so much to me, that I could do something like that and threaten to take the whole thing, knowing that neither one of us are going to get straight, maybe just get the edges taken off. If I'm going to keep that up, she can get somebody a whole lot better than me.

"A while ago we had an argument and she got scared and started running up these stairs. And her being afraid of me like that, that got me mad. She ran up to the sixth floor—as sick as she was—and ran into a bathroom and locked the door and tried to hide from me. You do something like that with an animal. You hide from an animal. She wouldn't open the door. I threatened to kick the panel out and she finally opened it. And she was in the shower stall, crouched down like a real refugee. You see them picture posters of refugees crouched down, and the *fear* that she had on her face, and the *shaking.* She was actually, really shaking. Afterwards she couldn't hold the cooker steady. I tell you, I'll leave her for good before I keep putting her through that. I don't want her to be afraid."

"When you were pushing, Johnny, what's the largest amount you ever bought—to put into bags and resell?"

"Three pieces, three ounces."

"How many bags will that make?"

"That depends how many times you cut it. Some connections used to cut it four to one, maybe five to one. But I only cut mine three and a half times. That way it would be very strong. And I put the rest of the connections in my neighborhood out of business.

"I used to get very good stuff. I went up to this guy's house and he cut it for me. You stretch a nylon stocking over a wire hanger, put the stuff on it and run over it with a spoon. And it flows through the nylon and gets fluffed up. And after that you cut it with quinine and milk sugar. And after it's mixed you have these stamp collectors' bags, little glassine envelopes, and you have these baby measuring spoons, like a mother uses with her kids. You put the stuff in one of the small spoons and run a razor over the top to flatten it out. Then you put it into the bag, wrap it up, put tape on it and you've got yourself a bag. And then you go out and sell it."

"How much does your habit cost you a day?"

"I'll tell you, when people tell you, like they're using $50 a day, they can't tell you that. They don't really know how much heroin they're using. Like I might find old Joe Schmo today and buy three bags from him and find that one bag straightens me out. Now, okay, so I'll time my shots and get away with $15 today. Tomorrow I can't find Joe Schmo so I go and find Larry the Jerk, and I buy three off him and one don't straighten me out, and maybe three won't straighten me out. So, actually how much you use depends on the quality of the stuff.

"Like right now the stuff is so weak that to find somebody on the streets that you can really say has a real bad habit would be doing something. I mean, it's not like it used to be. I've seen guys come into jail and, like the expression goes, they kicked their habit on the elevator. In two or three days they're eating, sleeping, doing pushups.

"So it depends on the quality. I can't say I use this much or that much. I used to use a lot. Even today, if I have ten bags in the morning, I won't have anything left that night, or maybe not even that afternoon. I just can't hold onto stuff without shooting it. I won't actually get greedy and shoot it all at once but like, whenever it enters my mind to get off, I just get off. I can't hold onto it."

"Johnny, when you go to a hospital or to jail and you get clean, why do you always go back on drugs?"

"Well, the longest I ever stayed clean on the street on my own was when one of my older brothers died of an overdose. I didn't want to use drugs. I think it was like two weeks, three weeks. I thought I would really do it—stay clean—because of my brother. And then, one day I was with one of my other brothers and I saw this kid I knew standing on the corner. He was sick. I was leading a good life. I was happy. He was sick. So I said to him, 'What are you shooting, what's your fix?' And he says, 'Two bags.' So I give him $6.00. And I know where he's going and what he's going to do, and I know the feeling he's going to get.

"It must have hit my mind all the way back. I looked at my brother. He knew what was on my mind and he like shrugged his shoulders, like to say, 'I don't care.' So I said to the kid, 'Look, here's another $6.00. Get two more.' So we got up to the bathroom in some hotel and the kid got off first because he was sick, and my brother got off and then I drew up the stuff and I just kept sitting around with it in my hand. And I kept thinking about my dead brother. And I didn't want to use it because of what happened to him. Then I says to myself, only it was like to him, 'I hope you'll understand. You know what it's like.' And I got off. After almost squirting it on the floor maybe four or five times. But finally I shot it. And ever since then . . ."

"What do you think of junkies in general, Johnny?"

"Well, I wouldn't put my money in another junkie's hand unless I really, really trusted him. I've been beat by my own brother, and if my brother's going to run around and beat me, who can I trust? I can't trust nobody out there. Even Karen has gotten off behind my back. Like all the times I've stayed sixteen, seventeen, eighteen hours without a fix and she disappeared someplace, and I *know* she's not going to go that long without a fix. She can tell me anything she wants, but I know Karen. And she'll come back and tell me she hasn't gotten off, but she's high. A couple of times she's been gone all day and if I didn't do anything I'd be sick when she came back. But when she came back, she'd have a bag of stuff to get me straight and I'd get off first before I even started arguing with her. And then I'd be happy I was straight and I'd only give her like half an argument.

"You can't trust junkies. But after using drugs for so long, they're like my people. That's what I call them, my people. I can't get along with square people. If I'm walking in the streets, anywhere, I walk pretty fast and if somebody's in front of me I get very, very aggravated with them. I'll shoot around them and I might say something under my breath or I might say, 'Move it the hell out of the way.' I don't like people. Maybe if I got back off drugs and got a job, I might try to force it from myself. Maybe in a week or two it'll just come back."

"What do you think is going to become of you, Johnny?"

"I don't know what's going to happen. But I've had it with drugs. I'm going to stop. I've had enough of it. If I want to go back to it ten years from now, it will still be out there. I can always get it. And if I can't make the square life, if I find it too rough—which I doubt—the stuff will always be on the corners, the connections will always be there. It's been there for hundreds of years, and it'll be there for another hundred years."

"Well, Johnny, what is it that keeps you around Needle Park?"

"Nothing, I just don't have anyplace else to go. That's the whole thing in a nutshell. I could go to my parents upstate. Like, Monday I'm going home. I want to clean up. I want to get a job. I want to be square again. I'm tired of this life. I've had it. I'm ready to stop. And I'm ready to take on responsibilities of all kinds that I should be able to—as a man. Instead of using escapes, all kinds of escapes."

"How long has it been, Johnny, since you've had a fix?"

"Two or three hours."

"How long do you think it will be before you get off again?"

"Maybe right after I leave here."

"Well, then, why do you say that you've had it with drugs?"

"Well, after Monday, anyway."

SEVEN

BEFORE HE SHOT HIMSELF, OTHER DETECTIVES liked to give Bob Kenney nicknames. Mostly, they called him Sam Huff because he had the build and temperament of a middle linebacker—big, tough and very, very determined. He knew the streets and he knew violence, and he knew you couldn't write a book of rules to tell someone how to handle either. He handled both with common sense and a lot of muscle, and he knew his bosses were behind him, maybe a little bit to one side but back there somewhere behind him.

Kenney's partner in the rough New York streets around Times Square was George Barrett. Seven years before Kenney's death, Barrett had sat in a Times Square bar, in amongst the hoodlums, pimps and off-duty muggers, and told a reporter why he liked to work with Sam Huff. "If you're standing outside a door with Sam and there's a real bad guy inside and you say, 'Okay, Sam, let's go,' he's going to hit that door and go right through it. Whereas most guys would start reciting sections of the penal code to you. They know there's a bad guy in there,

but they want to try the case out in the hall before
they go in."

Going through doors before the case is tried can
be a dangerous way of doing things. Sometimes it
can get you shot, and sometimes it can get you pros-
ecuted. "Old-school" detectives like Kenney and
Barrett took the risks.

The slug Bob Kenney used to kill himself was
what cops call a "boon stopper," a lead bullet cut off
flat at the end. It's what you want when you go
through a door. It'll stop anything—a truck, a
baboon, a very large and determined man.

Kenney lay in an open coffin at his wake—civilian
clothes, his gold shield pinned proudly to his jacket
pocket. The entrance wound in the front of his head
was clean and neat and expertly covered with cos-
metics. The hole torn out of the back of his head by
hot, expanding, splattered lead was mercifully out
of sight. Kenney's wife and teen-age daughter sat
composed and dignified by the coffin, quietly greeting the lines of police officers who came to pay respect.

Barrett stood around with the other cops and remarked quietly that some of their wives had come
to him privately since Kenney's death and asked
that he try to talk their husbands into retiring. He
left and went across the street to a tavern to have a
drink with some other detectives, old friends of
Kenney. Talk turned, as it inevitably does, to the
continuing investigations of police, to the use of
cops to set up other cops, to police who wear eaves-
dropping equipment while encouraging fellow officers to speak incriminatingly. A twenty-three-

year-old detective was there, one of the so-called
new breed. He was tall, good-looking, very bright,
had a master's degree in criminal justice. The department had put him in an intelligence unit working against organized crime. Lately he'd been
spending a lot of time looking over his shoulder.
"You go all day worrying about two things," he said.
"Who your partners are and where you're going to
have lunch."

Of course he knew who his partners were supposed to be, who they said they were. But who were
they really? Who did they work for really? Were
they "wired"? Was someone playing back recordings of his conversations, searching for something
that could "make a case"? Even a place to have
lunch was a problem. Is something going on in this
restaurant that I might be associated with if I'm
seen eating there? Is it bugged? Is it watched?

Another detective gave him some advice. "Don't
worry about your partners," he said. "Don't *have*
partners. Work alone."

"Right!" a third man said. "When I'm with my
partners I just go through the motions. Don't do
nothing. Forget it. When I work, I work by myself."

Another detective walked in, a bright, cheerful
man who'd been a cop for twenty-five years and
used to work with Kenney and Barrett. He moved
quickly down the bar, frisking the other cops.
"Okay," he said finally, "who's got the wire? There
can't be this many of you here and no one's got a
wire."

A few nights later, Barrett was back in Times
Square. He'd been retired for several years and his

old station house had been torn down. Barrett had one of the bricks on the bar in his home. This night he had just come from a dinner meeting of the police Honor Legion, an organization of cops who've been decorated for bravery. He was with Mike O'Dowd, a huge, broken-faced longshoreman who was once Rocky Marciano's sparring partner. When they needed someone with a toughest-man-in-the-world face to play in *On the Waterfront,* they went down to the docks and picked out Mike. Since then he's done TV commercials and movie bit parts.

Barrett was recalling anecdotes about his work with Kenney. "We had this big guy in the cage, and he was really giving it to Sam Huff." The prisoner, a mugger with a long record, was in the squad room's wire-mesh detention cage, yelling and swearing at detectives, complainants and other prisoners. He started in on Kenney, suggesting that Kenney perform a sex act upon him. Kenney took the abuse stoically. Then, as he was walking past the cage, the man placed his penis through the wire and again told Kenney what he could do. Kenney turned and kicked the man on the only part of his body he could get to.

Later, in court, the man's attorney tried to use the incident to discredit Kenney. "What did the defendant say to you in the squad room?" he yelled at Kenney. Kenney told him. "And what did the defendant then do?" Kenney told him. "And after he had done that, what did he say to you?" Kenney said the man suggested that he perform an unnatural act. The lawyer, triumphant now, closing in for the kill, demanded, "And *then*, Detective Kenney, what did you do *then?*"

Kenney smiled. "I declined, naturally."

The laughter continued so long the judge had to recess the trial.

Kenney had retired from the department less than six months before his death. He was only forty-four, not an easy age to jump into retired life after twenty-plus years as a New York detective. When George Barrett left the force, he softened the blow by taking a security job in a large company. But Kenney didn't do that. He wasn't working at all. "You leave the job," Barrett said, "and whatever you do it's like going from the Yankees to the Newark Bears. But you can't think about it. You've got to go on to something else."

A long time ago Barrett said that what he really wanted in life was to be a sheriff out in Wyoming, "where people still know the difference between the cops and the robbers." He remembered that now. "I'm still going to do that," he said. "I've got some money saved and I'm going to find some county that needs a sheriff for a few thousand a year. You can't think about when you were on the job. You've got to forget it and move on to bigger and better things."

When they got in a cab at the end of the evening, Mike O'Dowd sat in front. The driver got a look at Mike's face and hulk, then turned to the back seat and said, "Is he safe?"

Barrett laughed. "Just don't pull on his leash."

In a restaurant in Queens, a detective who never knew Bob Kenney talks about a nightmare—a week-long period when he thought corruption investigators were trying to set him up. A lawyer had told a client that he needed money to give to the detective as a bribe. Unaware that the lawyer intended to keep the money for himself, the client, an accused thief, reported the case to the Internal Affairs Division, a police unit that investigates cops. The detective got wind of the report and, while pursuing his regular investigations, he kept an eye out for signs that he was being watched. He found signs. He became convinced. "I *knew* I was being set up." He stayed awake nights trying to figure out how to protect himself. Finally he decided to report his suspicions to his squad commander. "I walked in to see him, and there was another lieutenant in his chair. Like he's replacing the regular guy for a couple of days." Fearful that the new man was a plant, the detective decided not to trust him and said nothing. "I knew they were setting me up. I was so scared. And, you know, you think about your family, about the disgrace, and really—I really started to think about the Dutch act." The Dutch act is suicide.

Later the detective made his arrest, proved his case and the investigation against him halted.

How does this detective feel about the new department, the investigations, the retirements, the morale? "A lot of good men . . ." he says, and then stops. His face contorts—half pain, half contempt. "A lot of good men, their hearts just"—his hands make an exploding gesture—"went like this."

He sits quietly for a moment. "Did you see the papers?" Stories ran that morning about police department proposals to forbid detectives from eating, drinking, socializing or shopping in stores, bars or restaurants within their command (a particularly tough order for police assigned to midtown Manhattan) and from eating on duty in any place with a liquor license. The "brown bag order," as cops quickly named it, also prohibits detectives from holding "apparent secret conversations" among themselves and suggests that detectives "be encouraged to have their meals in their office."

"The city's getting screwed, you know that?" the detective says. "Police work. There's not a cop left. They're all afraid to work. They all do their eight hours straight down the middle and never get involved."

A middle-aged man—dark suit, tieless, red-striped shirt, red handkerchief in his pocket—stops at the table. "Tony," the detective says, "tell me something. Before, before this—if I need to know something, I'm going to know it or not?"

"You're gonna know it," Tony says. "Before." He laughs. "Not now. Now you talk to a guy. He's got a stickpin. It's a microphone. You don't say nothing."

He leaves. "That guy's a bookmaker," the detective says. "In the old days, you had a homicide. Who knows the area? Such and such a bookmaker knows it. You talk to him. The old 887 Sub 4. Vagrancy. Then you get a phone call. 'The guy who did this is so-and-so.' You get a picture. Witnesses identify him. The newspapers say, 'The case was solved as the result of confidential information.' Today? Talk to a bookmaker? No chance. The IAD'd be down all over you."

The detective takes a few bites of his dinner, and goes on. "You never know who you're going to meet in a place like this. So you smile at everyone. Scum. Smile at everyone. They love it. 'Who's this her?' 'Oh, this? Say hello to Sonny.' So Sonny's a stickup man. Beautiful. Someday it all gets used. But not any more. Not any more."

The detective stares unhappily into his plate. "They don't have detectives today." A long, sad pause. "I'm not a detective." Another pause. "I'm as useless as tits on a ball."

Bob Kenney's friends wonder what could have driven him—or could drive themselves—to suicide. Could it have been the sudden withdrawal from years of violence and danger? Or the sorrowful spectacle of a once-proud job reduced to paranoia, brown bags and uselessness? Kenney himself left no clues. One Sunday morning he drove his wife home from her job at the telephone company, went for a walk up the street, stopped at a brick wall and, having given no indication to anyone of what he was about to do, drew his .38-caliber Detective Special and fired a bullet into his head.

EIGHT

MARTIN ERDMANN THINKS HE MIGHT BE ANTISO-
cial. When he was six he liked to sneak across his
family's red-carpeted, spiral-staircased entrance
hall to the potted palm, and spit in it. At Yankee
Stadium, he rooted for the Red Sox. When he went
to Dartmouth, he cheered for Yale. He didn't make
a lot of friends. He says he doesn't need them. Today he's fifty-seven years old, an unmarried millionaire lawyer, and he has defended more criminals
than anyone else in the world. Because he is one of
the five or ten best defense lawyers in New York, he
gets those criminals turned back into the streets
months or years earlier than they have any right to
hope for. His clients are not Mafia bosses or bank
embezzlers or suburban executives who've shot
their wives. He defends killers, burglars, rapists,
robbers—the men people mean when they talk
about crime in the streets. Martin Erdmann's clients *are* crime in the streets.

In twenty-five years Martin Erdmann has defended more than 100,000 criminals. He has saved
them tens of thousands of years in prison and in
those years they have robbed, raped, burglarized

and murdered tens upon tens of thousands of people. The idea of having had a very personal and direct hand in all that mayhem strikes him as boring and irrelevant. "I have nothing to do with justice," he says. "Justice is not even part of the equation. If you say I have no moral reaction to what I do, you are right."

And *he* is right. As right as our adversary judicial system, as right as jury trials, as right as the presumption of innocence and the Fifth Amendment. If there is a fault in Erdmann's eagerness to free defendants, it is not with Erdmann himself, but with the system. Criminal law to the defense lawyer does not mean equity or fairness or proper punishment or vengeance. It means getting everything he can for his client. And in perhaps 98 per cent of his cases, the clients are guilty. Justice is a luxury enjoyed by the district attorney. He alone is sworn "to see that justice is done." The defense lawyer does not bask in the grandeur of any such noble oath. He finds himself most often working for the guilty and for a judicial system based upon the sound but paradoxical principle that the guilty must be freed to protect the innocent.

And Erdmann does free them, as many as he possibly can. He works for the Legal Aid Society, a private organization with a city contract to represent the 179,000 indigent defendants who flood each year into New York City courtrooms. He heads the society's supreme court branch, has fifty-five lawyers working under him, makes $23,500 a year. Next to the millions left him by his father, a Wall Street bond broker, the money means nothing.

Twenty-five years ago, until the accounting office told him he was messing up their books, he kept his paychecks stuffed in a desk drawer. In private practice he could have a six-figure income and, probably, the fame of Edward Bennett Williams, or F. Lee Bailey, or Percy Foreman. He is disgusted when people accuse him of dedication. "That's just plain nonsense. The one word that does *not* describe me is dedicated. I reserve that word for people who do something that requires sacrifice. I don't sacrifice anything. The only reason I'm any good is because I have an ego. I like to win."

Martin Erdmann does not look like a winner. He is slight, unimposing, with balding hair cut short every Monday on his way to work, custom-made suits that come out baggy anyway and a slightly stooped, forward-leaning walk that makes him look, in motion, like Groucho Marx. His face is lean, bony, taut-skinned, with thin lips and bulging eyes. He lives in a one-bedroom co-op on Manhattan's East Side, has no television set and rarely answers his phone ("I learned that from my father—he could sit in a room for hours with a ringing phone"). He plays chess by postcard, buys Christmas presents from catalogues and seldom goes out except to work and eat. Defendants who ask him for loans get them. He finances black student scholarships and is listed as a patron of New York's City Center. His only self-indulgences are a seventy-five-acre weekend Connecticut retreat and a one-month-a-year fishing trip, alone, to the Adirondacks. "I discovered a long time ago," he says, "that I am a very self-contained person."

Like most men who are alone without loneliness, Martin Erdmann is emotionally compact: self-centered, stubborn, at times perverse. He is also a failed idealist. "I had an English professor in college," he says, "who read an essay I wrote and told me, 'Martin, you are looking for better bread than is made of wheat.' I've never forgotten that."

Martin Erdmann gets up at 4:45, reads till 6:30, then subways three miles downtown to the Criminal Court Building. He moves through the dark, empty hallway to his office and unlocks the door. He is there at 7:30, two and a half hours before the courts open, and he is alone. In another ten or fifteen minutes Milton Adler will arrive, his boss, chief attorney in the criminal branch. Then, one or two at a time, come the phone operator and clerks, the other lawyers, the defendants on bail, mothers of men in jail, sick-looking junkies with vomit-stained shirts, frightened people who sit quietly on the seven wooden chairs along the wall, angry people mumbling viciously, insane people dressed in costumes with feathers in their hair.

Before the rush begins, Martin Erdmann sits at his desk in a side office and goes over the folders of the day's cases. Anthony Howard, a twenty-one-year-old Negro, is accused of using a stick and knife to rob a man of his wallet. Howard's mother visits him in jail, brings clean clothes and takes out his laundry. She doesn't know that the greatest danger to her son is not the robbery charge, but the man who sleeps above him in the eight-by-six-foot cell. Robert Phillips, Howard's cellmate, escaped from a state mental hospital seven years ago, was recaptured, released, then arrested for the murder of a twenty-two-year-old girl and an infant boy. After three more years in a mental hospital, he has been declared legally sane and is now awaiting trial for the murders. Erdmann looks over the file. "Prisoners who've been in mental hospitals," he says, "tell me they keep them there until they admit the charges against them. Then they mark them sane and send them down for pleading." He decides to give the Anthony Howard case to Alice Schlesinger, a young lawyer who can still believe her clients are innocent. She's good at what Erdmann calls "hand-holding," giving a defendant and his family more time than the case might need.

Adler walks in, starts to say something, and the phone rings. Erdmann answers it. The call is from a woman out on bail on a charge of throwing lye on her husband. Now she wants Erdmann to help her get a shotgun license. She says she needs it for protection.

"Okay, Mable," he says, "but don't shoot too many people." He hangs up smiling and says to Adler, "Mable's switched from lye to shotguns."

Adler says something about a meeting he went to yesterday with DAs and judges to discuss ways of getting more prisoners out on bail. Erdmann listens and says nothing. What's left of his idealism, the wreckage, he defends against the day's events by affecting an air of playful cynicism. He smiles and laughs and pricks the pretty little bubbles of naïveté that rise around him from other lawyers. Listening to Adler, his face flashes now with the playful-cynic smile. "If they do reduce bail," he says, "it'll be the last they see of the defendants."

Alice Schlesinger appears in the doorway, a small young woman, about thirty, with long black hair. She wants to know what she can do to pressure the DA to start the trial of a bailed defendant charged with robbery. "Can't we put the screws to them a little? My client is very nervous and upset. He wants to get the trial over with."

"Well," says Erdmann, "of course you can always make a motion to dismiss for lack of prosecution. Say your client is suffering great emotional stress at having this dreadfully unjust accusation hanging over his head."

"Don't *smile* like that," she says. "He *is* innocent, this time."

Erdmann gets rid of the smile. "Well, you know," he says, "maybe the DA is having a little trouble locating the complainant, and your defendant's on bail anyway, so why urge them to go right out and track him down? Because if they find the complainant and go to trial and if from some extremely unfortunate occurrence your client should be convicted, then he's going to jail and he'll be a lot worse off than just nervous."

She agrees reluctantly and leaves. Erdmann sits silently at his desk, staring into the piles of papers. Then he says, "She has a lot to learn. She'll learn. With some tears, but she'll learn."

Erdmann gathers up the folders and takes the elevator to a courtroom on the thirteenth floor. He sits in one of the soft upholstered chairs in the jury box and takes another look at the thirty folders of the day's cases: a forgery, robberies (mostly muggings), burglaries, drug sales, assault with a gun, arson, sodomy, an attempted murder. He arranges them on the shelf in front of the jury box and sits back to await the DAs and the judge. He is alone in the courtroom, a dimly lighted, solemn place—meant to be imposing, it is only oppressive. Brown walls, brown tables, brown church-pew seats soak up what little light the low-watt overhead bulbs surrender.

A few spectators walk in and Erdmann calls the names of his bail cases. No one answers. "That's not surprising," he says, "they couldn't possibly get up this early."

A DA comes in and Erdmann asks him about a kidnapping case that's approaching trial. "The DA on that one's on trial on another case, Marty. He won't be finished for a month at least."

"Wonderful." Erdmann laughs. "I hope he stays on trial until the complainant's thirty. Then it won't look so bad. She was eight when it happened and she's already eleven." The DA shakes his head and walks away. Two more DAs arrive and Erdmann talks to them, joking with them, making gentle fun of them, establishing his presence: twice their age, more experienced, more knowledgeable, more cunning. "There's no question that my reputation is much too high," he says. "It's been carefully cultivated. Myths are very important in this business."

The judge enters: Mitchell Schweitzer, tall, thin, gray-haired, on the bench twenty-six years, sixteen of them working closely with Erdmann. He flashes a look around the room, greeting private lawyers, Erdmann and the two assistant DAs.

The clerk calls a name: "José Santiago!"

Erdmann fumbles through his folders and pulls one out. "He's mine," he says. An assistant DA looks at the rows of folders on his table and picks one up. Erdmann and the DA walk slowly toward the judge's bench, pulling out papers as they go. Erdmann has, among other things, a copy of the complaint and a handwritten interview another Legal Aid lawyer had earlier with the defendant. The DA has a synopsis of the grand jury testimony and a copy of the defendant's record. With these documents, in the next three or four minutes, while the defendant himself sits unaware in a detention pen beneath the courtroom, the judge, DA and Erdmann will determine the likelihood of guilt and the amount of time the man will serve.

Trials are obsolete. In New York City only one arrest in thousands ends in trial. The government no longer has time and money to afford the luxury of presuming innocence, nor the belief that the truest way of determining guilt is by jury trial. Today, in effect, the government says to each defendant, "If you will abandon your unsupportable claim of innocence, we will compensate you with a light sentence." The defendant says, "How light?"—and the DA, defense lawyer and judge are drawn together at the bench. The conference there is called "plea bargaining," and it proceeds as the playing of a game, with moves and countermoves, protocol, rules and ritual. Power is in the hands of the prisoners. For as increasing crime has pushed our judicial system to the crumbling edge of chaos and collapse, the defendant himself has emerged as the only man with a helping hand. The government needs guilty pleas to move the cases out of court, and the defendants are selling their guilty pleas for the only currency the government can offer—time. But no matter what sentence is finally agreed upon, the real outcome of this bargaining contest is never truly in doubt. The guilty always win. The innocent always lose.

To play the game well, a lawyer must be ruthless. He is working within, but *against,* a system that has been battered to its knees. He must not hesitate to kick it when it's down, and to take every advantage of its weakness. No one is better at the game than Martin Erdmann.

Judge Schweitzer glances through the grand jury extract handed him by the DA, a young bespectacled man named Jack Litman. Then the judge looks up over his glasses. "What are you looking for, Marty?"

Erdmann isn't sure yet. His client is accused of robbing a man on the street after stabbing him in the face, neck, chest, stomach and back. The victim was held from behind by an accomplice. "They have a big identification problem," Erdmann says. He is looking at a copy of a police report. "The DD-5 says the complaining witness refused to look at pictures in the hospital the next day because he said he wouldn't be able to identify the assailants from photographs."

"Your honor," Litman says, "they put sixty-five stitches in him."

"Just a minute," says the judge, and proceeds to
read quickly to Erdmann from the grand jury extract: "They fled into an apartment house, the cop
asked the super if he'd seen them, the super said
they went into apartment 3-A, the cop went in,
placed them under arrest and took them to the
hospital where they were identified by the victim."
He looks up. Erdmann has never heard the grand
jury testimony before, and it hasn't exactly made his
day. "So, you see, Marty, it's not such a bad case."
He leans back. "I'll tell you what. A year with credit
for time served." Santiago already has been in jail
for ten months. With time off for good behavior,
that sentence will let him out today. Erdmann
agrees. The DA nods and starts stuffing papers back
into the folder. "Bring him up," he says.

Santiago's accomplice is brought in with him.
Both men are twenty-one, short and defiant-look-
ing. The accomplice, Jesus Rodriguez, has his own
lawyer, who now joins Erdmann in agreeing to the
sentence. The lawyers explain the offer to the defendants. They tell them that the offer can be made
only if they are in fact guilty. Neither the judge nor
the DA nor the lawyers themselves would permit an
innocent man to plead guilty. Santiago and Rodriguez look bewildered. They say they are innocent,
they did nothing. Much mumbling and consterna-
tion at the counsel table. Then Schweitzer says,
"Would you like a second call?"

"Yes, your honor," says Erdmann. "A second
call." The defendants are led out and downstairs to
a detention pen. Erdmann looks at Santiago's interview sheet, a mimeographed form with blanks for

name, age, address, education, employer, and then
at the bottom, space for his version of what happened. Santiago's statement begins, "I am not
guilty. I did nothing wrong." He has never been
arrested before. He says he and Rodriguez were
asleep in their apartment when the police charged
in and grabbed them. At his arraignment some
weeks ago, he pleaded not guilty.

"Talk to them," Judge Schweitzer suggests.
Erdmann and his co-counsel walk over to the door
of the pen. A court officer opens it and they step
from the court's dark, quiet brownness into a
bright, noisy, butt-littered hallway. The door slams
shut behind them. From somewhere below come
voices shouting, and the clang of cell doors closing.
A guard yells, "On the gate!" and precedes them
down a dark stairway to a barred steel door. An
inside guard unlocks the door and they walk into a
yellow, men's-room-tiled corridor with windows on
the left and a large bench-lined cell on the right.
Twenty men are in the cell, almost all of them dirty
and bearded, some young and frightened sitting
alone on the benches, others older, talking, standing, as at home here as on a Harlem street corner.
Suddenly the voices stop and the prisoners, like animals expecting to be fed, turn their heads toward
Erdmann and his co-counsel. Three other lawyers
walk in, too, and in a moment the voices begin again
—prisoners and lawyers arguing with each other,
explaining, cajoling, conning in the jailhouse jargon
of pleas and sentences: "I can get you one and one
running wild [two years consecutive]. . . . I know
a guy got an E and a flat [a Class E felony with a

year]. . . . So you want a bullet [a year]? You'll take
a bullet?"

Erdmann walks to the far end of the cell and
Santiago meets him at the bars. Erdmann puts his
toe on a cross strip between the bars and balances
Santiago's folder and papers on his knee. He takes
out a Lucky Strike, lights it and inhales. Santiago
watches, and then a sudden rush of words starts
violently from his mouth. Erdmann silences him.
"First let me find out what I have to know," he says
calmly, "and then you can talk as much as you
want." Santiago is standing next to a chest-high
steel-plate partition. On the other side of it, a toilet
flushes. A few steps away, Rodriguez is talking
through the bars to his lawyer.

"If you didn't do anything wrong," Erdmann says
to Santiago, "then there's no point even discussing
this. You'll go to trial."

Santiago nods desperately. "I ain't done nothing,
I was asleep! I *never* been in trouble before." This is
the first time since his initial interview seven
months ago that he has had a chance to tell his story
to a lawyer, and he is frantic to get it all out.
Erdmann cannot stop the torrent, and now he does
not try. "I never been arrested," Santiago shouts,
"never been to jail, never been in *no* trouble, *nothing*. We just asleep in the apartment and the police
break in and grab us out of bed and take us, we ain't
done nothing, I *never* been in trouble, I never saw
this man before, and he says we did it. I don't even
know what we did, and I been here ten months, I
don't see no lawyer or nothing, I ain't had a shower
in two months, we locked up twenty-four hours a

day, I got no shave, no hot food, I ain't *never* been like this before, I can't stand it, I'm going to kill myself, I got to get out, I ain't—"

Now Erdmann interrupts, icily calm, speaking very slowly, foot on the cross strip, drawing on his cigarette. "Well, it's very simple. Either you are guilty or you're not. If you're guilty of anything you can take the plea and they'll give you a year, and under the circumstances that's a very good plea and you ought to take it. If you're not guilty, you have to go to trial."

"I'm not guilty." He says it fast, nodding, sure of that.

"Then you should go to trial. But the jury is going to hear that the cop followed you into the building, the super sent him to apartment 3-A, he arrested you there and the man identified you in the hospital. If they find you guilty, you might get fifteen years."

Santiago is unimpressed with all of that. "I'm innocent. I didn't do nothing. But I got to get out of here. I got to—"

"Well, if you *did* do anything and you are a little guilty, they'll give you time served and you'll walk."

That's more like it.

"Today? I walk today?"

"If you are guilty of something and you take the plea."

"I'll take the plea. But I didn't do nothing."

"You can't take the plea unless you are guilty of something."

"I want the year. I'm innocent, but I'll take the year. I walk today if I take the year?"

The papers start to fall from Erdmann's knee and he grabs them and settles them back. "You walk if you take the plea, but no one's going to let you take the plea if you aren't guilty."

"But I didn't *do* nothing."

"Then you'll have to stay in and go to trial."

"When will that be?"

"In a couple of months. Maybe longer."

Santiago has a grip on the bars. "You mean if I'm guilty I get out today?"

"Yes." Someone is urinating on the other side of the partition.

"But if I'm innocent, I got to stay in?" The toilet flushes.

"That's right."

It's too much for Santiago. He lets go of the bars, takes a step back, shakes his head, turns around and comes quickly back to the bars. "But, *man*—"

Back upstairs at the bench, Erdmann says to Schweitzer, "He's got no record, your honor, and I've had no admission of guilt. You know I'm very careful with people who have no records—"

"And I am, too, Marty, you know that."

"He says he hasn't had a shower in two months, he's in a twenty-four-hour-a-day lockup and he wants to get out, and I don't blame him."

"Marty, I'm not taking a guilty plea just because he wants a shower."

"Of course not."

"Do you want me to talk to them?"

"I think it might be a good idea, your honor."

Santiago and Rodriguez are brought up again and led into a small jury room adjoining the courtroom.

chweitzer reads the grand jury extract to the defendants, making sure they know the case against hem.

Now Rodriguez says he'll take the plea. Schweiter asks him to tell what happened the night of the obbery. Rodriguez says he and Santiago were on he street and they ran into the complainant and poke with him and the complainant had a knife in is pocket and ended up getting cut, "but I didn't lo nothing."

This departure from the original story, the admission that they had been with the victim and that here was indeed a knife, is enough for Erdmann. He looks at Schweitzer. "Now I'm convinced he's guilty." Schweitzer and Litman go back to court. Erdmann says to Santiago, "Do you want the plea?"

"Yes, man, I *told* you that, I got to get out—"

"Then the judge will ask you certain questions nd you have to give the appropriate answers." He 1ods towards Rodriguez. "He held him and you tabbed him. Let's go."

They return to the courtroom and stand before he bench. Schweitzer asks Santiago if he wants to :hange his plea. Santiago is still not buying. What if his whole routine is just a trick to extract a confesion from him? "One year," he says.

Schweitzer is patient. "That's not what I asked ou. Do you want to change your plea?"

"One year."

Erdmann talks with him, explains that he will get he year but first he has to answer certain questions. 5antiago starts off again with just wanting to get out. Erdmann quiets him down, and they try again.

Schweitzer: "Do you now wish to change your plea?"

"I want one year."

Schweitzer is exasperated. Erdmann is angry. Santiago leans over to Erdmann and again starts talking. Erdmann says strongly, "Look, do you want the plea or not? Just yes or no. Answer him. Don't make speeches. You'll *get* the year. Just answer him."

Schweitzer asks again. Santiago turns to Erdmann and starts to talk. Erdmann grimaces and covers his ear with the folder. "I don't *want* any more speeches. I'm losing my patience. You'll *get* the year, but *first* you have to plead."

Schweitzer gives up and moves on to Rodriguez. Rodriguez quickly pleads guilty. Schweitzer asks him to tell the truth about what really happened. Rodriguez says he held the man from behind while Santiago stabbed him. Schweitzer immediately sentences him to a year. Erdmann is leaning against the clerk's desk, his arms crossed over his chest, his eyes burning into Santiago. This ignorant, stupid, vicious kid has been offered a huge, heaping helping of the Erdmann talent, the experience, the knowledge, the myth—and has shoved it away. Erdmann's face is covered with disgust. Through his eyes, way beyond them, is fury, and unclouded, clear contempt.

The defendants are led from the courtroom. Erdmann walks to his seat in the jury box. As he passes the bench, Schweitzer looks down helplessly. "He wants me to sentence him before he pleads. How can I do that?"

The clerk calls a case for a private lawyer, and

Erdmann takes advantage of the break to get a cigarette. He goes into a small side room the court officers use for a lounge. The room has lockers, a desk,
a refrigerator, toaster and hot plate—all of them old
and beaten and scarred. Cops' jackets hang from
the chair backs. Erdmann has forgotten Santiago.
He stands by the window with his foot up on a
radiator and looks across at the Tombs, one of the
worst jails in the country, home of many of his clients, a desperate place of rats and rapes, beatings,
murders and, so far this year, six suicides. Eighty per
cent of the 1,800 men locked up in the Tombs are
clients of the Legal Aid Society. One of them, a
twenty-five-year-old homosexual named Raymond
Lavon Moore, will eventually come to the fleeting
attention of Martin Erdmann. At this moment,
however, he sits in a small iron box whose only
openings are a barred window at the back and a
four-inch-wide glass slit in the door. He is doing
twenty days in solitary for hitting a guard. Charged
with shooting a policeman in a bar, Moore has been
in the Tombs ten months, made twenty-four appearances in court and steadfastly refuses to plead
guilty to anything more serious than a misde-
meanor. He came in weighing 205 pounds, and is
now down to 155. He has never been in jail before.
He has never been physically examined in the
Tombs, but is nevertheless getting frequent heavy
doses of tranquilizers. The Tombs doctor, a graduate of the Eclectic Medical College of Cincinnati, is
seventy-seven years old (jail records say he's sixty-
nine). Moore has been removed to hospitals for
mental observation five times, and each time he has

been returned to the Tombs. He has twice tried to kill himself. Not long ago some Tombs prisoners, angry at the overcrowding, vermin and lack of official attention, decided to find out what could be accomplished by rioting. The riots were followed by avalanches of studies, committees, investigations and reports—some helpful, some hysterical. None did anything to help Raymond Lavon Moore, the man in the iron box.

Erdmann is looking at workmen on a Tombs setback clearing away shattered glass and broken furniture from beneath burned-out windows. "It will never be the same," he says. "Once they've found out they can riot and take hostages, it will never be the same. Today defendants are telling the judges what sentences they'll take. They say to me, 'Go back and tell him I'll take six months.' I had a guy the other day who told me he knew the system was congested and that they needed guilty pleas, and he was willing to help by pleading guilty for eight months. The judge would only come down to eleven. He wouldn't take it. He was willing to help out for eight months, but not for eleven. The leniency feeds upon itself. They start out settling for a year, then others want six months, then three months, then parole. The guilty are getting great breaks. But the innocent are put under tremendous pressure to take a plea and get out. The innocent suffer, and the community suffers. It's all just get the cases out of court—move the calendar, move the calendar, move the calendar. That's all they're interested in—everyone."

He unwraps another pack of Luckies, forgetting the opened one in his pocket.

"If the defendants *really* get together, they've got the system by the balls. If they all decide to plead not guilty, and keep on pleading not guilty, then what will happen? The offered pleas will get lower and lower—six months, three months. If that doesn't work, and they still plead not guilty, maybe the court will take fifteen or twenty and try them and give them the maximum sentences. And if *that* doesn't work—I don't know. I don't know. They have the power, and when they find out, you're in trouble."

Two workmen standing on a plank are lowering themselves on ropes down the side of the Tombs. "Fixing windows," Erdmann says. Then he smiles. "Or escaping."

Forty minutes have been wasted with the stubborn Santiago, and now comes another problem. An Erdmann client named Richard Henderson says he was asleep in a Welfare Department flophouse when another man "pounced" on him with a stick. The other man says he was trying to wake Henderson when Henderson "jumped up like a jack rabbit" and stabbed him in the chest. Henderson is charged with attempted murder.

Erdmann talks to him in the pen hallway just outside the courtroom door. It has started to rain. A casement window, opaque, with chicken wire between the plates, has been cranked open and cold air and rain are blowing in and making things miserable for Henderson. He's a twenty-one-year-old junkie—wire-thin, with deep, lost, wandering eyes, and a face sad and dead, as if all the muscles that could make it laugh or frown or show fear or anger had been cut. He stands there shivering in a dirty white shirt, no socks, no shoelaces, the backs of his shoes pushed in like slippers, hands stiff-armed down into the pockets of beltless khaki pants. Quietly, he tells Erdmann he wants to go to trial.

"Well you certainly have that right. But if you're guilty, I've spoken to the judge, and he'll give you a year with credit for time served. How long have you been in?" Erdmann turns the folder and looks at a date. "Six months. So with good behavior you'll have four left. It simply depends on whether you're guilty of anything or not."

Henderson nods. "Yes, that's why I want a jury trial."

"Why?"

"To find out if I'm innocent or not."

"Don't you know?" Erdmann takes another look in the folder. Henderson was psychiatrically examined at Bellevue Hospital and returned as legally sane.

"No. I don't know. But I have an opinion." His eyes leave Erdmann and begin to examine the hallway. He has withdrawn from the conversation. Erdmann watches him a moment, then brings him back.

"What is your opinion?"

"That I am."

"Well if you go to trial, it may be four months anyway before you *get* a trial, and then you'll be gambling zero against five or ten years. And even if you are acquitted, you'll still have done the four months."

Henderson moves his feet and shivers. "I understand," he says meekly. "So I think I'd better do that."

"What?"

"Go to trial."

Erdmann just looks at him and walks back into court. "Ready for trial," he announces. "Don't even bother bringing him out." Litman makes a note on his file and they move on to another case.

Erdmann sits down in the jury box. The next few defendants have private lawyers, so he just waits there: watching, smiling, his bulging eyes gently ridiculing those around him who have failed to see as clearly as he into the depths of this charade, and to have found the joke there.

The judge is asking a defendant where he got the loaded gun. "He found it," Erdmann whispers before the man answers.

"I found it," the man says.

"Where?" asks the judge.

"Someone just gave it to him," Erdmann says.

"Someone walked by and handed it to me," says the defendant.

Erdmann smiles. "It's amazing," he says, "how often people rush by defendants and thrust things into their hands—guns, watches, wallets, things like that."

One of the two DAs is Richie Lowe, a black man—young, tall, slender, double-breasted, mod, Afro haircut. Black defendants coming into court glance quickly around, and they see a white judge, white defense lawyers, white clerk, white stenographer, white guards and then, over there, at that table over there, a black, the only black in the room, and he's—the *enemy*.

Now Lowe, the black kid with a law degree from St. John's, sits down next to Erdmann, the millionaire with a Wall Street father and Dartmouth and Yale law, and no one can help but notice the ironic reversal of their roles. Prosecutor and defender. But the irony is superficial—inside, Erdmann's character belies his background. He says he was "far to the left" of his parents, and he spent much of his youth trying to radicalize them. His father was quiet, shy, conservative, "difficult to get close to." His mother he remembers fondly as "a very determined lady, a person of strong likes and dislikes." But not so strong that her son could not attack them. When he was twenty-two, he decided to bring a friend home to dinner. The friend was a black assistant DA. He smiles as he recalls her reaction. "It was very difficult for her. She told the elevator man and all the maids what was going to happen. She behaved admirably even though I'm sure she hated every minute of it." He reminisces silently for a moment, and then adds, "I read about him years later. I think he ended up marrying the daughter of the Yale registrar and then shooting someone in Detroit."

After law school Erdmann went to work in "a stuffy Wall Street law firm" where his first assignment was discovering whether or not a Florida gambling casino had acted legally in denying admittance to a female client's poodle. He quit, spent World War II in the Army and then joined the Legal

Aid Society. "When I run into someone I can't place, I just say, 'Good to see you again, when did you get out?' That covers college, the Army and prison."

A guard leads a black defendant toward the pen door. He's wearing a black headband, a gold earring and a wad of white paper is stuffed up his left nostril. "Can I ask you one thing?" he whispers to the guard as they head for the door.

"Yeah, ask me anything."

"What'd I get?"

"You got a year, a year in jail." The door slams behind him.

In the seats next to Erdmann, a prisoner is being allowed a visit with his wife and small son. "I heard about your commotion in school," the father whispers. "Now you better be good or I'm gonna get you when I get out."

Guards bring in an old, toothless black man with wild white hair and an endless record of rapes, assaults, sodomy and armed robbery. He's accused of trying to rape a four-year-old Puerto Rican girl. Some people driving in a car saw the man sitting on a wall with the girl struggling in his lap and rescued her. Erdmann, Lowe and Judge Schweitzer talk it over. Schweitzer suggests a year. Lowe runs his eyes again over the grand jury extract. He usually goes along with Schweitzer, but this time he balks. "I can't see it, your honor. I can't see it."

Erdmann speaks a few urging words, but Lowe won't budge. "No," he says, "I just can't see it, your honor. If these people hadn't come by in the car and seen the girl, this could have been—it could have been anything."

Schweitzer, himself under great appellate division pressure to dispose of cases, now pressures Lowe, politely, gently. He points out that the girl was not injured.

"I just can't, your honor," Lowe says. "I just can't. This is abhorrent, this—"

Schweitzer breaks in. "It's abhorrent to *me*, too, and it's being discussed *only* in the light of the calendar."

"Your honor, we've been giving away the courthouse for the sake of the calendar. I can't do it. I won't do it." He stuffs his papers back in the folder. "Ready for trial, your honor."

He moves back to the prosecution table and announces for the record, "The people are ready for trial."

Erdmann has been saying nothing. As he passes Lowe's table on his way to the jury box, Lowe says, "Am I being unreasonable, Marty?"

Erdmann stops for a moment, very serious, and then shakes his head. "No, I don't think you are."

Lowe is upset. The next case has not yet been called. He moves around the table, fumbling folders. Then loudly he says, "Your honor, if he takes it *right now* I'll give him a year."

The judge fires Lowe a look. "You'll *recommend* a year. *I'll* give him a year."

Erdmann talks to the defendant at the counsel table. Lowe keeps shaking his head. He is suffering. He takes a step toward the bench. "Your honor," he says desperately, "he should get zip to three, at least."

"I *know* he should," Schweitzer says.

Erdmann now stands and for the record makes the customary speech. "Your honor, the defendant at this time wishes to withdraw his plea of not guilty, previously entered, and plead guilty to the second count of the indictment, attempted assault in the second degree, a Class E felony, that plea to cover the entire indictment."

Now it's Lowe's turn to make the speech of acceptance for the people, to accept the Class E felony, the least serious type of felony in the penal code. He stands. "Your honor, the people respectfully recommend acceptance of this plea, feeling that it will provide the court with adequate scope for punishment—" He stops. The next words should be "in the interest of justice." He sits down and pretends to write something on a folder. Then softly, as if hoping he might not be heard, he speaks down into the table, ". . . in the interest of justice."

He walks over to a visitor. "What do you think about *that?*" he demands. "That took a little *piece* out of me. He got a *year* for trying to *rape* a four-year-old girl."

Schweitzer recesses for lunch, and Lowe and Erdmann ride down in the elevator. Lowe is still upset. "What do I tell that girl's mother when she calls me and wants to know what happened to the man who tried to rape her daughter?"

Erdmann smiles, the playful cynic. *Better bread than is made of wheat.* "Tell her, 'No speeka English, no speeka English, no speeka English.'"

Because Manhattan's Criminal Court Building is on the Lower East Side, in the ethnic no man's land where Little Italy collides with Chinatown, it is surrounded by some of the city's best Italian and Chinese restaurants. But every lunchtime Erdmann ignores these and walks two blocks north to Canal Street, a truck-choked crosstown conduit littered with derelicts overflowing from the Bowery, and eats in the sprawling, Formica-filled, tray-crashing chaos of the foulest cafeteria east of Newark. No number of threats, insults or arguments can persuade him into any other eating place. He has, every day, one scoop of cottage cheese, a slice of melon and one slice of rye bread, buttered. (They give you two slices, want them or not, but he never succumbs.) Today he is at a table with a friend, not a lawyer, who asks how he feels when he goes to trial with a man he knows is guilty and gets the man freed.

"Lovely! Perfectly beautiful! You're dancing on air and you say to yourself, 'How could that have happened? I must have done a wonderful job!' It's a euphoric feeling. Just to see the look of shock on the judge's face when the jury foreman says 'not guilty' is worth something. It's the same sense of greed you get if a horse you bet on comes in at fifteen to one. You've beaten the odds, the knowledgeable opinion, the wise people." He laughs. "The exultation of winning dampens any moral feelings you have."

"But what," he is asked, "if you defended a man who had raped and murdered a five-year-old girl, and he was acquitted and went free and a year later was arrested for raping and murdering another five-year-old girl? Would you defend him again with the same vigor?"

"I'm afraid so."

"Why afraid?"

"Because I think most people would disapprove of that."

"Do you care?"

"No."

"It doesn't concern you?"

"I'm not concerned with the crime committed or the consequences of his going free. If I were, I couldn't practice. I'm concerned with seeing that every client gets as good representation as he could if he had $200,000. I don't want him to get screwed because there wasn't anyone around to see that he not get screwed. If you're a doctor and Hitler comes to you and says you're the one man in the world who can cure him, you do it."

"How much of that is ego?"

"Ninety-nine per cent."

Erdmann eats his cottage cheese. An old derelict —bearded, toothless, with swollen lips—puts his tray down next to Erdmann and sits slurping soup and eying the untouched slice of rye.

In the courthouse lobby after lunch, Erdmann stops to buy a candy bar. Someone says he saw a story in the *Times* that five thousand of that brand had been recalled after rodent hair was found in some of them. Erdmann smiles and buys two more.

A court officer sees Erdmann coming down the hall. "Hey, Marty," he yells, "he's on the bench, he's starting to call your cases."

"So what do you want me to do," Erdmann says, "break into a run?"

A defendant's name is called and Erdmann and Lowe approach the bench. Erdmann looks at Lowe. "Your move." He smiles.

"Your honor," Lowe says, looking over his file, "this is a robbery, no weapon, two victims. It's a woman who beats up old people in the subway and robs them. One of the complainants is eighty-one years old." He hands Schweitzer her three-page record of drugs, prostitution and assaults.

"Injuries?" Schweitzer asks.

"Just light, your honor. Nothing serious."

"In these times," Erdmann says, "people ought to be grateful when they're not injured while being robbed."

Schweitzer looks up. "What about a year and a year consecutive?" Erdmann and Lowe agree. The defendant comes in—short, fat, built like a cannonball. She starts right in on Erdmann. "I ain't takin' no plea. I didn't do nothin'. I'm innocent and I ain't takin' no plea."

Erdmann is not going to waste his time. He writes on the folder: "NG—ready for trial." He looks back at the woman. "Don't you even want to know what the offer is?"

She's been around. "I know what the offer is. One and one consec."

Erdmann turns away, and they take her out.

Guards bring in a twenty-year-old girl charged with robbery with a knife. Erdmann is talking to her at the counsel table when Lowe strolls over and says, "Marty, an E and a flat?"

The girl looks at Lowe. "What's he saying, who's he?"

Lowe starts away. "Don't listen to me, I'm the enemy."

She wants to know why she has to go to jail. "Well, rightly or wrongly," Erdmann tells her, "people think they shouldn't be robbed. So when they get robbed, they give a little time." She asks if the year can run concurrent with another sentence pending against her. Erdmann asks Lowe and he agrees. She still hesitates, and finally refuses the offer.

"What's wrong?" Lowe says. "She wanted a year, I gave her a year. She wanted it concurrent, I made it concurrent. It's unreal. They tell us what they want and we're supposed to genuflect."

"José Sanchez!" the clerk calls. A drug-sale case.

"Your honor," Erdmann protests, "he hasn't even been interviewed. I haven't seen him."

"Well, just let's look at it, Marty," the judge says. He goes over to Lowe's file. "It's one sale, Marty. He doesn't have any robberies. Burglaries, petty larceny. Mostly drugs. I'll tell you what, Marty. I'll give him an E and a flat." Lowe agrees.

Erdmann walks into the pen hallway, and they bring up a defendant. "They're offering an E and a flat," Erdmann says to him. "For a single sale, that's about the—"

The defendant looks mystified. He says nothing. The guard interrupts. "This isn't Sanchez, Marty, it's Fernandez."

Erdmann drops his arms in disgust, and without a word he turns and goes back into court and sits down in the jury box. A defendant has in effect been

tried, convicted and sentenced before his lawyer
even knew what he looked like.

After court, Alice Schlesinger comes into
Erdmann's office to brief him on a client of hers, a
woman, who will be in Schweitzer's court tomorrow. "She's absolutely not guilty," Alice says. When
she leaves, Erdmann's smile turns wistful and nos-
talgic. "It must be wonderful," he says, "to have an
absolute sense of who's guilty and who isn't. I wish I
had it."

Adler walks into the office. "What can I tell
them?" he asks Erdmann. "Jack says he's leaving
because the job's making a cynic of him. He says he
thought he was going to defend the downtrodden
and he finds out they're hostile and they lie to him.
So he's leaving. Alice comes to me and says, 'The
system's wonderful for the guilty, but for the innocent it's awful. Some of them *must* be innocent.'
What do you *say* to that?"

"You say nothing," Erdmann answers, "because
it's true."

"No. You say that in a good system of government
the vast majority get fair treatment, but there are
bound to be a few who don't." He looks at
Erdmann. "You think that's sentimental."

"I think you're a Pollyanna."

Adler turns to another man in the office. "He's
called me sentimental, and he's called me a Pollyanna. And you know what? It's *true.*"

Erdmann laughs. "What difference does *that*
make?"

That night Erdmann goes home, has three
scotches on the rocks, meets a former judge for

dinner, has a double scotch and thus fortified appears before the judge's evening seminar at the New York University Law School. Ten students are sitting in upholstered, stainless-steel swivel chairs in a red-carpeted conference room—all very new and rich and modern. Erdmann is supposed to tell them about jury selection and trial tactics, subjects on which he is a recognized master.

He unwraps a pack of cigarettes, lights up and leans close over the table. Two of the students are girls. Most of the men are in jeans and have long hair. Erdmann knows the look in their eyes. They think they will have innocent clients, they think they'll be serving their fellow man, the community, justice. They don't know that what they'll be serving is the system. He wants to give them some of the facts of life. "You are salesmen," he begins, "and you are selling a product that no one particularly wants to buy. You are selling a defendant who in all likelihood is guilty." They give him looks. "So you are going to disguise the product, wrap it in the folds of justice and make it a symbol of justice. You have to convince the jurors that you're sincere, and that the product you are selling is not really this defendant, but justice. You must convince them that your defendant is not on trial. Justice is on trial."

He takes a long drag on the cigarette, inhales and then blows it out toward the ceiling. The students are cautious. No one has taken any notes. "Your job is at the beginning and the end of the trial—the jury picking and the summation. In between comes that ugly mess of evidence. In examining prospective jurors you have to sell your product before they get a look at him, before they hear the evidence. You want also to plant the seeds of your defense, and soften the blow of the prosecution's case. If you know that a cop is going to testify that the defendant stabbed the old lady eighty-nine times, you can't hide from it. You might just as well bring it out yourself, tell them they're going to hear a police officer testify that the defendant stabbed the old lady eighty-nine times and then when the testimony comes you will be spared the sudden indrawing of breath. And maybe you can even leave the impression that the cop is lying."

A girl mentions the Tombs riots and asks Erdmann what could be done to give the prisoners speedy trials. During the riots, inmates' demands for less crowding, better food, extermination of rats and vermin were supported even by the hostage guards. But their demands for speedy trials, though they found strong support in the press, were less sincere. Virtually every prisoner in the Tombs is guilty, either of the crime charged or of some lesser but connected crime. He knows that he will either plead guilty or be convicted in a trial, and that he will serve time. He knows, too, that delays will help his case. Witnesses disappear, cops' memories fade, complainants lose their desire for vengeance. As prosecutors see their cases decaying, they lower and lower the pleas. Meanwhile, time served in the Tombs before sentencing counts as part of the sentence. Erdmann wants to explain that to the students, but he knows he will not find many believers.

"Let me disabuse you," he says, "of the idea that the prisoners in the Tombs want speedy trials. Most of them are guilty of something, and the *last* thing they want is a trial. They know that if every case could be tried within sixty days, the pleas of one-to-three for armed robbery would be back up to fifteen-to-twenty-five."

"What about the defendants out on bail?" a student asks.

"People out on bail almost *never* have to go to trial. If you can get your client out on bail, he won't be tried for at least three years, if at all. The case will go from one DA's back drawer to another's until it either dissolves into dust or the DA agrees to a plea of time served."

A student asks about the defense lawyer's responsibility to be honest. That triggers Erdmann's smile. "My *only* responsibility," he says, "is to my client. And not to suborn perjury, and not to lie personally. My client may lie as much as he wants."

Since the case of Richard Henderson, the junkie who didn't know if he was guilty, was marked ready for trial, he has been returned each day to the detention pen beneath Schweitzer's courtroom—on the almost nonexistent chance that his lawyer, and the DA assigned to the case, and a judge and courtroom might all become simultaneously available for trial. Each day he sits there in the pen while upstairs in court his case is called and passed, with no more certain consequence than that he will be back again the next day, so that it can be called and passed once more. After several days of this, Erdmann speaks to him again to see if he has changed his mind. He is the same—same clothes, same dead expression, same mad insistence on trial. Erdmann tries to encourage him to take the plea, "if you're guilty of anything."

Henderson still wants a trial.

"What will happen today?" he asks.

"Nothing. They'll set another date for trial, and that date will mean about as much as any date they set, which is nothing. You'll just have to wait in line."

Henderson picks at some mosquito-bite-size scars on his arm. "The other prisoners intimidate me," he says. "They keep asking me about my case, what I did, what I'm in for."

"What do you say?"

"I don't answer them. I don't want to talk about it."

Erdmann leaves him and goes back to court.

Erdmann's disrespect for judges (Schweitzer is a rare exception) is so strong and all-inclusive that it amounts at times to class hatred. When one of his young lawyers was held in contempt and fined $200, Erdmann left Schweitzer's court and rushed to the rescue. He argued with the judge and conned him into withdrawing the penalty. Then, outside the courtroom in the corridor, Erdmann's composure cracked. "He's a bully," he said angrily. "I'll put Tucker [one of his senior lawyers] in there a couple of days and tell him, 'No pleas.' That'll fix *that* wagon." He makes a note, then crumples it up. "No. I'll take it myself—and it'll be on the record this time." Erdmann remembers that two days earlier the judge's car was stolen in front of the courthouse. "I should have told him not to let the theft of his Cadillac upset him so much."

"There are so few trial judges who just judge," Erdmann says, "who rule on questions of law, and leave guilt or innocence to the jury. And appellate division judges aren't any better. They're the whores who became madams."

Would he like to be a judge?

"I would like to—just to see if I could be the kind of judge I think a judge should be. But the only way you can get it is to be in politics or buy it—and I don't even know the going price."

Erdmann is still in the hallway fuming over the contempt citation when a lawyer rushes up and says a defendant who has been in the Tombs five months for homicide has been offered time served and probation—and won't take it. Erdmann hurries to the courtroom. The defendant and his girl friend had been playing "hit and run," a ghetto game in which contestants take turns hitting each other with lead pipes. He said he was drunk when he played it and didn't know how hard he was hitting the girl. They both passed out and when he awoke the next morning she was dead. He had no previous record, and the judge is considering the extraordinarily light sentence agreed upon by the lawyer and DA. Neither the judge nor the DA is in a mood for any further haggling from the defendant. Erdmann talks with the defendant and gets the plea accepted. Five months for homicide. As he leaves the courtroom, a DA says, "Marty, you got away with murder."

Erdmann is gleeful. "I always get away with murder."

He goes down to his office. Alice Schlesinger walks by his desk and Erdmann remembers something he saw in the *Times* that morning about Anthony Howard, the man with an insane cellmate whose case he assigned to her three weeks ago.

"Hey, Alice," he calls to her, "congratulations on winning your first case."

She shrugs. A lawyer named James Vinci walks in and Erdmann says to him, "Don't forget to congratulate Alice. She just won her first case."

"Really?" says Vinci. "That's great."

"Yeah," Erdmann laughs. "Anthony Howard. His cellmate strangled him to death last night."

Every evening Martin Erdmann walks crosstown to a small French restaurant in the theater district. He sits always at the same table in a rear corner, with his back to whatever other customers there are, and he is happiest when there are none. The owner and his wife are always pleased to see him, and when he does not come they call his apartment to see if everything is all right.

Not long ago he reluctantly agreed to allow a reporter to join him for dinner. When they sat down, the reporter asked if Erdmann could be positive, after twenty-five years, that he had ever defended an innocent man.

"No. That you never know. It is much easier to know guilt than innocence. And anyway, it's much easier to defend a man if you know he's guilty. You don't have the responsibility of saving him from unjust punishment."

"What do you think about the courts today, the judicial system?"

"I think it's time people were told what's really going on. Everyone's so cowardly. Nobody wants to tell the public that the mini-measures proposed to clear up the mess *won't* do it. If you only had two roads going in and out of New York and someone said, 'What can we do about the traffic problem?' the answer would be, 'Nothing—until we get more roads.' You couldn't help it by tinkering around with the lights. Well, tinkering with the courts isn't going to help. We need more courts, more DAs, more Legal Aids, more judges—and it's going to cost a massive amount of money. I wonder how much money you could raise if you could guarantee safety from mugging and burglary and rape for $50 per person. Eight million people in New York? Could you get $20 million? And if you asked for $20 million to provide a workable system of criminal justice, how much would you get? People are more interested in their safety than in justice. They can pay for law and order, or they can be mugged."

"So what's the solution?"

"I've never really felt it was my problem. Everything up to now has benefited the defendant, and he's a member of the community, too. When you say, 'The people versus John Smith'—well, John Smith is part of the people, too. As a Legal Aid lawyer, I don't think it's my problem to make things run smoothly so my clients will get longer sentences. That's the courts' problem."

He stops talking and thinks for a minute. Something is burning inside. "That's the wrong attitude, I suppose, but then the appellate division has never approached me and asked me what can be done to improve justice for the *accused*. They *never* ask *that* question. It's just how can we clear the calendars. It's how can we get these bastards in jail faster for longer. Not in those words—*certainly* not. They *never* in all the years asked, how can we have more justice for the defendants. That's why I'm not too concerned about the system."

He has become angry and impassioned and now draws back. He concentrates on a lamb chop. "I'm loquacious when I'm tired," he says.

After several minutes he begins again. "You know, I really don't think there *is* any solution to the problem, any more than there is to the traffic problem. You do what you can within the problem."

"Is the day coming when the traffic won't move at all?"

"Yes. If every defendant refused to plead and demanded a trial, within a year the system would collapse. There would be three-year delays in reaching trial, prison riots, defendants would be paroled into the streets."

"What's Martin Erdmann going to do when that happens?"

"That's an interesting question. It would be too late by then to do anything. It's going to be too late very soon."

Every Friday, Erdmann assigns himself to a courtroom with a half-day calendar and catches the 1:35 bus for Danbury, Connecticut. From there he drives to his estate in Roxbury and spends the weekend walking, gardening "and talking to myself." He

has a three-story house with a junk-jammed attic, a
cellar filled with jarred fruit he preserved years ago
and never ate and a library cluttered with unread
books and magazines. A brook runs down from the
acres of Scotch pine, past his garden and under a
small bridge to the country below. He walks along
the brook, and stops on the bridge to stare down at
the trout. He never fishes here. "These are my
friends," he says, "and you don't catch your
friends."

Most of the weekend he spends coaxing co-opera-
tion from the flowers and vegetables. "I worry most
about the tomatoes because I like to eat them. The
most difficult is what I don't grow any more, roses.
They demand constant care and that's why I don't
have them." Tulips he likes. He spent a recent four-
day weekend putting in four hundred bulbs sent by
a friend from Holland. "They're not difficult. You
just dig four hundred holes and put them in and
they come up in the spring. The only problem is
moles. The moles make runs to eat insects and then
the mice use the mole runs to eat the tulip bulbs.
Years ago I used to be out with spray guns. And then
I figured, what the hell, this is nature, the mice
don't know they're not supposed to eat tulip bulbs.
So I gave up the spraying. I can't be hostile to something that's just doing what comes naturally."

The tulips are all in, it's 9 A.M. Monday morning
and Erdmann is back in his office going through the
Times. He is stopped by an item about a Legal Aid
client, a twenty-five-year-old named Raymond
Lavon Moore, the man in the iron box. Last weekend, while Erdmann was on his hands and knees

digging the four hundred tulip holes, Moore stripped the white ticking from his mattress, knotted it into a noose and hanged himself from the barred window.

Erdmann slowly folds the paper around the clipping and without expression hands it across his desk to another lawyer. He says nothing.

That noon Erdmann is back talking through the bars of the detention pen beneath Schweitzer's courtroom. He's asking a drug pusher if there's someone who will make bail for him.

"I can't get in touch with no one from in here, man."

"Can I?"

"Yeah. My mama in Cincinnati." He is about to give Erdmann the phone number when Erdmann moves aside to allow a guard to open the door and insert more prisoners. One of the prisoners is Richard Henderson, the junkie who wants to go to trial. He walks in, foggy and listless, and his momentum carries him to the center of the cell. He stops there, staring straight ahead. For three minutes he does not move or look around. Then he takes two steps to the bench, sits down and puts his hands between his knees. He sits there, rubbing his palms together.

Five hours later, Judge Schweitzer is almost at the end of the day's calendar. The spectators have all left, and no one remains but court personnel. Everyone is tired. To speed things up, Schweitzer has told the guards to bring up everyone left in the pen and keep them in the hall by the door. Five come up. Their cases already have been adjourned and what's happening now is more or less a body count to make sure no one is missed.

The last is Henderson. A guard walks him in, holding his arm, and someone says, "That's Henderson. He's been adjourned."

The guard, just four steps into the courtroom when he hears this news, quickly wheels Henderson around and heads him back out the door. Something in the wide, crack-the-whip arc of Henderson's swift passage through the court, something in his dead, unaware, zombie-eyed stare as he banks around the pivoting guard, strikes everyone who sees it as enormously funny. It's strange and it's pathetic, and no one can keep from laughing.

AFTERWORD

AFTER *Life* MAGAZINE PUBLISHED A LONG ARTICLE of mine about two heroin addicts named John and Karen, Assistant Managing Editor Ralph Graves suggested that the method used in that article—two months spent around the clock with the subjects—might also work for a story about a detective. We discussed, in fact, the possibility of examining the entire criminal justice spectacle by spending several months with each of its major participants—not only lawbreakers and a detective, but with a judge, defense lawyer, prosecutor, jail guard and complainant. I pursued the idea, and seven years later, in its last regular issue, *Life* published what has become chapter seven of this book, a story about the suicide of a New York City detective.

Shortly after my discussion with Graves, I mentioned the book idea to Sam Vaughan, an editor (now publisher) at Doubleday. I said I wanted to call the book *On the Edge* because that was how these people lived—flush up against the tragic, often violent realities of life and death. All these men and women were quite properly impressed by the seriousness of their work. Their conversation contained little small talk.

Few of the people who became the subjects of this book welcomed at first the intrusion of a writer. But eventually their self-censorship fell away, replaced by a tacit pact: "We're friends, you're going to know it all, don't hurt me."

Time spent with the subjects varied between two and five months. I spent nine months with a prosecutor, but the material was so voluminous it went into a book of its own. Only a piece is represented here: the story of a professional killer assassinated by the Mafia. It is told with tape recordings, stenographic transcripts and interviews of my own. A New York hoodlum named Sonny Franzese and three of his lieutenants were tried for that murder and acquitted.

While it took time, often weeks, to penetrate the subject's initial reserve, it sometimes took that long as well to break away when the story was over. It is addicting, I think, to have someone constantly with you who wants nothing more in his life at that moment than to observe your actions, listen to your thoughts, know your problems, your secrets, your dreams. Men said things I am sure they had never said to their wives, or analysts, or colleagues, or best friends. When the day-and-night research was over, the break sometimes came reluctantly. "You should have been here yesterday. Where were you yesterday? Listen to what you missed, what happened yesterday. This guy . . ." And I'd run back and hang around a few more days.

The people in this book felt very strongly about

what they were doing. Offered an opportunity to
express themselves to a large audience, they spoke
with dangerous candor. Their passion and honesty
invited attack. Some of the material about Detective George Barrett was so damaging—his critical
statements about police, his striking of prisoners—
that I offered to leave out his real name. He read the
final manuscript and said he'd talk it over with his
wife. A few days later he told me to leave his name
in. "Everything you say I said, I said. Everything
you say I did, I did. It's true. So the hell with 'em."

The story was published, and immediately Barrett's superiors launched an investigation. He was
called to headquarters and told to explain himself.
He took a few days off from work. Newspaper col-
umnists, referring to one of his remarks, called him
"the I've-got-to-win cop." When it became clear
that his promotion to first grade was in jeopardy, I
went to George Hunt, *Life*'s managing editor.
Hunt, a six-foot-four former Marine captain with a
Navy Cross, listened to my account of Barrett's
troubles, then stood behind his desk and said, "The
day hasn't come when a man gets into trouble for
telling the truth to *Life* magazine." A few weeks
later Barrett had his promotion.

Legal Aid lawyer Martin Erdmann sat across
from me in a little French restaurant off Broadway
and said honestly what he thought about judges.
Appellate justices, he said, "are the whores who
became madams." He must have known the effect
that would have, but he said it anyway because it
was what he believed. When the story was printed
the justices asked the Bar Association's grievance

committee to investigate the possibility of disciplinary action against Erdmann. The Bar recommended that no action be taken. The justices ignored that negative recommendation, the first time
they had ever done so, and started disciplinary action of their own. Word was conveyed to Erdmann
that a full apology, a disavowal in fact, might fix
things. He refused. In a hearing in which they
themselves acted as complainants, prosecutor and
judge, and which neither Erdmann nor his attorney
were permitted to attend, the justices censured
him. They censured him not only for his own words,
but for co-operating with the writer in the first
place, and for opinions in the story that were not
Erdmann's but mine alone. Erdmann appealed the
censure and months later a higher court reversed it.
By then, however, he was out of court, no longer
representing defendants, tucked safely away in an
administrative post.

I am indebted to many people at *Life* magazine,
principally to George Hunt, who was responsible
for my doing the story about John and Karen, and
who helped thereafter in many, many ways; to
Ralph Graves, who gave much encouragement and
edited parts of this book; to Steve Gelman, *Life*'s
articles editor who with Ralph Graves is the best
text editor alive; to Joe Kastner, *Life*'s copy editor,
who taught me more than even he imagines. I also
owe a large debt to Gene Haggerty and other editors during my two years at United Press International.

Some passages in this book were not published in
Life magazine and appear here for the first time.

222   JAMES MILLS

The longest of these is the chapter about prisoners
in the Tombs. I had almost finished two months with
Captain Dom Ghezzi when I asked the then correc-
tions commissioner, George McGrath, if I could
spend twenty-four hours locked in a cell. He'd had a
big lunch and two martinis and said okay. I picked
one in the special OBSO section where they kept
the lunatics, homicidal and/or suicidal. None of the
prisoners knew who I was, and few of the guards. (I
do not, of course, imagine for a moment that the
experience for me, there by choice, even approached what it was for the inmates.)

In the years spent researching and writing this
book, some details have changed. The face of New
York is not quite the same. Barrett's old station
house has been torn down. The Tombs has been
closed, temporarily at least. But the crimes are the
same, regrettably, and so are the violence and neglect, the apathy and the suffering. This book is
about people, and they have not changed.

I want to say, while I am at it, that after eight
years working on this book, I do not agree that
America's criminal justice system is as bad as some
people like to claim. Taken as a whole—from the
commission of a crime, through investigation, apprehension, trial, confinement, parole—it is one of
the least inhumane in the world. Which of course is
saying very little. Human beings have never cared
much for what they can't see, and since crime and
those associated with it are for most of us invisible,
we care little about them.

Which brings me to an apology. I never found a
way of including in this book a study of a complain-

ant. Short of walking unarmed through Harlem at 2
A.M., I know of no way to be present at the commission of a crime and follow the victim throughout his
ordeal. So the book neglects the victim. I find that
fitting in a way, for our judicial apparatus neglects
him too.

Public Works

Public
Works

STUDENT WRITING
AS PUBLIC TEXT

Edited by

Emily J. Isaacs & Phoebe Jackson

Boynton/Cook Publishers
HEINEMANN
Portsmouth, New Hampshire

Boynton/Cook Publishers, Inc.
A subsidiary of Reed Elsevier Inc.
361 Hanover Street
Portsmouth, NH 03801–3912
www.boyntoncook.com

Offices and agents throughout the world

Library of Congress Cataloging-in-Publication Data
Public works: student writing as public text / edited by Emily J. Isaacs and Phoebe Jackson.
    p. cm.
    Includes bibliographical references.
    ISBN 0-86709-571-7 (pbk.)
    1. English language—Rhetoric—Study and teaching. 2. Report writing—Study and teaching (Higher). 3. College students' writings—Publishing. 4. Academic writing—Publishing. 5. Authors and readers. 6. Peer review. I. Title: Student writing as public text. II. Isaacs, Emily J. III. Jackson, Phoebe.

PE1404 .P83 2001
808'.042'071—dc21   00-069659

Editor: Lisa Luedeke
Production service: Denise Botelho, Colophon
Production coordinator: Vicki Kasabian
Cover design: Joni Doherty
Manufacturing: Steve Bernier

Printed in the United States of America on acid-free paper
05 04 03 02 01 DA 1 2 3 4 5

Contents

Part III: The Pedagogy of Public Writing

Acknowledgments

We thank Anne Herrington, Amy Lee, and Louis Palmer for their useful feedback early on in the conceptualizing and writing of this project. As well, we thank Montclair State University for support through the separately budgeted research fund. Finally, we thank the teachers at the University of New Hampshire's 1996 October conference who inspired us to develop this collection.

Introduction

What's the Issue with Student Writing as Public Text?

The title of this collection, *Public Works: Student Writing as Public Text,* seems simple enough. *Student* writing, compositionists have been arguing for some thirty-plus years, must be seen as *writer's* writing, just as *students* must be seen as *writers.* By extension, as teachers of writers, albeit teachers of student-writers, it is reasonable to assume that we would seek opportunities for students to go public with at least some of their writing, just as other writers do. Indeed, as Charles Moran discusses in Chapter 5, the founders of the process-writing movement were quite explicit in their advocacy of pedagogies that include students going public through peer groups, in-class magazines, and even mainstream outlets like local and college newspapers. Today, the demand for public writing reaches beyond the confines of the classroom experience. Service–learning projects, for example, frequently call upon students to write for organizations with broad and diverse audiences. Moreover, the Internet has increased our zeal for public exposure with the profusion of "personal" and class Web pages and the posting of material for an infinite virtual audience. These new trends in the field of composition, and in higher education more broadly, suggest that writing teachers will feel pressure to make public writing a part of their composition curriculum and pedagogy.

To repeat, it all seems rather easy and simple: Writing teachers must be, with increasing frequency, developing courses that enable and perhaps mandate public writing. To read the literature across various theoretical perspectives—from so-called expressivism to critical pedagogical approaches to service–learning approaches, and so on—one can trace a consistent and even increasing call and rationale for public writing. Among the many differences we might have, the value of writing for audiences beyond the teacher seems almost universally valued. In a moment we briefly, and selectively, trace this history, both to demonstrate the widespread advocacy for public writing, and also the much less visible traces of contradictions to these pedagogies that make going public challenging and potentially problematic.

Interestingly, while many scholars argue for public writing quite forcefully, few discuss critically the values behind the call for public writing, the ethics involved with asking students to write publicly, or the pedagogical

approaches and strategies that are employed when students are asked to engage in public writing. There has not been enough attention to the ethics of assuming that students will necessarily benefit from such practice; there has been little discussion about the problems teachers face trying to institute such a practice; and finally, sometimes these practices have unintended, even negative, effects on students and their writing or the audience for whom they are writing. The need exists for more critical reflection on a practice that has been taken for granted by many compositionists who underscore the common-sense and theoretical aspects of public writing rather than interrogate the complexities inherent in such a practice.

From various perspectives, the writers in *Public Works: Student Writing as Public Text* examine and reflect on what has become a tacit assumption in many writing classrooms: Students and their writing benefit from having a readership beyond that of the teacher, in short, of going public. We define the term *public writing* broadly, from sharing writing with just one person other than a teacher (i.e., with a peer) to writing for a very public audience (i.e., on a Web page or in the print media). In the current–traditional writing classroom as defined by James Berlin (1982, 1987), teachers ask students to write for their almost exclusive perusal, while in the student-centered, process, or even "post-process" classrooms students are, theoretically anyway, expected to assume that their teacher, peers, and, in some cases, an audience outside of the class will read their material. We say "theoretically" because, as our discussion below reveals, the pedagogical literature in our field is clear about advocating public writing. But what about practice? What seems to be missing from the discussion are the very real ethical and pedagogical problems that teachers and students have encountered when a larger reading audience is assumed.

The authors included in this collection endeavor to think through the implications of asking students to go public with their writing. First, they explore the range of what constitutes public writing: in-class oral presentations of student writing, in-class publications (print or electronic), and printed materials resulting from service–learning projects. In each case, the essays balance the description of particular practices of having students go public with critical theorizing and reflection on the issues that such practices raise. From their critical reflection, the contributors offer readers ways to go about rethinking their own classroom practice in order to successfully implement and integrate public writing. However, in order to think through the current implications of public writing, it seems necessary to understand the historical and pedagogical context from which it derives. A review of the widespread support and advocacy for public writing not only demonstrates the continuing relevance of the topic, but also suggests the need for a sustained reflective discussion of pedagogical considerations that incorporate the newer practices of public writing.

Advocacy of Public Writing: From 1970's Process Pioneers to 2000's Service–Learning and Web Pedagogues

Process Pioneers and Social Constructivists

The newer practices of public writing came out of a rich tradition of composition scholarship that began in the late 1960s and early 1970s with Peter Elbow's peer writing groups.[1] In two texts that are now canons of our academic field but were originally written for writers, not students or composition specialists, *Writing Without Teachers* (1973) and *Writing with Power* (1981 originally), Elbow argues for sharing writing just as he argues for free writing and other private writing experiences, all for the purpose of producing clearer, more meaningful, and more satisfying product for the writer. While Elbow is always cautious about readers and going public at the wrong time and to the wrong people (teachers being among those who can be most "dangerous"), in these early texts particularly, Elbow values going public as one of the essential, albeit painful and risky, parts of the writing ("cooking") process:

> If you are stuck writing or trying to figure something out, there is nothing better than finding one person, or more, to talk to. . . . I write a paper; it's not good; I discuss it with someone; after fifteen minutes of back-and-forth I say something in response to a question or argument of his and he says, "But why didn't you *say* that? That's good. That's clear." I want to shout, "But I *did* say that. The whole paper is saying that." But in truth the whole paper is merely implying or leading up to or circumnavigating that. Until I could see my words and thoughts refracted through his consciousness, I *couldn't* say it directly that way." (1973, 49)

In this quote from *Writing Without Teachers,* Elbow is suggesting that if students write like "real" writers—unfettered by teachers and educational institutions—students will want to write, and write well. Real writers, Elbow and other early process-writing pioneers argue, ultimately write for readers, because reaching others is the assumed point of (most) writing; therefore, despite all their thorns, readers are sometimes the only ones who can give the information that writers really need.

Although Elbow in many ways has remained the dominant voice from this early period and pedagogical school, the legacies of others, including Donald Murray, who represented the "real" writer quite literally (as popular journalist turned academic), and James Moffett, who approached the business of teaching writing from a decidedly developmentalist perspective, reveal an early inclination toward and faith in the value of public writing for students. Murray (author of *A Writer Teaches Writing,* 1968) highlights the significance of public writing's "real work/real audience" perspective, thus emphasizing the prac-

tical value of readers and the belief that students are best served when they imitate his almost-glorified "real writer," rather than the damaged, uninspired, student writer. Moffett (*Teaching the Universe of Discourse,* 1968), a developmentalist, also underscores the importance of the dialogic and trans-actional element of public writing on the grounds that such writing enables students to write for readers other than the teacher. Notably, Elbow, Murray, and Moffett espouse student-centered classrooms and pedagogies that deemphasize teacher authority. In this environment, public writing is pre-sumed to flourish by positioning student writers as authorities, countering the force of "truth" that teacher comments necessarily carry.

Early expressionists and process-oriented theorists were joined by writing teacher–scholars who come from social constructivist and poststructuralist per-spectives. Advocating a collaborative approach to learning, Ken Bruffee, in *A Short Course in Writing* (1980), published first in 1972, emphasizes the value of the social nature of public writing, a condition he identifies as common in nonacademic settings. In this work, Bruffee argues strenuously for students to go public with their writing to receive feedback, on the grounds that public writ-ing in classrooms deemphasizes teacher authority and promotes student-writers' abilities to see themselves as responsible writers and to view writing as a social activity. As he comments, "Knowing each other's work helps writers develop responsibility for what they have to say, and the courage to say it, through the immediate response of a community of sympathetic peers. . . . Immediate re-sponse also helps to give writers a sense of a real and alive audience" (107).

In 1984, Ede and Lunsford focused our attention on audience with publi-cation of "Audience Addressed/Audience Invoked." Their exposition of the ways that audiences affect writers, even when they are writing alone, further served to push compositionists to require students to practice some form of public writing. This landmark work on audience led to explicit calls to do more than invoke audience by providing students with addressable audiences that could and would respond back to writers. Marilyn Cooper (1986), in concert with others who critique a model of writing as a solitary endeavor (Brodkey 1986, and other feminists), encourages teachers to seek ways to encourage community and sharing of writing among student writers, noting that we need not ask our students to invoke an audience when they have, at their disposal, a roomful of very real writers; her argument for public writing through peer sharing rests on the principle, "Students learn about how to deal with their readers' by developing the habits and skills involved in finding readers and making use of their responses" (372).

While writing pedagogues advocate the benefits of expanding the student's writing audience, recently Elbow has given a closer look to the feed-back that students receive under such circumstances. In the introduction of the most recent edition of *Writing with Power* (1998), Elbow doesn't back away entirely from the value of feedback (he retains these sections), but he does ar-gue for the more certain and clear value of going public *without* feedback,

what he calls "sharing": "The more I teach and write, the more I value what could be called a third mysterious dimension of my book, the minimal but powerful process of mere sharing. . . . The feedback process can misfire in many ways (for instance, when we get responses that confuse or intimidate us), but mere sharing can't go wrong" (xxi–xxii). Elbow, one might surmise, has run up against some of the same problems that other teachers have had with having students go public with their writing. Elbow has had to figure out how to fit the public role of writing into his own writing pedagogy, a pedagogy that is, in the end, about writers, not readers: ". . . my larger self wants [students] to feel themselves as readers and academics, but this goal seems to conflict with my more pressing hunger to help them feel themselves as writers. That is, I can't help wanting my students to have some of that uppitiness of writers toward readers" (1995, 77). It appears that Elbow, recognizing that the primary goals of his own writing classroom are poorly suited for more readerly-based public writing, has moved more and more toward a public writing pedagogy of "sharing" and away from feedback.

For social constructivists, the problems are somewhat different. Here the problem is not with protecting the writer from difficult readers, but with creating the engaged and critical student-readers that student-writers need. In discussions of peer review, this is perhaps the most frequently expressed lament: Student-readers can do nothing more than express enthusiasm for their peers' texts! It becomes a kind of liking game; I like you, I like your paper. Further, having students go public—through peer groups, as is most frequently suggested by social constructivists of this period—does not in and of itself change student-writers' beliefs about writing and knowledge construction. In "Habits of Mind: Historical Configurations of Textual Ownership in Peer Writing Groups" (1998), Candace Spigelman quotes a student who has demonstrated herself to be an effective and engaged peer respondent, writing, "I like the writing groups, but I don't use the advice because then the paper would not be *my own*. I feel that my writing is *my writing* and should not be based upon what advice is given by others" (234, Spigelman's emphasis). Spigelman goes on to make a persuasive case for how this student, as well as most others raised in Western culture, is bound to hold tightly to individual perspective, and therefore will rigorously resist using public writing as an opportunity for revision. In her conclusion, Spigelman suggests that it is not enough to teach and require public writing and peer response; in addition, we need to address the issues of intellectual property and textual ownership directly in the content of our courses. Spigelman's suggestion reveals that public writing may require more than a change of classroom activities; it may require a change in curriculum as well.

Critical and Feminist Writing Pedagogies

In the late eighties and into the nineties, the influence of critical educational theorists and critical feminist pedagogues made its mark on mainstream com-

position studies. For feminists and critical pedagogues who focus on ways to disrupt and rearrange socially constructed power dynamics in the classroom, public writing serves to reduce teacher authority and provide room for a multiplicity of voices, including women and other minorities, who are frequently not heard in open discussion.

Grounded within the work of such critical educational scholars as Freire (1970), hooks (1989, 1994), and Shor (1980), critical and feminist pedagogues call for, in the words of Henry Giroux and Peter McLaren (1989), "taking seriously, as a crucial aspect of learning, the experiences of students mediated by their own histories, languages and traditions. . . . teaching students how to identify, unravel, and critically appropriate the codes, vocabularies, and deep grammar of different cultural traditions" (xxiv). As Susan Jarratt (1991) underscores in "Feminism and Composition: The Case for Conflict," making space for student voices is not simply a matter of providing a student-centered classroom that focuses on students' words and writings; rather, it is essential to "confront and explore the uneven power relations" that are represented in our classroom and the culture at large (113). For many of us, class discussion provides only so much opportunity for students to articulate and engage conflicting positions. Thus, for critical pedagogues, public writing offers teachers and students opportunities to observe and discuss the ways that the very ideologies of domination that they study outside the classroom also operate within their own classroom.

For critical pedagogues, public writing serves as a "teaching tool" to reveal to students "thoughts-in-process" (Dixon 1995, 108) and facilitate teachers' efforts to have students see the ways that they themselves are both reflections and *producers* of cultural artifacts (Gutjahr 1995). Giroux (1995), in a discussion of his own classroom practice, writes of the importance of public writing; in his class, student papers are "duplicated" and "used as a basis for class discussion" (14). For Giroux, having students go public with their writing facilitates his goal of giving students more control and authority for their learning, enabling students to learn from each other, and furthering his goal of getting students to "theorize their own experiences" (11). Moreover, such a practice encourages students to "bring out and examine the contradiction and conflicts" (Jarratt 1991, 116) that expressions of the "differences of gender, race, and class amongst students and teachers provide" (113).

Feminists concerned with the silencing of women see public writing as helping students transition "from invisible silence to public writers" (Hollis 1992, 343). Rooted in the early feminist literary critical tradition of unearthing and valuing women and people of color who have historically been excluded, Hollis and other feminists (e.g., Cayton 1990; Frey 1987) seek to preempt the process of silencing student writers by providing opportunities for students to write for audiences while they are still in school. Importantly, entering the public sphere not only allows students to express themselves, but also provides the opportunity for students to see their classmates and them-

selves as positioned socially by their race, class, gender, and other social formations. Min-Zhan Lu (1998), for example, seeks ways to help students perform analyses "where the self is not used as an end in and of itself but as an opening of a perspective that allows [students] to conceive of transforming [them]selves with the aid of others" (243). While Lu, like some other critical and feminist pedagogues, does not speak specifically to the value of public writing, the aims of her inquiry suggest the value of supporting the transformative agenda of critical and feminist pedagogy through having students go public with their writing.

Critical feminist educators Magda Gere Lewis (1993) and Elizabeth Ellsworth (1992) both write of the challenges of implementing critical and feminist pedagogies within their courses. Lewis writes of a female student's presentation on violence against women being interrupted by "a frustrated young man" asking why she didn't offer "'the other side of the story'" (165). Lewis points out that this young man's strategy reflects his effort to deflect one of the purposes of the course, to self-reflect on the benefits he has received from a patriarchal society. Lewis finds this moment, and moments like it, as presenting a pedagogical challenge for teachers: Should the teacher step back and see how the questioned student (a member of the relatively oppressed group) handles it (Lewis says no); if we step in, how do we do so in a way that the silent student can feel empowered and the silencing student can understand his actions? For Ellsworth, critical pedagogy's reliance on the magical power of "sharing" is dangerous, or as she says, "Acting as if our classroom were a safe space in which democratic dialogue was possible and happening did not make it so" (107). In sum, when calls for students to go public are couched within a curriculum and discourse of critical examinations of the self in relation to existing oppressive formations, we must expect selective and strategic self-presentation, hurt students, and, in the end, new pedagogical and ethical challenges.

The "Real World": Service Learning, New Technologies, and Other Intersections Between the Classroom and the World Outside of the Ivory Walls

Compositionists have argued for public writing on the grounds that it prepares students for the "real world." In the words of Margaret Mansfield (1993), "real world" writing "can be done in contexts of practical and political necessity, in contexts where what you write will be read by 'real people' and will be used to gain essential information, complete tasks, evaluate proposals, make policy decisions, and so forth" (70). Accordingly, public writing gives students experience with writing for multiple constituencies, for broadening definitions of what constitutes "real writing," for developing rhetorical strategies, and finally, for becoming more precise writers. Paul Sladky (1997) has made student writing "real writing" quite literally, publishing *Free Falling and Other Student Essays*, a collection of student writing, in a mainstream press. On a less

grand scale, Paul Popken (1995) notes that many colleges and universities now publish their own student-writing magazines, with the aim of providing students a place for expository writing. Dutton and Fils-Aime (1993) suggest that institution-wide magazines work to provide students with an incentive to write "pieces worthy of publication," while also helping students understand audience. Most importantly, Dutton and Fils-Aime believe that the university publication inspires their students "to produce publishable pieces" that will be "taken seriously" (86–87).

Another avenue for "real" writing has been through the use of service–learning projects, in which students write in conjunction with providing services to community organizations. Bruce Herzberg (1994) notes that community service writing offers students occasions for "real application" (308) of their writing skills. Aaron Schutz and Anne Ruggles Gere (1998) argue that service learning not only gives students the opportunity for "different modes of presentation of the self and the group" (144), but also increases students' contact with those who exist "outside the exclusionary walls of the university" (145).

Finally, technology has opened up yet another area that promotes public writing. Through the use of technological resources, student writing can be made public quickly, widely, and (despite the considerable costs of buying and servicing of equipment, as Moran [1998] notes) cheaply. Proponents of computers and composition contend that interchange between writers and readers is facilitated through the use of technology (discussed in Duin and Hansen 1994; Johnson-Eilola 1994). Additionally, advocates of technology in the writing classroom argue that the classroom experience of public writing with technology provides students with experience and skills that are transferable to jobs outside of the academy. Compositionists who embrace this new technology encourage student postings on list-servs and network discussion groups, desktop-published magazines, student-authored Web pages, as well as the sharing of student writing through the more traditional (though electronic) peer review groups and collaborative writing groups.

Pedagogical and Ethical Negotiations of Public Writing

In these latest developments in writing pedagogy—writing for the "real world," service–learning writing, and Web-based instruction—public writing has been embraced seemingly without question. To have students write publicly and to think critically and intellectually, teachers need to prepare their students, and themselves, for the responses that articulation of one's views entails. As we commit ourselves more fully to the teaching of public writing, we need to consider how to prepare students and ourselves for discussion of student public writing and how to appreciate and make productive analyses and use of public response. The assembled authors help us to consider ways that writing for the public has repercussions that we, as teachers, have the opportunity to mediate and help our students analyze critically. While that frequently referred-to real

world may not provide such opportunities for mediation and critical thinking for writers who go public, the academy offers unique opportunities not only to prepare students for public writing, but also to aid them in strategizing for, coping with, and responding to the repercussions of going public.

The Collection

The first section of this book, "Pedagogical Negotiation of Public Writing," addresses the pedagogical negotiations that occur between students and students, teachers and students, and institutions and teachers when students are encouraged to go public with their writing. Stover begins the section by examining how we define public and private writing in the composition classroom. Because there is little agreement, even historically, about defining *privacy,* Stover concludes that students should participate in discussions of what constitutes private and public writing. Lee argues that students' writing is always socially mediated by other members in the class. While it would appear that a public writing component to our classes provides writers with the freedom to narrate and *own* their personal experiences, in fact student writers find that readers "rewrite" not only experiences represented by a text, but also the writer as well. Stenberg is also concerned with the ways that stated pedagogical aims of inclusion and reduction of teacher authority can be undermined and contradicted by subtle patriarchal teacher modeling, resulting in exclusion and silencing, rather than inclusion. More specifically, Stenberg uses her own experience in an undergraduate cultural studies course to argue that teachers must be attentive to moments when public writing does not guarantee students a receptive audience. Finally, Goodburn discusses how public writing in a service–learning course can inadvertently misrepresent a community. In response to recent zeal for service–learning courses, she cautions professors to reconsider the politics and ethics of sending student writers out to locales in the community to represent the experience of "Others" in texts that are neither written with nor shared with members of the community.

The writers of the second section of the book, "The Virtual Public," investigate the use of the Web as the latest medium with which to go public with student writing. In an overview of the early history of process writing in relation to public writing, Moran explores how the "new world of Web publishing exacerbates and therefore makes more visible, the problems inherent in a writing program that incorporates publishing and sharing." Mauriello and Pagnucci, through a narration of two experimental forays into Web-based composition classes, discuss the ethical dilemmas that are raised when students are required to write on the Web. They found that students feared their Web-posted writing would be misunderstood, stolen, and might even put them into personal danger. By exploring some of the problems that their students faced, Mauriello and Pagnucci hope to offer suggestions that might help in making "future Web-based writing courses more equitable." Derek Owens, situated at an urban

multiethnic university, examines how the posting of student essays on the Web implicitly suggests certain shared cultural expectations about the public nature of writing that he had not anticipated. He argues that teachers need to consider and discuss these cultural assumptions, especially in light of changing student populations, which might hold values different than those of the instructor. Jonathan Benda, through an analysis of course-related student Web pages, examines proponents' claims that Web-texts promote interactivity. A user and advocate of the technology, Benda aims to provide readers with data about the effects of Web-based publishing that neither the technology nor traditional rhetorical and composition theory can fully account or provide for.

In the last section of the book, "The Pedagogy of Public Writing," authors share the conviction not only that public writing is of value and is a practice that is here to stay, but also that this practice requires that we reconceive the traditional process-writing classroom. Wendy Bishop introduces this section with a call for us to reconsider the role of product in a process-writing classroom. Situated firmly within a process framework, Bishop affirms the role of peer response in creating a classroom environment of authentic writers and audiences. Daum and Palmeri, undergraduate student writers, make the case for the development of student-led writing groups outside the domain of the composition classroom. They assert that the hierarchical evaluative context of a teacher's writing classroom inhibits students' efforts toward self-determination in their own writing. Palmeri and Daum describe the nonevaluative, teacherless, peer writing groups they have developed, and discuss the ways that these groups help student-writers deal with particular problems. The chapters by Benson and Latchaw and Hewett and McRuer offer perspectives on the value of writing for real audiences beyond the classroom. Benson and Latchaw, for example, argue that students who write manuals and pamphlets for real discourse communities become more self-motivated and efficient and learn the value of collaboration. Hewett and McRuer examine how writing for a public audience helps students understand how they can actively engage in constructing the world around them. A cultural studies model, in which students participate in actual conferences with their writing, allows students to learn that "recognition of the writing self as social does not immobilize students, but rather empowers them to participate in the shaping and reshaping of the public sphere."

As the writers of this collection make clear, going public with student writing involves more than the mechanics of writing publicly. To have students write publicly and to think critically and intellectually, teachers need to prepare their students, and themselves, for the responses that articulation of one's views entails. As we commit ourselves more fully to the teaching of public writing, we need to consider how to prepare students and ourselves for discussion of student public writing and how to appreciate and make productive analyses and use of public response.

Emily Isaacs and Phoebe Jackson

Note

1. Of course, the history of writing groups predates process-writing pedagogy, as Anne Ruggles Gere makes clear in *Writing Groups: History, Theory, and Implications*. We focus on the ways that having students go public with their writing has been conceptualized, valued, and articulated from the late 1960s to the present, as it is composition theorists and pedagogues from this period who influence writing teachers of today.

Public
Works

1

Redefining Public/Private Boundaries in the Composition Classroom

Andrea Stover

My main goal as a teacher is to promote the desire to write. In my experience as both a writer and a teacher, this desire is fragile because it requires a delicate balance between privacy and exposure. A writer needs to feel private enough to feel safe, yet public enough to be heard. Depending on how people conceive of identity and audience, this balance can be achieved anywhere along the private/public continuum—from writing in a private diary to writing for large public audiences. Some people write daily without sharing their writing with anyone, not even themselves—they don't reread what they have written. Other people feel more comfortable writing for someone else, always anticipating that their words will be read. Some of these people may also keep a diary, but they conceive of a public audience while composing. Both types of people, along with those who fall somewhere between the two extremes, enter our composition classrooms. Each requires a different degree and type of privacy to keep their desire for writing alive and healthy. But, because successful academic writing requires a well-balanced (though variable) mix of the public and the private, students who are very private need to risk exposing more of their thoughts to others. Similarly, students who are very public, always writing for somebody else or to fulfill somebody else's requirements, need to learn how to write for and to themselves. How are composition teachers to structure an environment that is both private enough to be safe and public enough to engage students in the academic community?

I would like to envision the composition classroom as a place that mediates between people's private and public selves. Several difficulties arise with such a conception. As a composition teacher, my own ideology of *public* and *private* shapes the environment of the classroom, puts students in a position of assimilating to or resisting the practices I promote, and may in fact violate the very sense of comfort and safety I find essential to writing. For instance, in my attempts to build a stronger, more trusting classroom community, I once

1

critiqued a paper (gently) in class. Though my usual style involves one-on-one discussions with students, I thought public discussion would help them realize that we all make the same mistakes and that we can learn from one another and celebrate each other's successes. I also wanted to encourage students to help each other openly and confidently, while lessening dependence on my private feedback. Much to my dismay, the student responded, "But I thought you liked it." Even though I had offered the same critique in a private setting, my public commentary felt like betrayal. The same signals of praise were read differently (or not at all) in the more public forum. In another instance, I assigned a private journal in which students were free to write whatever they wished. I counted pages only to make sure students were fulfilling the assignment. Some students found this private writing exceptionally helpful; others found it useless and did whatever they could to avoid (or subvert) the assignment. For these resistant students, private writing had no place in a public classroom. As these examples show, because my boundaries of privacy are different from my students', and theirs from each other's, I face the dilemma of how to conduct public and private teaching practices that promote growth without stimulating resistance.

I wish to examine what we mean exactly by the terms *public* and *private* when it comes to teaching the writing process. Because these terms call up associations that have blocked my own writing, I hesitate to make any claims on what constitutes private or public writing. It seems to me that the ideas of public and private are largely invented. For some students, journal writing feels public even though we promise not to read it. After all, the writing is demanded by someone else, and the students' once unarticulated and hence untraceable thoughts are now made manifest on a page. It is difficult for some students to imagine an assignment of any kind as private. Other students, no matter how often we tell them that private writing is loose and free, feel constricted by the genre because they have difficulty inventing an audience who matters to them. We often make a mistake in assuming that naming the audience "oneself" puts writers at their ease. In fact, it is a very odd concept for students who conceive of writing as a transmission of ideas to someone else.

On the other hand, we may confuse students when we call writing *public*. The actual process of producing a written text, even for a class publication, requires large chunks of private time—sitting alone, testing the words against oneself and one's experience to see if they sound right. In reality, a great deal of writing that underscores the drafting process is private. In my own writing, and in my teaching, I have experienced a boundary-crossing between the terms *public* and *private*. I no longer see them as two discrete zones that elicit two distinct kinds of writing.

As we walk into a classroom, whether as teachers or students, we tacitly understand that a mix of our public and private lives is expected. The tension comes as everyone waits to see exactly how that mix will be concocted. In composition classes, we require students to draw from their personal lives and

private experience to write their public essays. The classroom is a site of mediating the private lives of each student with the public, written expression of ideas. Any space or genre that is recognized as a mediating space faces several challenges. As Nancy Walker (1988) so eloquently says, "There is a point at which a life lived primarily in the mind or imagination encounters and must be translated for the world outside the mind, for other people—a public, however limited. The medium of this encounter, if one is a writer, is words" (273). Though the contact point between the private life of the imagination and the public life of the world outside is words in a diary for Walker, I see this same contact point enacted in the composition classroom. Both require that private thoughts be made manifest in written words, whether we name those words *private writing, journals, essays,* or *peer responses.*

In trying to get a handle on how other teachers manage the public/private mix in composition classrooms, I turned to the work of Sharyn Lowenstein, Elizabeth Chiseri-Strater, and Cinthia Gannett (1994). Refuting scholars and commentators who claim that the journal promotes self-centeredness, these scholars look to "historical and cultural traditions, from which school journal practices have developed" to show that journals can effectively connect individual, private reflections with communal, public knowledge: "We want to re-envision the academic journal as a mediator through which students can engage in larger academic and social conversations both within and outside the academy" (142).

Enthused by their theoretical savvy, and encouraged by their practical suggestions for ways to use journals in the classroom, I imagine myself revamping my teaching style to make room for the journal. But something stops me. Though I love the idea of a collaborative class journal where "students could be invited to respond to course content or to the events of the class itself" (151), I realize, if I were a student I would not write in such a journal because I would feel too exposed. If I were to participate in such a journal, I would play it safe by not revealing too much of what I really thought. Hence I would write things I didn't care much about. Consequently, I would lose interest in the project and it would lose its connective value for me.

If a person's emotional and intellectual responses to a theory or practice are at odds with one another, the emotional response will almost always win out. And in my experience, issues of privacy provoke more intense emotional responses than intellectual ones. People are unlikely to initiate a teaching strategy that makes them emotionally uncomfortable, no matter how much they intellectually value it. If I had an easy relationship with the journal, journal keeping would be central to my teaching. I would use it to help students move between what they perceive as their personal/private lives (in writing) and the more professional public life of the classroom—making connections and using the insights of one to inform the other. But because my relationship with journal writing is conflicted, I am ineffective in selling it as a useful tool for students. Rather than arguing against journals in school, or against private

writing, it seems more honest to acknowledge that one person's point of comfortable and fruitful mediation between the public and the private is not necessarily another's.

So, how can composition teachers mediate between public and private lives when no one has a clear, agreed upon understanding of what constitutes the private as opposed to the public (in politics, sex, law, writing . . .)? We are trying to bridge the public/private gap without knowing exactly what we are bridging. People argue fervently about rights to privacy, yet their passionate stands are not based on any stable, culturally accepted foundation.

American cultural formulations of privacy have been unstable since before the turn of the century. The 1890s in America mark a time of dramatic increase and fascination with the technologies of publicity along with a simultaneous draw toward interiority and new legal protections of privacy. Growing technologies of publicity (e.g., photography and publishing) in the late nineteenth century helped to define and construct a newly contested space for privacy, a space still in confusion today. We find this reconstruction in the law (Warren and Brandeis), literature (Henry James), painting (Eakins), and architecture (Wright). The tension, and subsequent need for negotiation, between the realms of privacy and publicity, and the roles each plays in constructing personality, erupt again and again in late Victorian America.[1]

Not until 1890 was the "right to privacy" introduced to the courts. Samuel D. Warren and Louis D. Brandeis, harassed by reporters and photographers, wrote an appeal, "The Right to Privacy," which for the first time in American history differentiated between laws that protected privacy from those that protected property. Prior to that, only property was protected by law, but Warren and Brandeis articulated the concern that while property is alienable from the human being who possesses it, privacy is an inalienable part of one's personality and therefore needs a different set of laws to protect it.[2] Historian Robert Mensel (1991) explains that though the appeal gained widespread support, and though several people felt that their privacy needed legal protection (especially from amateur photographers who took people's pictures and sold them without permission), it wasn't until 1903 that actual legislation was established in the name of privacy rather than property (41). Throughout the decade, judges "turned down defendant's claims to privacy . . . because the protection of feelings was said to be beyond the practical, tangible business of the courts" (26). The difficulty stemmed, not from theoretical formulations of privacy and privacy rights, but from the practical applications of them.

E. L. Godkin (1890), editor of *The Nation,* also made attempts to differentiate between a public and private identity. He distinguished *character* from *personality,* seeing character as a "measure of one's reliability in such matters as credit transactions, professional practice, and business in general," whereas personality "was a complex of feelings which existed in the private confines of the mind" (quoted in Mensel 1991, 26–27). Although Godkin was distressed about new intrusions of the media on privacy, he did not advocate, or

see the possibility for, legal protections of privacy per se. As Mensel explains, "As a practical matter, the cure would be worse than the affliction, because legal vindication of the right of privacy would occur in a public courtroom" (27). In defining laws of privacy, people found that though the distinction between a public character and a private personality was clear enough in theory, it was nearly impossible to defend in practice.

I offer this brief historical sketch to illustrate its remarkable parallel with the 1999 Clinton–Lewinsky affair and to suggest that the dilemmas and issues about how to define and protect rights of privacy in a public context are as unsettled and contested now as they were then. In the comic strip *Life in Hell,* Matt Groening (1998) offered "Sex Tips from Your Moral Superiors," saying, "We believe that sex is a private matter between a husband, a wife, the government, the media and the American people." His satiric commentary epitomizes the confusion and contradiction that saturates our culture. If we have not decided the role of public and private boundaries in our courts, government, or media, how are we to enact them in our classrooms?

The public and the private frequently collide in my classroom, and I worry about it. Because we are in the business of language, we know that the way we name things shapes our reality. The very word *private,* at times and in certain contexts, invokes positive associations (personal, intimate, safe) and at other times and contexts invokes negative associations (exclusive, secretive, asocial). But because these associations change with personality, context, previous experience, and perhaps maturity level, they are difficult to pin down, talk about, or translate into teaching practices.

The following teaching scenario provides a cautionary tale for those who aim to break down public and private boundaries in the classroom without providing careful safeguards. In her *Linguafranca* article, "The Man Who Knew Too Much," Ruth Shalit (1998) tells the devastating tale of a teacher who fell from tremendous popularity to public disgrace because of his strategies for connecting difficult academic material to students' personal, private lives. Adam Weisberger, a professor at Colby College in Maine, asked his students to "reflect on the class readings [classical works of social theory] and discussion by means of analyzing an important part of your lives—namely, your family" (33). In having his students analyze family life, he hoped to show how our most private lives are determined by shared public cultural values.

Weisberger did not make this assignment optional (unless students made a persuasive case to write about something else), and he used it as the central means to evaluate the students' understanding of course material. Furthermore, he downplayed the need for empathy or sympathetic understanding. He says, "I didn't want any of this boohoo, I'm a victim stuff . . . that's bullshit. I've heard it a million times. . . . Why should I, as a teacher, simply accept formulaic kinds of self-insight, whether it comes from male or female, left or right?" (33).

Weisberger's justification for such a hard-edged approach stems from his ideological understanding of public/private boundaries. In Weisberger's view,

what students deem private, personal, and self-reflective comes from a clichéd, public script. Rather than respecting what they considered private, he felt it his job to disabuse them of their illusions:

> I wanted students to see that that which we believe to be most personal is where the categorical lives most deeply. I was striving against pat formulas. Maybe I didn't do it successfully but I tried. (quoted in Shalit 1998, 33)

Clearly, however, many of Weisberger's students believed that their "most personal" experiences and self-reflections belonged to them, and had more private meaning than some public "pat formula." As one student says, "Not everyone is ready or able to get deep into their family stuff. . . . How do you grade something like that? No one can assess the value of my pain" (32). For Weisberger, her pain reflected sociological forces that could be analyzed and hence graded. For the student, her pain was hers, private, none of his business.

In this case, teacher and students clash on where they draw the public/private line. But the story goes on to illustrate the more confusing clash that took place within the students themselves. Many who enjoyed the class initially, and willingly opened up their private lives for scrutiny while enrolled in it, later felt that they had been manipulated and their privacy violated. Jamie Geier, one of Weisberger's most hostile accusers, had once been an ardent supporter of his teaching style. A year after the course ended, she filed charges against him, claiming that he "had pressured her to write papers about the (nonparental) sexual abuse she had suffered as a child" (35). Earlier, while in the course, she had written, "Adam has made social theory interesting and has taught me to apply my major to what happens in everyday life" (36). Similarly, another student, who "liked Weisberger initially," says, "He was trying to relate sociology to a personal level. . . . I thought it was a good idea" (34). However, this student ultimately grew "disgusted" by the papers she wrote for the course: "They were awful and wrong, . . . I was exploiting my family members for a grade. I didn't realize that until about two thirds of the way through the course" (34).

Because ideas about privacy, and more importantly, feelings about privacy, change over time, Weisberger had no guarantee that his pedagogy, once so popular and heartily embraced, would continue to have the positive, educational effects he intended. He also failed to recognize the issues of power at play. In his own defense he says, "They're saying I crammed these assignments down their throats over their protests? These students uttered not one word of protest the entire semester!" (34). But as one student retorts, "Adam thought that because he criticized social hierarchy, and how unfair it was, somehow it didn't apply to him. . . . And that's where he made his major goof. Authority relationships don't dissolve after six weeks of class" (34).

Interestingly, just as Weisberger was unable to fully acknowledge his own power to impose an ideology of public and private boundaries on others, so too was he caught short when the Chair of his department, then the Dean, and then the tenure committee imposed their own ideas of public and private boundaries

on him. Both the Chair and the Dean entertained students' complaints, keeping their own reactions private from Weisberger. When student letters were included in Weisberger's tenure review before being fully investigated, the head of the tenure committee felt uncomfortable. Worried about the consequences of such a procedure, she asked the Dean, "Who told students they would have the option of airing their complaints by writing letters to Weisberger's tenure committee?" He replied, "I did" (37). The level of privacy deemed appropriate and fair for any given individual in this entire chain of events depended on the discretion of the person in power. In the end, Weisberger was fired. Consequently, with the most ironic twist of all, he decided to sue Colby College for (among other things) "invasion of privacy" (38)! Ultimately, the matter rested in the court's hands, and the courts (as we know from the contested establishment of privacy laws in 1903, and contradictions that haunted legal proceedings in the Clinton–Lewinsky affair) are as confused as the rest of us.

Weisberger's experience highlights points of contact and conflict between one person's private boundary and another's. Conflict and confusion arise for five central reasons: (1) Anyone's boundary of privacy is susceptible to change with context or over time; (2) a person's intellectual and affective understandings of privacy may be at odds with one another; (3) a teacher's concept of "private life" and its role in the public classroom may clash with a student's concept; (4) teachers have more power than students, and therefore exert more control over the public/private boundaries established in class; and (5) private boundaries are invisible, flexible, often indeterminate, yet vulnerable, and so it is difficult to trace the consequences of their violation.

In discussing the ethics of implementing a pedagogy that "involves a high-degree of self disclosure," Elizabeth Grauerholz and Stacy Capenhaver assert the value of such a style—both intellectual and therapeutic—while also noting the danger: "If we encourage students to think about the connections between their personal lives and the world around them . . . we are putting some students at risk" (quoted in Shalit 1998, 39). As composition teachers, we must encourage students to make these connections, but as the example of Weisberger shows, in doing so we put both our students and ourselves at risk.

Weisberger's experience points out the dangers in enforcing self-styled, seemingly preordained definitions of *the public* and *the private* in classroom writing practices. Weisberger required students to adapt to whatever public/private boundary felt comfortable or appropriate to the teacher. This sort of manipulation of students' values fostered resentment and resistance to writing.

My own experience as an undergraduate student contrasts sharply with the Weisberger scenario. In my case, and in the experiences of many students I have talked to, teachers did not invite too much of the personal and private into their classrooms; rather, they invited far too little, giving the impression that anything personal or private would somehow taint academic learning. In either case, the subtle and invisible movement of authority between students and teachers is vibrantly alive with power dynamics that can potentially promote

or hinder the desire to write. As an undergraduate student, I internalized this academic disdain for the private, and it has blocked my ability to find the appropriate public/private balance necessary for writing ever since.

For most of my writing-life, it has been my habit to leave my private life, my personal reflections, my self out of my writing, and I have been rewarded for my efforts. I came to understand that such private matters belonged to diary writing. But I had no interest in separating my self from my brain in this way, relegating things that matter to me to private writing that no one would ever see, and things that were utterly inconsequential to me to public writing that people who measured my worth (or at least my intelligence) would see. The message seemed to be, "Anything personal and private is trivial, nonintellectual, and not worth reading. If you must write such tripe, keep it to yourself; write it in your diary." So I held contradictory views: Diary writing was important because I could write out my own thoughts, but my own thoughts were considered so trivial that they were not worth reading. This message promotes self-doubt, not self-expression. On the other hand, public academic writing was important because it involved me in a community of thinkers beyond my own limited experience, but it came to feel trivial to me because I left myself out of it and was no longer invested in it.

Rather than trying to embrace either one practice or the other (each useless in isolation from the other), I stopped writing. I never realized that writing as I now understand it, and wish to teach it, needn't be divided into two neat categories whose boundaries remain distinct from one another—one public, one private. Indeed, if a person wants access to her own thinking, those boundaries must merge and overlap. If we do not encourage such an overlap, students will find writing as useless, stale, and alien as I once did. If we do encourage it, we must learn to deal with the risky situations that will inevitably occur. Just as writing genres are really neither purely public nor purely private, neither are composition classrooms. In some ways, the classroom serves as a spatial metaphor for the mix of public and private writing required in academia.

We teachers can't help designing our courses, assignments, and classroom exercises according to our own previous experiences and current comfort with public exposure and private reflection. There is no abstract, inherent value in going public or remaining private with one's writing. The value fluctuates depending on each writer's needs, desires, and goals at the time of writing. It's not for me, or any teacher, to decide when, how, and in what form a student goes public or remains private. What I can do is provide opportunities for all sorts of writing outside the basic requirements of the course, such as publication on the Web, publication in class magazines, private journal writing, collaborative journal writing, and so forth, without ranking these modes from least to most important, and without requiring that students participate in publication before they are ready to do so.

Even more important than providing a variety of opportunities for public or private writing, we must make our own understandings of public and private

boundaries explicit to our students (even if we suspect they are misperceptions), and we must invite our students to make their understandings explicit to us. In my experience, both the desire to publish and the desire to keep a private journal grow from witnessing others participate in, and enjoy, these practices. After the first class publication is distributed, most students want to be included in subsequent publications. Similarly, after lengthy discussions about the value or drawbacks in using private journal writing in school, many students revise their original objections to journal writing and decide to take up the practice. In addition, we can invite open discussions based on how and why people make the choices they do about when to go public and when to remain private. Such self-reflection helps students, and teachers, understand their own motivations and valid reasons for whatever choices they make. Essentially, it gives them the control over their own writing processes that students in Weisberger's class were denied. When students are allowed to control when to engage in private writing and when to go public, they take themselves and the writing class more seriously. Furthermore, they are in a stronger position to think critically about handed-down, dogmatic pronouncements concerning writing.

Notes

1. See essays by Philip Fisher and Brook Thomas for a fuller overview of nineteenth-century constructions of privacy in literature, culture, and law.

2. For a fuller explanation of this historical moment in American legal development, see works by Hofstadter and Horowitz, E. L. Godkin, and Robert E. Mensel.

2

Embodied Processes

Pedagogies in Context

Amy Lee

Traditionally, *pedagogy* is understood as theories and practices of teaching. At one moment, we think about teaching writing (or we think about teaching writing "critically," so as to empower students as writers); in the next, we go and do it. Such a conception is deeply problematic, similar to suggesting that the act of composing can be distinguished from the composition itself. What about all the time spent thinking about writing before we actually begin; what about drafts, assessment, readers' feedback, and critique; what about honing a sense of the operative rhetorical context, of the effect we intend our text to have and how to achieve it; what about revision? *Writing,* as we generally understand it in the discipline of Composition, is a process that requires reflection and action, a process that results in a "product," but is one that necessitates thinking about what we're doing, how we're doing it, and why. Often, this reflexive thinking cannot occur until we have done some writing. It is not a sequential or linear process of thinking and then doing, but a recursive one. *Pedagogy,* and the development of a pedagogical process, whether it is informed by feminist or humanist or expressivist or radical pedagogy, is also constituted by reflection and action. Pedagogy, like writing, develops in multiple and sometimes simultaneous spheres of action and requires not simply practice, but also engaged reflection and revision, as well as critical attention to the contexts in which our pedagogy operates. And, as we try to foster in our student-writers, developing as *teachers* requires ongoing inquiry into what, how, who, and why we are teaching.[1]

Making students' writing public, through peer critique and class publications, has come to hold the place of a familiar piety in writing pedagogy. While we talk often about the intended effects of such strategies (provides readers beyond the teacher; enables richer, dimensional contexts for writing; generates students' confidence by allowing them to have their texts read, responded to,

10

and celebrated), we don't often reflect on the unintended, sometimes invisible effects of our methods, the results we don't anticipate and so may not acknowledge or register. This is not to suggest that all unintended results are negative or to be avoided. Nonetheless, no single strategy or praxis, once taken up in specific sites of practice by complex and active participants, can be contained or controlled absolutely. Perhaps, we would do well to provide richer, more textured representations reflecting on how our strategies get taken up and made meaningful. That is, instead of treating them as unconditionally "good" practices abstracted from material sites ("peer review works!!"), we might theorize these activities from complicated and conflicted classroom sites.

Composing Maria: Going Public with "Personal" Narratives

During my first semester of teaching Basic Writing, Maria wrote an essay that was both a narrative and cultural critique. In this piece, as the following opening line suggests, Maria reflects on how, "In my own time and in my own way, I have dealt with my rape, recognizing that it has shaped and mis-shaped me." She narrates the moments directly preceding being raped and then shifts her attention to its subsequent effects (her long, self-imposed silence and internalized shame; her mother's unsupportive response; her experience of contending with images and attitudes that circulate in our culture around rape and rape victims). In her essay, Maria shifts from a personal voice, when she presents and examines her experiences and interpretations, to a more public voice, in which the "I" takes on more social authority and directly addresses her readers, posing questions to them, offering "public" evidence, calling attention to and critiquing cultural images.

The final draft of Maria's essay, along with those of her classmates', was published in a class magazine. Since I began teaching writing, I have published all final drafts in a bound booklet, with a cover and a table of contents. I originally did this because it was required by the Writing Program in the institution where I taught; the rationale, we were told, was to present students' writing as "professional," worthy of formal collection and celebration.

During our discussion of the class publication, it was evident that Maria's text had had an impact on her readers. Her writing produced discomfort in readers, who did not like how they were positioned or represented by or in the piece. As I attempted to facilitate responses centered around the formal and rhetorical aspects of the text, I was aware that we were not able to focus on the writing itself, the formal product, the choices Maria made as a writer (instead of as a rape victim). These were ignored or glossed over as students focused instead on her topic, on how it made them feel, on how they felt the piece assumed a position for them that they did not want to occupy. Similar to Richard Miller's (1994) recounting of the discussion about "Queer, Bums, and Magic," this powerful piece of writing left us unable to talk about the power

of the writing. We were affected not simply by the writing, but by the text. By *text*, I am referring to that intersection of writerly and readerly processes, the interchange between the rhetorical, formal features with which the writer composes her subject into a written product, and what readers bring with them to this produced version of the subject. In this case, we were situated in specific ways in relation to larger circulating cultural narratives about rape, discourses of gender and victimization and of privacy, and discourses of and cultural narratives about rape. It was this intersection, and not simply Maria's essay, that made the experience of responding to this text so powerful.

Maria's piece was from the first essay assignment of the semester. Students were asked to inquire into an experience, value, or belief so as to reflect, through the writing process and within the final product, on the significance it had come to hold. They were not asked to write a "personal narrative"; we were not, that is, focusing on that particular rhetorical form, nor were we working to convey an experience or feeling. As part of the project, we talked about what it means to inquire into one's history. We had read a variety of texts—poems, short fiction, memoir, essays, and cross-genre pieces—to consider the various rhetorical and poetic strategies available for representing this intellectual work, but no rhetorical form was specified for this assignment. Since I had begun reading in critical and feminist pedagogies, my aim was not to use this assignment as a forum for radical self-expression, but rather as a way of enacting Gramsci's call for a "self"-inventory. According to Gramsci, "The beginning of the critical elaboration is the consciousness of what one really is, . . . as the product of the historical process which has left you an infinity of traces gathered together without the advantage of an inventory" (1987, 58–59).

In Maria's case, writing the essay seemed to be a powerful experience; having chosen not to tell anyone except her mother about the rape, her decision to tell a classroom of strangers can be interpreted as her decision to refuse their inscription of her as damaged, guilty, or helpless. And yet, after the power of the composing experience, she was faced with a feeling of potential disempowerment when considering how her essay would be received once it was made "public." Obviously, we could choose to ignore such social tensions and discursive conditions, creating assignments and setting rules, as if to prevent such "distractions" from entering our classrooms. Yet, this hardly seems an adequate response. Among others, Sedgwick (1990) calls our critical attention to how discursive ignorance "can bring about the revelation of a powerful unknowing as unknowing, not as a vacuum or as the blank it can pretend to be but as a weighty and occupied and consequential epistemological space" (77). It seems to be our responsibility, then, to contend with our own and our students' unknowing.

On the day my students discussed the class magazine that included Maria's essay, Maria was absent. I note this because her absence likely had an impact on the kinds of comments some students made. First, a student told the class Maria's was her favorite essay and began to describe why it had moved her. Next, a student admitted that, while he found the piece to be well written

and gripping, he also found it to be "too personal." He had peer edited this piece and said his unspoken response at that time was to question her motives for writing it, as he felt uncomfortable while reading it. Three other students, all male, agreed. They didn't feel it was an appropriate topic for class. Because all three of them had earlier cited their favorite essay as a piece detailing a boy's escape from Vietnam, I asked what made the rape essay somehow more personal than the escape story. One student claimed it was because the former was a "touchy" subject, while the latter was "a success story. He made it here to America, against all those odds."

In other words, Buu's story of survival against the odds, of being beaten, hungry, lost, and arrested, was somehow different from Maria's story of survival in spite of the odds, of being beaten, silenced (during the experience and afterward, in terms of not telling it), and raped. Buu's story confirms our myth that America means freedom; "making it here" (whether physically immigrating or economically ascending or educationally succeeding) is upheld in his narrative as the dream. The dream is realized, attained, and the survivor lives to tell the story, so we can all celebrate. I am not discounting or devaluing Buu's experience. Indeed, his narrative and his history were remarkable. But I wondered why we couldn't read Maria's story through the same lens. Perhaps Buu's narrative was more pleasing not only because it so forcefully sustained the myth of the American dream, but also because the victim and the perpetrator were clearly "others." The class members could distance themselves on the basis of geography, ethnicity, even formal governing practices. Maria's essay did not reiterate a comforting myth or present us with familiar "others" from whom we had already learned to distance ourselves. The rapist was a friendly acquaintance; the person who blamed and silenced Maria was a mother; the person who was raped was one of us. It wasn't a story of a woman attacked by strangers lurking in the bushes. If it had been, perhaps the students would have felt more comfortable responding to it in the supportive ways Maria had hoped they might, but believed they wouldn't be able.

Another woman in the class had written of a time when she was sitting close to a girlfriend on a park bench and was physically attacked (left bleeding and bruised) by three kids who were screaming "you f*@# dykes! (sic)." She used the story to reflect inwardly on her own internalized homophobia. She claimed Maria was "brave" and asked why her own story about being beaten was "okay" but Maria's story about being raped was not acceptable. I pointed out that, in the essay, we learn that Maria didn't tell anyone about the rape for a year and a half because she felt guilty and ashamed. Her mother's response, upon finally hearing of the attack, was to urge Maria not to tell anyone else and not to repeat "whatever she'd done to ask for it." I asked the class whether there were something powerful about choosing to tell a roomful of strangers a secret that even your own mother had used against you and that society in general cannot adequately respond to.

My narrative of this discussion represents the forces at play in our classrooms, whether we invite, acknowledge, or ignore them. Our students are not

reading or writing in a vacuum, and they bring cultural constructions and social myths to their readings of one another's texts. Of course, they don't have
to read or engage each other's texts, and it's easier to pretend that politics are
elsewhere when they don't. But, when all texts and responses are praised
equally because they are student-generated, there can be no distinguishing
among texts (or readings of or responses to texts) that recount or reenact violence and oppression within the classroom. Obviously, the students responded
to Maria's as a powerful piece of writing, and yet the power they identified was
a slippery and confusing one, making them feel privy to matters some of them
would have preferred to ignore and forcing them to confront, as a real and
painful experience, an event they had known previously only as an abstraction.

Many colleagues who have heard versions of this chapter have responded
by noting that because Maria's piece was "personal," this was not really a
"critical" endeavor. Or they have pointed out that radical pedagogy is disinter-
ested in personal experience or individual stories. But these responses evade
the fundamental question, which this story brings to my mind: How might we
effectively contend with powerful pieces of writing in our classrooms? It
seems that no piece of writing is powerful if it doesn't appeal to, move, or
touch us in some profound personal way. That doesn't mean it can't be an essay about governmental terrorism in Guatemala or the use of capital punishment on teen-aged offenders in the United States. But it seems too simple, and
a willful evasion of the point, to dismiss Maria's story or this moment in my
class because it was personal to the writer. Would Maria's text have been easier
for us (me, her classmates, my colleagues) to respond to it if it had maintained
a strong condemnation of our culture's inability to substantively deal with rape
but hadn't revealed her "personal experience"? And if so, what does that say
about us? The challenge is this: How, in making writing public, can we enable
critical, self-reflexive reading so that texts, and positions, are not dismissed or
silenced out of hand, but engaged. How can we use the occasion of making
students' writing public in order to teach alternative or reflective/critical reading habits to our students?

Perhaps it is easier to imagine our writing classrooms as places where the
differences that mark us outside can be held in temporary abeyance, except as
we choose to reveal them through our texts. Perhaps we prefer to envision our
classrooms as places where our "differences" make us unique and are to be celebrated; maybe we aim to create classrooms in which we can depoliticize diversity, without consideration of how those differences may not be individually
elected but socially inscribed on our bodies and our texts with dehumanizing or
marginalizing effects. However, to subscribe to the idea that classes are ideol-
ogy-free in their "natural" state is to assume that the instructor has the power to
introduce or prohibit the entry of "politics" into the classroom. Giroux (1986)
characterizes this pedagogy as informed by "ideology of positive thinking." In
this approach, "difference no longer symbolizes the threat of disruption. On the
contrary, it now signals an invitation for diverse cultural groups to join hands

under the democratic banner of integrative pluralism." Further, such a pedagogy assumes that, "in spite of differences manifested around race, ethnicity, language, values, and lifestyles, there is an underlying equality among different cultural groups that allegedly disavows that any one of them is privileged" (53).

Unless we restrict students not only in what they write, but also in how they write about it and in how they respond to one another's texts, I fail to see how we can invest ourselves with the power to control the entry of politics into the classroom. Nor am I clear as to why we would want to. Here one might insist, "But we are teaching writing, after all"; to this I would respond that writing and reading are cultural practices bound up in discourse, power, and material conditions (it isn't a teacher's choice whether or not to make them so). Unless we decide to stick to drills-and-skills exercises, or to turn process practices into another kind of empty drill-and-skill exercise (express, edit, revise, celebrate!), the questions and issues that emerged during our reading of Maria's text are not exceptional, but to be expected.

The moment Maria and I decided to make these texts public, the moment readers were introduced into the equation, Maria and her text were opened to the effects of others' being situated differently in relation to discourse and experience. Maria and her text were exposed to the effects of her readers' certainty, not only about what they knew, but also about what they refused to know or to know differently. This was not caused by the fact that Maria had written a "personal" or experience-based essay, for Maria's piece was precisely not personal in that it did not aim to simply describe or effectively render one individual's experiences and worldview. Rather, her purpose, one represented also by critical pedagogy and feminist pedagogy, was to reinsert her experience into the social realm in order to challenge how it and she were named, understood, "made sense of." She was holding the "personal" up to scrutinize its linkages to, and its representation of, the social.

Pedagogies in Process

[D]ialogue cannot occur between those who want to name the world and those who do not wish this naming (between those who deny others the right to speak their word and those whose right to speak has been denied them. (Freire 1970, 69)

The narrative thus far exposes the gap that sometimes exists between the way I intend my instructional practices to work and the effects they actually generate when enacted within the complicated, multilayered context of a classroom. Clearly, process-oriented strategies (drafting, self-assessment, revision, peer response) are useful, and were even empowering for Maria as a writer. Like other students, she talked about this essay as something she "needed" to write, but had lacked the occasion and confidence to do so. It is not these practices I am rejecting, but the common-sense assumption that they inevitably produce

specific effects, extratextual results. We need to reflect on, not simply employ, these practices.

Although the literature about critical pedagogy provides useful and energizing accounts of how this theoretical framework should inform our teaching, it provides few representations of how our teaching might change in light of subscribing to this pedagogical vision. I found that it took many "drafts" and much deliberation to begin to forge a pedagogy, not simply a theory, about the possibilities of teaching a critically oriented writing class. As Linda Brodkey (1989) suggests, arguing for a truth, vision, or idea is different from enacting it, taking it up as a praxis:

> What . . . poststructuralists have been arguing for the last fifteen or twenty years is considerably easier to state than act on: we are at once constituted by and unified as subjects in language and discourse. . . . [T]his means that since writers cannot avoid constructing a social and political reality in their texts, as teachers we need to learn how to "read" the various relationships between writer, reader, and reality that language and discipline supposedly produce. (125)

How can we enact, not simply imagine, a pedagogy that acknowledges and makes use of the ideology embedded within texts, whether those texts are written by Adrienne Rich, Richard Rodriguez, or one of our students? How can we contend with the fact that reading is also a situated, ideological process and engage in it constructively with our students? When we ask students to "edit" or to provide "sayback" for one another's texts, we are asking them to perform a certain kind of reading, to act as a particular sort of reader. These methods do not preclude ideology; they assume instead that the best way to contend with it in our writing classes is to ask students to ignore their situatedness from time to time.

We need to be wary, however, of assuming an equal-opportunity vision of power in which it is available to all through the same means. Maria sought an alternative to normative narratives about women who are raped; she sought to resist popular discourse. Maria felt written on, written about, as a rape victim; her decision to write about the experience was an attempt to control its telling, to compose herself more complexly: at once a victim of rape as well as the agent of how that experience would be represented to others. Yet she knew that writing did not guarantee that she could avoid the discourse students brought with them to her text, the discourse that informed the very narratives she sought to challenge, to revision. Foucault (1990) suggests, "We must make allowances for the complex and unstable process whereby discourse can be both an instrument and effect of power, but also . . . a point of resistance and a starting point for an opposing strategy. Discourse transmits and produces power; it reinforces it, but it also undermines and exposes it, renders it fragile and makes it possible to thwart it" (101). Maria's experience of writing into an existing discourse, one that situates rape victims, rapists, men, and women

in particular ways and ascribes to them specific identities, was also, and simultaneously, an effort to write outside of that discourse, to take it up in order to deform it and reform the identity it posited for her. Inside or outside of school, claiming a powerful voice was a tricky process of negotiation in this instance.

Revisioning Critical Processes: Learning from Our Teaching

Classroom moments such as those involving Maria's essay raise questions not simply about the texts that are produced in our classes, but also about the readings that are produced and what effects they might have. These moments have taught me that, if I intend to continue making texts "public" because I value the potential in such a practice, I need to foreground the teaching of critical, reflective reading. Unless we pay conscious and critical attention to the process and effects of reading (an activity that is central to peer review and publicizing students' writing), our classrooms might function to inadvertently resecure the burden on the writer who works from marginalized knowledge, subject-position, and suppressed discourses. That is, the outlier who wants to speak within and to the culture of power might indeed get her piece read, but this does not ensure the kind of engagement she seeks.

Attending to the role of the reader, and to the need for writing teachers to consider how they are teaching reading (as an active process and product), seems particularly essential in classrooms in which we want to allow writers to write against the grain and to provide an arena in which we can, as writers and readers, represent, inquire into, and revise our assumptions and values. Asking writers and readers to critically engage the texts before them, whether those texts are personal narrative, political essays, newspaper articles, or commercials, seems a legitimate and necessary process in a critical writing class. Simply asking students to generate writing or asking them to edit one another's work does not go far enough in exposing them to the way discourse works on and through us. We can and should question the writer-centeredness of our process pedagogies in order to find ways to ask readers not simply to express their responses to texts, but also to understand, reflect on, and critique those responses, so as to have the power to *re*read.

Note

1. Jennifer Gore (1993) usefully articulates a distinction between the pedagogy argued for and the pedagogy of argument. Without reproducing a hierarchical and binary distinction between theory and practice, she conceptualizes pedagogy as both necessitating reflection on the theories, which animate our work in local sites, and drawing on those sites as a basis for critical revisioning of our theory.

3

"Why Didn't You Speak Up?"

When Public Writing Becomes Public Silencing

Shari Stenberg

Henry Giroux (1995) argues that the concept of critical pedagogy must be used with "respectful caution," as there are not only different versions of what constitutes critical pedagogy, but also no generic definition of the term itself (7). Still, he argues that there are important "theoretical insights" and problems that hold together various approaches to critical pedagogy, and one of these is the notion of student agency and empowerment. In both critical pedagogy and composition scholarship, making student writing and knowledge central is an oft-cited and relied upon practice for enabling agency and empowerment. That is, asking students to share texts with one another, granting student texts an "equal" status to published texts, and making student voices as important as the teacher's voice are practices often linked with "student-centered" or "critical" pedagogies.

As Mimi Orner (1992) points out, however, calls for student voice often assume that students, voices, and identities are "singular, unchanging and unaffected by the context in which the speaking occurs" (80). "Liberatory" pedagogues too often assume that as long as the call is made for student voices, students will be able to answer it. With Orner, I agree that there has not been enough consideration given to the subjects of our pedagogies, and the contexts that impinge upon what is sayable and doable in a classroom (81).

Though I am deeply committed to the aims I have just named—to fostering student voice and encouraging students to go public with their work and ideas—I am concerned that we have focused too much on voice and not enough on the unsaid, or the silence, in our classrooms. As Patti Lather insists, "We must be willing to learn from those who don't speak up in words. What are their silences telling us?" (quoted in Orner 1992, 81). In order to examine this question in relation to my teaching practices, I begin by looking back to my history as a student. With Jennifer Gore (1993), I believe it is necessary to

18

reflect not only on our current realities as educators, but also on "how we have come to be this way" (148). It is my contention that if we make it a priority to revisit the classrooms in which we were students, we will be more likely (and better prepared) to inquire into the way students are experiencing our teaching. For instance, if I work to remember how I experienced certain "student-centered" practices as a learner, it is not so easy to simply assume the effectiveness of my own practices.

In what follows, I theorize out of my experience as an undergraduate student in a course that sought to make student writing and knowledge central, but inadvertently created a silencing atmosphere, particularly for female voices. In doing so, I have two concerns: (1) the dissonance that exists between the aims of "critical" or student-focused pedagogies and how students experience them; and (2) the way female students might experience liberatory pedagogies, and in particular, going public with one's words and ideas. From this examination I argue that we need to examine the ramifications that "going public" might have on particular students in particular contexts, since our liberatory aims can too easily silence the very students we hope they will empower.

Looking Back: Re-collecting Pedagogical Contexts

Rhetorics of Knowledge was a course developed within our new cultural studies program at a small, private Midwestern university. Though still in its nascent stages, the program was already being talked about by students and professors as highly "rigorous," relying on theoretical texts and pedagogical approaches often reserved for graduate courses. While this was exciting, it was also intimidating. Would I, a junior in college, who had just declared myself an English major, measure up? What would it require to succeed in such a climate?

On the first day of class, we were told that the course would examine how knowledge is produced and disciplined, and that our own textual inquiries—as much as the texts we studied—would occupy the center of the course. The writing workload, on top of the reading, seemed overwhelming: two "traditional" papers, three "Storyspace" documents, and two in-class presentations. The professors explained that Storyspace, a hypertextual word-processing program, would be used as a means to interrupt traditional writing practices. The software allows one to write in a nonlinear, layered fashion by composing in "boxes," which can be linked to one another to create multiple paths. Consequently, we would be asked to think not only about what our texts argued, but also how they were constructed. These documents would be projected on a screen and made public to the class at various points throughout the semester.

Because of the combination of texts read in the course (beginning with Deleuze and Foucault), the amount of writing and presenting required, and the way in which the course was talked about—there was a great deal at stake in participating in this rigor with "competence." One of the professors of the course insisted that it would be treated "like a graduate course," and though

his words may have been intended to acknowledge the capability and potential of the students, it also made the course "count" more. It also made fitting
into the arena, behaving as a successful participant, even more important.

A precedent was set when the professors requested that a male student—
whom we all knew to be adept at working with theoretical discourses—present
his document first, while the rest of us signed up for presentation dates. This
student came to class on that second week and projected on the screen a
twenty-page hypertext. His level of performance, combined with his ability to
make use of theoretical language that seemed not only difficult, but alienating, set up a "model" with which many would attempt to compete. Many students read this text (and this student) as an ideal intellectual product, engaging
with the "right" kinds of knowledges and in the "right" ways. Because we
knew he was "chosen," we read his text as "correct" and thus "legitimate."
From the beginning, then, the act of going public in this classroom was a
gendered one, steeped in traditionally masculine notions of mastery and performance. Rather than using these presentations to begin a dialogue or to
collaboratively share in an ongoing writing process with other students, the
student and his/her writing were to assume the role the teacher usually does—
presenting a seemingly "finished" knowledge. So even if the practices were
different from the traditional classroom, the effects were not.

For instance, even though women made up half of the class, they rarely
spoke. In sharp contrast, many of the male students seemed to easily create a
space in which they joked, debated, and steered the social and theoretical
agenda. My primary mode of participation in this classroom—which
foregrounded student voices—ironically, was silence. Because of my assumption that I should be able to speak—since the pedagogy encouraged, even expected it—I had difficulty discerning whether I was "failing" in the class, or
the class was failing me.

During the several weeks we spent reading Foucault's *Discipline and
Punish,* I began to think differently about the class and my role in it. Engaging this text enabled me to understand my own self-monitoring in new ways.
Each time I wanted to speak, I interrogated myself, determining whether my
comment would be deemed relevant to the current discussion. I had become
what Orner (1998) names as one's own "gender overseer," "observing, judg-
ing and disciplining every aspect of [myself]" (279). As I sought out feminist
responses to Foucault, I began to understand how disciplining worked not just
on the body, but on the "voice," as well.

Unfortunately, these connections did not make their way into the classrooms. We discussed disciplinary tactics abstractly, as if they existed only in a
culture outside of the classroom. Theory and culture were so rigidly defined that
speaking from lived experience seemed directly antithetical to the "rigor" required of the class. As Linda Brodkey (1987) writes, "The academy has traditionally demonstrated a limited tolerance for lived experience, which it easily
dismisses as 'anecdotal' or 'stories' and in some quarters that intolerance is so

great that any ethnographic narrative would be an affront to scholarly sensibilities" (40). Rather than risk seeming intellectually "deficient," I remained silent.

I did, however, begin to talk to other women outside of class about their experiences, and discovered that I was not alone. Even so, interrupting the dynamics themselves remained extremely difficult. Still, another female student, Tracy, and I decided that rather than leaving our astute readings of the gender dynamics outside of the classroom, we might find a way to disrupt them. In attempting to do so, we sought out ways to make use of Foucault's work for our own project. In the end, we prepared a Storyspace document examining women's internalization of the panopticon and its effects on the female body.

Shaping the boxes of our story space in a corset—perhaps a metaphor for how we ourselves felt in the class (small, contained, restricted)—we wove together feminist theory, narrative, and popular discourse as a means of revealing the disciplining of women's sexuality, reproductive organs, and (excess) flesh. We had much at stake in this project, as we hoped that projecting our multilayered text, which made use of and challenged Foucault, would serve both to interrupt the trajectory of the class and allow us a space to speak. But on the day we were to speak, to intervene, the presentations were overscheduled and we ran behind and out of time before our turn came. Perhaps Magda Gere Lewis (1993) says it best: "While the experience of being consciously, deliberately, and overtly dismissed is painful, the experience of being invisible is brutalizing" (137).

I left the room in tears—an ultimate embarrassment in such a space. We later received an apology from our instructors, and a "Why didn't you speak up?" from a few of the male students when we later complained to them, but we never did present our document in the classroom that semester. The question of speaking up is an interesting one, of course, because underlying it is the assumption that we were positioned equally in the classroom, all of us feeling equally entitled to freely enter and disrupt the direction of the course. As well, the way the question is framed places the responsibility for silence on the individual not speaking—relieving all those contributing to the dynamic from having to examine their own complicity. The question that needed to be asked was: "Why aren't the women speaking?"

Because there was much at stake in speaking within this particular discourse, our document emerged from a contradictory location; we wanted both to disrupt the course and, at the same time, to be sanctioned by it. When our professors read the document, we received a great deal of praise not only for the "content" but for the "transgressive" ways in which we'd made use of the technology. They regretted, they said, that it had not entered the classroom so that other students could see the possibilities of Storyspace. While there is no question that Tracy and I felt a certain pleasure from the approval stamped on our work, this approval had to be negotiated with our feelings of "lack" in the classroom. The driving force behind our work was a shared desire to bring about different discussion in the classroom and to make public our ideas; the

fact that we were later praised for work that wasn't allowed to enter the class-room space made us question the place of feminist critique and whether its acceptance was contingent upon its containment.

As Tracy and I worked to interrupt the course dynamics with our writing project, another female student (one who spoke often in seemingly comfort-able ways) attempted to do the same through a public e-mail sent to the class distribution list. She explained that after speaking with another member of the class who felt her comments were being devalued, she felt compelled to "call" people on their classroom behavior and elitism. She made clear that she was "watching" people's responses to others' comments and that those who called themselves "theory boys/girls" better rethink their actions. Her message quite literally added another "gaze" to the complex ways in which spectatorship and surveillance were already at work in the classroom. In response to it, I received several phone calls that night—from both male and female students—asking, "Who do you think she means?" and "Do you think she means me?" While her message evoked a certain level of "terror" among her classmates, it made the subtle relations in the class crystal clear. Students had certainly learned to regulate each other—to "make choices, organize, and act on their own beliefs" (Giroux 1988, 115)—the problem is that we had learned to do so in ways that perpetuated unproductive and intellectually violent dynamics, allowing those who already felt entitled to speak to serve a judiciary and policing role.

The e-mail message remained on e-mail—it wasn't allowed to enter the classroom. Though it was intended as a "public" act—and indeed, had public effects—it was left to be internalized privately. Because this message wasn't engaged, it only reinforced the notion that discussion about the class was best left outside, or at least, was less important than the content we engaged. Bring-ing the text of the e-mail into the conversation of the course—as painful and risky as that may have been—might have enabled us to talk about the way in which power was being exercised, how we understood terms like *theory boy,* the goals of the course, and the ways in which silence was being read.

Even though the message was silenced in the classroom, and, in this case, made more powerful because of it, it stirred conversation about the class out-side of it. Some of us (privately) made the professors aware of how we were experiencing the course, and one of them made greater efforts to include women in the discussion. While these efforts were appreciated, inviting those who haven't spoken to add their voices without considering all that contrib-utes to who speaks and gets heard is not enough. As Lewis (1993) writes, "One cannot simply donate freedom from a position that does not challenge privi-lege" (144). She argues that "being 'given' time and space [has] its own op-pressive moments in that the power of control over such time and space [does not change]. . . . Being muted is not just a matter of being unable to claim a space and time within which to enter a conversation. Being muted also occurs when one cannot discover forms of speech within conversation to express meanings and to find validation from others" (142).

Just as empowerment cannot be given from teacher to student, entitlement to join a conversation cannot be donated. To assume it can removes practices from contexts and pretends that students all experience classrooms and the power relations within them in the same ways. In this class, silence was not only about some students speaking too much and leaving too little room for other students, so that altering this dynamic would only mean altering who speaks. It was also an issue of whether the female students perceived their knowledge to be valuable in such a space—whether their speech acts would even be heard.

As Simon (Lewis and Simon 1986) points out, liberatory pedagogy is not so much about making women (or other marginalized groups) the question of the course, but rather, establishing practices wherein women can enunciate the question. The problem with Rhetorics of Knowledge was not the subject matter—it was that knowledge had already been defined in ways that allowed only those who studied relations of power *in the abstract* (certainly a luxury, as I see it) to enunciate the questions. Those of us who wanted to speak about lived material effects of discipline kept our ideas to ourselves, or to the writing we knew wouldn't be made public.

My final paper for the course examined my own silence, with specific attention to how issues of gender perpetuated it. It was an important paper for me to write—both in allowing me to finally express my dissatisfaction with the role I had come to assume in the class, as well as in providing me a space to inscribe my experience with the social conditions informing it. I wrote this piece knowing that it would not be made public in the class. I did, however, find other ways to circulate it—sharing it with another teacher and other students—so as to get the feedback of those I felt might provide a different "reading" than the kind established in the course. I had come to value what "making writing public" (at least potentially) allowed, as I grew to understand writing as a crucial means of participating in cultural conversations, of adding the narratives and arguments that weren't often heard. Making this paper "public" to at least some other readers allowed me to explore what had been lost in trying to discover a place to speak throughout the semester. In making a choice about who my readers would be, I was enabled to construct an argument I wasn't sure would be valued within the space of the classroom. The act of excluding, then, was as important as including readers.

While the dynamics remained consistent throughout the course, I would argue that the real critical and collaborative engagement began when the class was over. Only then did we begin to discuss the pedagogy of the course—to heed Giroux's warning that cultural studies fails if attention is paid only to *what* and not *how* we teach and learn. The most obvious example came when our professors asked for volunteers to speak at a small sociology conference to be held at our campus that summer. Although the panel was intended to discuss our class' use of Storyspace, the "intent" was interrupted when one of the "silent" female students began her presentation, saying, "It's strange that I'm here now presenting on this course since I rarely spoke in class." Her disrup-

tion allowed for an examination of "going public" and how the Storyspace served as a means to display our work rather than to share and produce knowledge collectively. Most importantly, she insisted that we consider the lived experience of those who are "written on" by a pedagogy.

While it's interesting to consider what allowed for this interruption—perhaps including the post-course conversations and the attentive audience of mainly female teachers—it is also necessary to consider what might have facilitated interruptive practices in the classroom itself. How could the silence of the women in that classroom have been used in transformative ways—allowing us to learn from it and disrupt the conditions that gave rise to it? Gore (1993) suggests that "if pedagogy is not just received by students, but is 'unpacked' with students, the work of unpacking will occur at least partly 'outside the regime [of truth]'" (143). With this in mind, allowing room for the kind of work that was ultimately done outside of class during the course itself might have opened possibilities for momentarily getting "outside" to interrogate and critique what was going on within—and in this way, would have potentially allowed for interruption of the disciplinary practices working on student bodies and voices.

Moving My Reflections Outward

Like my professors in the preceding narrative, I want to make student writing public and student knowledge central. But this doesn't prevent silencing from occurring in my classroom. As Orner (1992) argues, "It seems impossibly naïve to think that there can be anything like a genuine sharing of voices in the classroom. What does seem possible, on the other hand, is an attempt to recognize the power differentials present and to understand how they impinge upon what gets said and heard in that specific context" (81). What also seems possible is to make productive use of those "silences" that do occur, so that a space is made for students to intervene in the pedagogy when they experience it as working problematically. But this space has to be made before the silences occur. To this end, reflective work on the course, itself, must be built into the pedagogy so that examining both the teacher's aims and how students experience them is valued as much as the "content" of the course.

In my class, I ask students to do a range of "reflective" assignments: reading my syllabus and its aims and values against their expectations for the course; accounting for their own participation—how they would name it and what it enables or hinders; considering what makes for "good" or "bad" learning situations; and collaboratively creating "ground rules" for workshopping. My hope is that these practices facilitate a shared sense of responsibility among all of us for the way the class is functioning—a student-centered class does depend on its students' contributions. But I also hope that such reflective work helps them to see the pedagogy, to consider how they are experiencing it in productive or unproductive ways, and to propose possibilities for revision.

This is not to say, however, that all runs smoothly or that this reflective work allows full participation or engagement. Nor does it allow everyone comfort in sharing writing or verbal comments. Recently, a female student, Loren, approached me after class, concerned that her and two other women's pieces were not discussed in her workshop group; they were, she felt, essentially being silenced. Loren had written an autobiographical piece in journal form about her difficult relationship with her father, and how that relationship was complicated by his failing health. The pieces that seemed to get workshopping attention, she said, were the men's pieces, which happened to be "light" and "jokey"—easy to respond to. After considering several ways of dealing with this situation, we decided that I would initiate a conversation during the next class period, discussing which pieces we neglect because of subject matter and which pieces seem easier to workshop. While the next morning's class was somewhat slow and awkward, we were able to begin a conversation about the difficulty attending to pieces that we assume are "personal" and the line between critiquing a piece of writing and a writer's life. We came up with few answers and perhaps even ended with more questions that we began with, but the conversation gave Loren a way to start a conversation about her piece with her group.

I realized later that I could have read this as a "failing" moment, when a female student in my class was being silenced. Instead, though, Loren (much to her credit) was invested in her piece and in getting a response to it, and so came forward in attempt to alter the current dynamics. What seems particularly important about Loren's interruption of the class as it was unfolding was her recognition of the contexts within which she was working. She didn't conclude that it was a lack in her piece that led to its dismissal; rather, she recognized that the piece wouldn't allow her readers the same comfort that other pieces had. And she saw the reading practices of her workshop group as worthy of discussion.

Because we can't guarantee that the pedagogical practices we enact will enable students to speak and be heard as we intend them to, we might rethink silence not merely as a sign of "failure" but as an important interruption calling for reflection. Instead of ignoring or attempting to diagnose and cure student silence, we might examine the relations of power within the classroom and how they contribute to who speaks and who is silent, as well as to who gets heard and who listens. Liberatory possibilities arise when we look carefully at the contexts of our practices, and when we make room for students to reflect on how they experience them. So when we ask students to go public, we must also be willing to go public with our pedagogies, and to make our classrooms public texts to be written and revised with students. In doing so, possibilities might emerge for questioning and interrupting those practices that work against our aims and, as a result, against our students.

4

The Ethics of Students' Community Writing as Public Text

Amy Goodburn

This chapter examines some of the ethical dilemmas I have faced when students make public their writing about community projects. Like many other compositionists (Bacon 1997; Herzberg 1994; Minter et al. 1995; Peck et al. 1995), I value community projects/service learning as a way for students to connect their academic learning with contexts beyond the classroom, and I view students' writing about their learning in these contexts as critical for helping them make sense of oftentimes confusing and contradictory experiences. One way that I value this writing in the classroom is by incorporating it as a public text, asking students to share their writing with other class members and placing students' writing in dialogue with assigned class texts. Thus, students' representations of their experiences become public texts that circulate in the classroom. It is this public nature of their writing that I discuss in this chapter. In particular, I focus on two ethical issues that have been raised for me with respect to the "public" nature of students' writing in these courses.

First, I am increasingly conscious of how student writing about community inquiry impacts fellow classmates and, by extension, the community members about whom they are writing, particularly when these representations are often unchallenged by class members and unmediated by the community members themselves. Second, I have been challenged in responding to and assessing the writing that students create for their community projects, particularly in terms of the tensions that "public" writing raises in relation to my "academic" expectations for what these texts should be. By focusing on one of my student's writing and experiences with community inquiry, I hope to show how distinctions between "public" and "private" texts are often collapsed when students do community inquiry, and that this collapse has implications for how composition teachers might more productively conceptualize and understand writing within such contexts.

To illustrate, I refer to a class that I taught in the fall of 1997, titled "Literacy and Community Issues." It was a mixed undergraduate and graduate student seminar that focused on theories of literacy and their relationship to community contexts. In addition to reading from texts such as *Toxic Literacies; Many Families, Many Literacies; Eating on the Street; Possible Lives*; and the collection *Perspectives on Literacy,* students participated in weekly community projects related to literacy, which they either designed on their own or selected from a list of ongoing community programs. The thirteen students participated in a variety of projects, predominantly tutoring partnerships (with women refugees, ESL high school students, at-risk fifth-graders, an adult working for a GED), but also writing documents for organizations, such as a pediatric clinic and a local literacy organization. Throughout the semester, students kept journals in which they described their experiences about their projects and which they shared in small groups and in full-class discussions. Half of each three-hour class was devoted to discussing issues that students were negotiating in their projects. As the semester progressed, then, students began to construct their writing as public texts, as writing that others would read and learn from and that provided them with opportunities to be authorities about their community sites.

From this class, I have chosen to focus on John, a white senior undergraduate Education major who worked in an Americorps-funded tutoring program for elementary-age students at the city's African American Community Center, for two reasons. First, throughout the semester, John's experiences at the Center—as represented through his writing and his oral contributions to discussions—became a primary public text with which the rest of the class engaged. Second, John's writing challenged me as a teacher to reconsider my pedagogical assumptions about what constitutes "reflection" and "analysis" in writing about community inquiry, particularly when this writing is made public to audiences beyond the teacher.

Representations of Community

The first issue I wish to discuss is John's representations of the community at the Center and the resulting impact of these representations on class members when his writing publicly circulated within the classroom. To do so, I begin with one of his earliest journals, which describes the connections he made between the class's reading of David Schaafsma's *Eating on the Street* and his tutoring experiences at the Center. Schaafsma's book describes a summer writing program for Detroit children and the ways that one incident—children eating food on the street while walking to a school program—raised tensions between and among black and white teachers about their expectations and actions toward black students in this program. While most of the black teachers felt that black students should be taught not to "eat on the street" (for fear of

perpetuating negative stereotypes), most of the white teachers saw nothing wrong with the children's actions. Schaafsma uses this incident as a springboard for exploring differences in the teachers' views toward culture, identity, and writing pedagogy. John's journal, written the week after the class had begun reading *Eating on the Street,* recounts a conversation he initiated with the Director of the Center about the book:

> I wanted to know his thoughts on eating on the street in a literal sense. I didn't want to ask him point blank, so I put him into a scenario and asked him how he would react. I told him that we were walking down the street, and we were heading to the park to eat lunch with the children. One of the children opened their lunch pails (sic) and began eating a sandwich. I asked him what he would do in this situation. He told me that he would send this person home for disrespecting himself. I knew why, but I wanted to hear him say it. He said that eating on the street is disrespectful and something that all children should know especially black children.
>
> I think that I couldn't have chosen a better internship than the . . . Center. I now can see what some of the elementary school teachers in *Eating on the Street* can see. I can make a judgment and see which students are going to make it and which cannot. I don't know if this is a good or a bad thing. However, it would enable me as a teacher to decipher between the students who are doing alright and those who need special attention. . . . It is really amazing to read some of the things in the book, and then live some things out in my internship. (Journal 10-28-1997)

This journal is an example of the type of writing that circulated publicly in my classroom. John's journal illustrates his individual satisfaction with his community project and shows the connections he is making with the academic content of the course (Schaafsma's book) and his community project. His journal also suggests that he is trying to engage the Director of the Center with his academic knowledge. Asking the director about his beliefs on "eating on the street" and then sharing Schaafsma's book with him reflects John's attempt to bring the class material into his community site in productive ways. As an individual "record" of his experiences, I was glad that John was satisfied with his project. In considering how John's text functioned as a public text in my class, though, I was a little less sanguine. I was concerned about the impact his journal might have for how class members might read the people at the Center.

Although student writing made public usually involves representations of others, when the writing is about community projects the stakes seem higher to me, especially when students are forced to rely upon their classmates' representations as the primary basis for their perceptions about these communities. In this case, John's journal represents the Director of the Center. Because only two other students also volunteered at this site, the rest of the class members were forced to rely on John's interpretations. While this journal represents the Director in a positive manner—receptive to John's suggestions and his ques-

tions—John's later representations of community members at the Center were not so positive, and thus the public nature of John's representations became more troubling for me. In particular, I became concerned with how John, a white student, framed his representations of the predominantly African American population at the Center to a class of all-white students within a town where African Americans comprise less than three percent of the total population.

Despite John's initial glowing account about tutoring at the Center, as the semester progressed he began to express frustration. In one class discussion, John, along with the other two students who tutored at the Center, described his feeling of being viewed as an outsider and criticized "other" Center volunteers who he felt were responsible for creating his outsider status. John's and the other students' complaints focused on two issues: (1) the Center's lack of organization for the tutoring program, with no orientation and few guidelines, and (2) tension between the "regular" volunteers (who were predominantly African American and working long-term at the Center) and volunteers like John, who were predominantly white and viewed as "drop-in university tourists" who did not care as much about the welfare of the children.

This public discourse of complaint made me uneasy because John's and the other two students' writing was viewed in terms of unmediated "truth" about their experiences rather than as motivated representations shaped by their own investments, interests, and privilege. Lu and Horner (1998) describe the tension teachers face in helping students understand their experiences as discursively constructed without "overwriting the students' experience" in ways that privilege the teachers' knowing. They argue that teachers need "to make productive use of, rather than dismiss, the challenges students' lived experience poses for the teachers' discursive understanding of that experience. . . . [and] explore as well how to use the teachers' own and others' lived experience to problematize the teachers' knowledge" (267). Yet, as Lu and Horner suggest, problematizing the teachers' discursive understanding can be difficult, particularly when teachers become caught "between the desire to teach a particular understanding of literacy and the desire to learn about literacy from the students' lived experience, between the desire to change students' literacy experiences and the desire to grasp their existing experience" (273). I felt this tension when I read and responded to John's journals and when class discussions about his experiences led his classmates to sympathize solely with his analysis. My discomfort about such representations surfaced again at the end of the semester when I was forced to assess and evaluate John's final project about his community experiences.

Assessing Public Texts

The parameters for students' final projects were broad: They were asked to synthesize their learning in the course either via a paper or some other type of project. In a conference with me, John and Sara, another student who tutored at

the Center, proposed writing a memo to the Center's Director to make suggestions for how to improve the experiences of volunteers. In addition to focusing
on the need for regular volunteer times and an orientation session, John and Sara
reiterated their perceptions that their work wasn't as valued because they were
white university students, and they discussed ways that such tensions could be
addressed. I was enthusiastic about their project because I saw it as an opportunity for the students to problem-solve about their experiences, to synthesize
their learning about the politics of race and literacy work, and to reciprocally
"give back" to the Center. Moreover, I was happy that these students selected
the Center as the audience for their memo rather than me or their classmates.

Two weeks later, Sara and John presented their memo to the class. They
described their final project as an attempt to improve the tutoring program for
future volunteers. However, they then stated that they had shifted the audience
of their text from the Director of the Center to me. In other words, they had
eliminated the public audience they had originally conceived for the memo. As
I listened to them read, I was conscious of how the text of their memo was de-
void of the analysis that we had discussed two weeks before in their conference. Indeed, their analysis of their positions as university volunteers versus the
full-term volunteers was absent. The following excerpts from their memo illustrate John and Sara's representation of the Center and their experiences in it:

> The Center is a place where the children in the neighborhood go to work and
> play with their friends. The Center is also a place where children can get
> love, support, and guidance from the people in their neighborhood who want
> them to succeed.
>
> The Director at the Center is . . . a great role model for the kids that go
> there and we truly believe he has a sincere interest in the children, their grades
> and the lives they lead. He is always telling the children to get good grades
> and to respect their teachers and others who try to help them. He has the re-
> spect of the kids at the Center and is always trying to teach them something.
>
> Since we began volunteering at the Center we have noticed some prob-
> lems. . . . We would like to discuss these problems *with you and suggest so-*
> *lutions to them* that would make the program a more successful one at the
> Center (emphasis mine).

Within these first three paragraphs, John and Sara seem to be writing for
two competing audiences—the Center's Director, whom they had originally
named as the audience, and me, the teacher. Despite their decision not to send
the memo to the Director, the first two paragraphs seemed directly geared toward him—beginning with the positive description of the Center's role in the
community and then focusing specifically on the Director as a "great role
model" for the children. It isn't until the third paragraph that their changing
notion of audience is reflected—with the statement that they want to discuss the
problems with me, their primary audience, so that they can suggest solutions to

"them," presumably those who work at the Center. These opening paragraphs suggest that while Sara and John want to make public their suggestions for improving the Center's tutoring program, they do not feel comfortable publicly discussing the problems that necessitate such suggestions. In a way, their memo functions to "test out" their ideas with me and their classmates in the public space of the classroom before moving to the public audience of the Center. The memo then identifies the problems that Sara and John see at the Center:

> We believe that part-time volunteers are not welcome at the center. . . . Even though it was never actually stated to us, it is clear to see that two distinct groups of volunteers exist at the center. There are many volunteers which appear to be part time. These volunteers are mostly students, *like us,* who are from UNL or other schools in Lincoln. These volunteers are probably there one or two hours a week and are volunteering to fill a requirement for a class.
>
> The other group of volunteers seem to make a full time commitment to the center. Most of *these people* appear to be part of the community. We have speculated that these volunteers are there because they want to help out the children in the community. They could be friends, family, or neighbors, but we feel that they have a demographic tie to the Center which leaves them with a sense of ownership.
>
> We believe that we are made to feel unwelcome at the Center because of the full-time volunteers. From the first day we arrived at the Center the full-time volunteers have not been helpful or friendly. Many of the volunteers have been rude and seem to resent us for being there. For example, we have asked questions and introduced ourselves to full-time volunteers only to be ignored and brushed off (emphasis mine).

Upon hearing these paragraphs, I was struck by the oppositional language of "us" and "them" and the ways that the memo does not address race as part of the writers' analysis. I was particularly surprised because during our conference John and Sara had theorized that most of the conflict between the volunteers was rooted in the fact that all of the university volunteers were white while the regular volunteers were African American. Yet, in this memo, race is not mentioned. There is no representation of why the full-time volunteers might resent their presence, nor is there any discussion about how differences in race might have had an impact on the children being tutored. There are a few coded references to race, such as the statement that the regular volunteers are part of the community that the Center serves and that they have a "demographic tie" to this community, but it is never explicitly stated what these demographics are. Such a context-free analysis allows John and Sara to interpret their experiences solely in terms of personality conflicts rather than in terms of racial tensions. In a sense, the issues of white privilege for which the university students were critiqued by the full-time volunteers became replicated in the text of John and Sara's memo.

The memo then concludes with an analysis of how the Center's tutoring program could be improved: A solution to both of these problems is very simple—an orientation program. If the Center were to hold an orientation program at the beginning of each semester, everyone would have a chance to get to know each other a little bit and know where each other is coming from.

After their presentation, students asked Sara and John why they chose not to write the memo to the Center's Director. They said that they planned to talk with the director face to face instead, because they felt that the memo would seem too formal in the environment of the Center and that they didn't want to be read as "big-time college students." In assessing this memo, I struggled with how it functioned as a quasi-public text and my relation to it as an audience. Because Sara and John had stated that I was the primary audience, my two-page response focused on the discourse that they had (and hadn't) used to interpret their experiences:

> One aspect of your paper I find interesting is that almost all mention of race is erased from your final project, even though in class discussions its relevance to understanding why you might not have been as welcomed by the full-time volunteers seemed to be central. . . . Given that we've talked all semester about relationships between literacy, community, and race, I was surprised that there is no mention of race as an issue within this paper, nor are there any explicit connections made between your experiences at the Center and many of the course readings that talk about these specific issues—such as the Smitherman essay, the Delpit essay, Denny Taylor's books, etc. Integrating what we've talked about in our class discussions regarding these issues with your experiences at the Center might have provided both of you with a broader lens to interpret and understand your experiences as tutors.

At the time, my response to John and Sara's memo made sense to me. But now, in reflecting more fully upon the public nature of their text, I wonder if John and Sara's memo illustrates more conscious rhetorical strategizing than I had originally given them credit for. I think my response failed to appreciate the ways in which these students might have been conscious of issues of power and representation with respect to the public nature of their memo.

As a public text, the memo's absence of discussion about race makes sense, particularly in terms of the concerns that these students had for being labeled *racist*. While John and Sara said in class that they changed the audience for their memo because they didn't want to appear like "big-time college students," they also might have feared that their memo would be misinterpreted by the Director of the Center, who is African American. My response to John and Sara didn't take into account how their memo could have had a negative impact on how the Director viewed them. Indeed, the original conception of their text as a public document for the Director can account for the memo's absent discussion of race. The fact that the students had originally conceived

of the Director as the audience is reflected in the paragraph that praises his efforts at the Center and the respect he has earned from the children (and, by extension, John and Sara as well). This paragraph serves to distinguish between the Director and other community members at the Center and alleviates some of the critique that is then rendered on the full-time volunteers who made them feel unwanted. Their decision to speak with the Director face to face about their suggestions shows their sensitivity to the community's rhetorical space in which they were operating. Perhaps Sara and John learned more about the relationship between public texts and community literacy practices than I had given them credit for. Rather than considering how these multiple audiences complicated the public nature of their text, though, my response focused mainly on what I would have preferred to see in the memo as the main audience—an integration of course material, more analysis and critical reflection, and so on, which probably wouldn't have been viewed as valuable by readers at the Center. Despite the fact that this course was designed to have students work in public contexts and to imagine writing as public texts beyond the sole teacher-as-audience, it was difficult to suppress my "teacher expectations" for what constitutes reflective and critical writing in this case.

As a teacher who intends to continue assigning community projects, I am led to consider how John's texts and experiences contribute to, revise, and complicate my pedagogical goals for how students "go public" with writing about community projects. Chris Anson (1997) suggests that teachers, like students, often go through developmental stages when incorporating service learning/community inquiry into their classrooms. He argues that teachers "need to approach our service learning courses with a critically reflective stance that models for students the kind of discursive explorations they should take in their journals and reflection logs" (177). While I agree that providing models of discursive exploration would be helpful for students, I also think that teachers need to question what such discursive exploration should look like and to consider how the public nature of texts can influence, shape, and even contradict the more academic genres of reflection that we ask our students to do.

While a teacher may desire students to analyze and synthesize course readings in a way that provides a critical interpretative framework for understanding community experiences, the student's own reflections about that experience don't necessarily need to be represented textually in such genres. Students might be hesitant to critique or analyze their community experiences, particularly when they feel allied with the community members and want to protect them from the sometimes harsh gaze of academic analysis. The public nature of their texts, even if circulated solely within the academic classroom, might pose ethical questions for them as they seek to fully and fairly represent others they have come to care about. Or, as Sara and John's memo illustrates, the process of reflection in which they engaged in conceptualizing the memo might not be reflected as critical reflection in the memo itself.

As Nora Bacon (1997) reminds us, teachers are often ill equipped to judge the communicative outcomes of texts that students write for community organizations. I believe this disclaimer extends as well to the texts that students write about community inquiry that are intended for teachers and classmates. My own experiences suggest that the binary often constructed between public and private audiences/texts becomes collapsed into distinctions of different types of public-ness in students' texts. While I remain committed to creating community projects for students in my writing classrooms, I am much more aware of the politics of how texts function publicly, in my classroom and beyond.

5

Public and Private Writing in the Information Age

Charles Moran

In this chapter I make four related points: first, that technology has made visible to me a deep conflict in my own pedagogy—the desire to have students write "from the heart" and the desire to have students publish their work; second, that this conflict has its origins in our particular writing program's history,[1] which is an aspect of the history of writing programs K–12 in America post-1980; third, that emerging technologies, as we have been using them, seem to be biased toward publication and against "writing from the heart"; and fourth, and finally, that as we bring our writing classes into the technological present, we need to make sure that we don't lose what we have so carefully constructed over the past thirty years—our focus on the student as writer, as learner, as something more than a publisher, a document processor, a writer of papers, a cog in a machine that produces language on demand.

To begin at the beginning, I need to explain how it is that in spring 1998 I felt clearly, for the first time in my thirty-plus years in writing classrooms, the conflict between two imperatives in my teaching: "write about things that have meaning for you" and "publish your work, because that is what real writers do." Seen in terms of pedagogical theory, it was as if I were watching two galaxies collide, the collision silent, distant, and without local consequence. Seen in terms of my students' writing, it was as if I were watching a smoothly functioning learning-and-teaching machine begin to break down, right there in my classroom, with the attendant noise and unhappiness.

Like many of us, perhaps most of us, I hope that my students will write honestly about their own experience, composing their lives, using language in the spectator mode, as James Britton (1970; Britton et al. 1975) and Nancy Martin (1976) urged us to do in the 1970s. I have wanted them to write authentically about what is most meaningful to them. I have tried to create a classroom atmosphere in which we trust one another, and in which we are therefore less likely to write what Ken Macrorie called "Engfish" and others have called "academic writing": the stuffy, voiceless prose that student writers must think we want to read.

As I have worked for honest, meaningful writing, I have also looked for opportunities for my students to publish their writing, following the advice of such theorists and teachers as Ken Macrorie, Peter Elbow, Donald Murray, and James Moffett. "Publication" in our university's writing program takes several forms, which together can usefully be seen as a set of concentric circles—ripples in a pond: first, sharing writing with one's response group; second, publishing writing in an anthology that is distributed to the twenty-four members of the class; third, publishing writing in one of the writing program's anthologies, with a press run of two thousand or so; and fourth, publishing on the World Wide Web. In our writing program, teachers regularly publish photocopied anthologies of student writing, as often as biweekly but at least monthly. In addition to the class anthologies, the Program publishes each semester an anthology of the best writing from its more than one hundred sections, and each year it publishes *Willing Wordswork,* an anthology of the best writing from the university's writing-across-the-curriculum program. We, of course, protect students' privacy, making sure that they can decide not to publish in these anthologies, as they can choose not to share their writing in response groups. This policy is designed to protect students who feel that what they have written should not be read by others. Yet the overall push of our program is toward publication. Every year in our orientation program for new teachers, someone asks, "What if a student refuses to publish all semester?" My answer has been, "This is an unlikely event; when it happens, let's talk about it."

So in 1998, when the Web came to our computer-equipped classrooms, I saw a chance to have students publish easily, quickly, and cheaply, and to a new, "real" audience. I asked them, therefore, late in the semester, to take one of their essays and post it on our class Web site. My goals in this were two: to give students practice in writing in this new "scene" and, secondarily, to introduce the Web to them as a place where they could write, as well as read. When I saw these essays on the Web, my heart first leapt up: My first-year students were colonizing the Web, putting their language up there with the others, asserting their place in the universe, mastering the technology and using it in the service of their own goals. But then, as I turned from reading the Web essays as technological and graphic achievement and read them instead as a writing teacher, I became troubled. The writing wasn't "bad," really, but it was more often than not lifeless, dutiful, something perilously close to Macrorie's Engfish. Here is a sample:

> In all of western music, one of the most difficult styles to master is the style of jazz. The performance of jazz requires a discipline of the player which is unlike European classical music and most of popular music. Jazz requires the player to bring to the music his own interpretation of the piece as well as his own emotional and mental spin at the moment of performance—it is a constantly changing art form, and no performance of the same song is ever the same twice.

The paper goes on to describe the emotional content and impact of jazz, and without a hint that the writer is an accomplished jazz musician. The writer asked that the piece be anonymous. Many of the other Web-published pieces were just as distant and careful: a piece on dieting, also headed "author anonymous," that gave no hint that the writer had herself attempted weight loss; and a piece on ethnic stereotyping that focused in a carefully distant way on the author's experience with bureaucratic forms that asked the writer to choose an identity. Even the pieces that had an "I" in them felt distant, somehow disconnected. Even the authors who put their names on their pieces seemed to hunker down, to write safely.

This reading of the Web anthology made me remember that in this same semester one of my students had begun talking to me about her childhood in what seemed to me an interesting way. I asked her whether she felt that there was something to write about here. She said that she would write it to me, but she did not want to put it in our virtual classroom, our local area network; and she absolutely did not want to write about this for the Web. I reflexively said that I thought she should not write just to me, and that maybe we'd better look elsewhere for topics, realizing as I formed the words that I had begun to assume, in our writing classrooms, that all writing was really public and that there should not be any transactions between teacher and student that were not public, at least to others in the class.

In our networked writing classroom, I have become accustomed to commenting on students' writing on-line, posting my comments to a file that is in our class "Comments" folder, a folder that anyone in the class can read. I have felt that this practice was valuable, that it meant that my comments to students were subject to some public scrutiny and were, therefore, somehow more responsible, and that students, by reading my comments on others' writing, might pick up something they could apply to their own writing. Even our local area network, then, has been a public place, though restricted to the small public of the class.

Now, in moving to the Web, we had moved to a larger public, the distant audience that Moffett saw as the most difficult for the writer, the most advanced. No wonder students hunkered down at the prospect of Web publishing. Here was the conflict made visible: In individual student conferences, I would try to steer students toward topics that they connected with at a deep level. Then, in class, I would put together editing teams and orchestrate a program of publishing student writing, both in photocopied anthologies and now on the World Wide Web. How had this conflict between public and private stayed submerged for so long? And was this conflict something that had been noted in the literature of composition studies, something that I had missed in what must have been a very long sleep?

To answer the first question, I'll argue that this tension is built into the work of our common "ancestors," the composition theorists who led us in the late 1960s from what has been termed a *current–traditional* mode of teaching

to what was first termed a *writing-process* model. Among the many who might be cited as ancestors, I choose three: Ken Macrorie, Peter Elbow, and Donald Murray. As I review the work of these three ancestors, I focus on the ways in which they have recognized and dealt with the conflict between the desire for "authentic" writing and the impulse to publish student writing.

Ken Macrorie

I begin with Ken Macrorie, because, with his three books, *Telling Writing* (1970), *Writing to Be Read* (1968), and *Uptaught* (1970), and through his editorship of *College Composition and Communication* in the 1960s, Macrorie defined *Engfish* as the enemy and made current what Tom Newkirk (1997) has called as "the traditional 'God terms' of the writing process movement— 'voice,' 'honesty,' 'truth-telling' " (xiii). In his work, Macrorie argues that students' writing should be risk-taking, should have an authentic voice, should be honest and fact-filled.

Macrorie not only called for authentic writing, but also published his students writing. In *Uptaught* (1970), he quotes this piece of student writing to demonstrate what happened on "the day we killed Engfish," an account of driving home after a party. "Then out of the fog loomed a red sign—STOP. The end of the road. I had miscounted. Sign, trees, ditch, fog, brakes, beer, that's all I remembered" (22). After my 1998 experience with students' Web publishing, I read this piece with new eyes. Yes, it is powerful. Yes, it is good writing. And would the writer publish this today? Under his name? Even among his classmates? The writer is telling us about a personal experience that might be actionable, perhaps DWI. Would the driver's parents read this? Others who were involved in the accident? In our increasingly litigious times, could this piece become evidence in a lawsuit? If Macrorie's student were to publish this piece on the Web, there would almost certainly be consequences.

It is interesting that when Macrorie does quote his students' writing in his books, he seldom names his authors. He publishes their work, but most often under the cover of anonymity. In his preface to *Writing to Be Read* (1968), Macrorie explains why it is that he has published most of them anonymously. "Originally," he writes, "I had intended to name all persons whose writing appears in these pages, but when I found that fairness, consistency, comprehensiveness, or discretion had to be disregarded again and again, I decided to name only writers of long pieces, and even then to omit some of those in the interest of protecting them from the perils of truthtelling" (vii). So it is that most student pieces are anonymous. Some have generic authorship—for example, "a third-grade girl" (1), or "a high school student writing freely" (196)—and others are signed "name withheld" (e.g., 3, 4). Macrorie has faced the dilemma squarely: Truthtelling and signed publication are not compatible goals.

Peter Elbow

In the preface to *Writing Without Teachers* (1973), Peter Elbow acknowledges Macrorie as his "ancestor," so it is not surprising that we find in Elbow's work the same tension between "writing honestly" and "publishing." For Elbow, writing is at times a transaction with the self. Freewriting "must be a piece of writing which, even if someone reads it, doesn't send any ripples back to you. It is like writing something and putting it in a bottle in the sea" (3). But still, writing is, for Elbow, more than a transaction with oneself: "Writing is also a transaction with other people. Writing is not just getting things down on paper, it is getting things inside someone's head. If you wish to improve your writing you must also learn to do more business with other people. That is the goal of the teacherless writing class" (76). Elbow is certainly aware of the dangers of going public with one's writing. The teacherless writing class requires, Elbow says, "bravery" and "willingness to risk" (112). The dangers of going public are simply, for Elbow, part of the scene: dangers to be recognized, but still to be faced and experienced. To gain power over one's own life, one needs to go public; one of the purposes of writing is "getting things inside someone's head."

Because of his twin emphases on private writing and publication, what he might term *contraries* that must be embraced, much of Elbow's advice to teachers has to do with creating a safe space for writing that matters. In *Sharing and Responding* (1995), which he co-authored with Pat Belanoff, the authors lay out a taxonomy of response that forecloses evaluation and teacher-like criticism. The responses that they lay out—for example, sharing (no response at all, just listening), pointing, movies of the mind, voice, summary, and sayback—are nonevaluative, nonjudgmental. The peer readers become "a thoughtful, interested audience rather than evaluators or editors or advice-givers" (5). The classroom becomes a community, "A place where people hear clearly even what is mumbled, understand what is badly written, and look for the validity even in what they disagree with" (6). Elbow and Belanoff clearly see that, in this classroom, the writer risks self-exposure. With their taxonomy of reader response, they have solved the attack-critic problem, but they have not, nor can they, eliminate the risks that writers take when they go public. In their view, the power gained by the writers and their writing is worth the attendant risks.

Donald Murray

Donald Murray is the theorist who pushed our University Writing Program most powerfully toward publication. As Tom Newkirk (1993) has written in "Locating Freshman English," "Murray's truly radical move was not to stress the writing process but to claim that the professional writer should be the ideal around which the course should be constructed" (4). Murray's pedagogy is

really quite different from the Macrorie–Elbow axis, much less oriented to the personal and expressive, and much more directed toward publication. In a Macrorie-esque exhortation in *A Writer Teaches Writing* (1968), Murray does say that students "must write out of their experience" (27); but Murray also urges the teacher to keep students at a distance: "The writing teacher cannot be a parent or an uncle, a psychiatric adviser or a social worker, he must keep his distance" (24). The relationship between teacher and student-writer, for Murray, seems more distant than it is for Macrorie and Elbow—less like the psychotherapist, and more like the editor who, in the newsroom, receives and comments on the writing of his cub reporters.

Given his model of the professional writer, Murray pushes us hard to publish our students' writing. In *A Writer Teaches Writing,* he argues that the writer who is not publishing "can be compared with the athlete who never gets into the game" (162). In the University of Massachusetts writing program, through our regularly published anthologies of student writing, we have enacted Murray's assumption that "the act of writing is not complete until a piece of writing is published and read, and the teacher should seek whatever ways he can in his own school to achieve a variety of publications for his students" (162).

Emerging Technologies: A Bias Toward the Public?

So it seems that the tension between writing from the heart and publication has been explicit in much of the writing in our field that I see as foundational. Why, then, did the tension seem suddenly visible, no longer transparent and "natural," when I asked my students to publish on the Web? To some degree, my sudden ability to see this tension is a function of the introduction of technology into the classroom. In this new place, the familiar seems strange. To some degree, the sudden visibility of this tension is a function of the medium itself.

My experience with Web publishing has made me consider a rather frightening possibility: that computer technologies, as we are presently using them, move all of us in our first-year writing courses toward the production and publication of "documents" that will live in the public sphere, and away from more or less private writing that will help us compose our lives. These emerging technologies move us toward the professional writer model of the early Murray, toward transactional writing and away from expressive writing, toward technical and professional writing and away from the teachings of such theorists and teachers as Macrorie, Elbow, Britton, Martin, Graves, Atwell, Rief, Calkins, and Romano. Hawisher and Selfe (1998) have speculated, "Writing at a computer in elementary school settings . . . may in fact transform school-based writing from a private to a public activity as students gather around the computers to read and talk about their writings" (7). To the extent that emerging technologies connect us with one another—with our classmates and with correspondents/collaborators outside our classrooms—they begin to crowd private writing into a rather narrow space.

It is emerging technologies that make the move toward the public possible. I'm not suggesting, of course, that technology is making us do what we are doing; it is only making it possible for us to do what we must have long wanted to do. And, of course, as we take advantage of these new possibilities, we introduce changes in every aspect of our teaching. I group the "new possibilities" under three headings: desktop publishing, e-mail, and the Web; and I look at the ways in which these three applications of technology move us toward publication and away from private writing.

Desktop Publishing

In 1986, as desktop publishing was just becoming possible for teachers and students, Stephen Bernhardt (1986) argued that we writing teachers needed to see our student writers as desktop publishers and consider widening our view to include a "rhetoric of visual design" (75). In the course of his article, he suggested that visual elements of the text might supplant such standard elements of our teaching as the topic sentence and the transition. In 1991, Patricia Sullivan argued that "word processing" was rapidly becoming "word publishing" (51). "Writers must become sensitive about how pages look, attuned to how readers will see pages, as well as with the text, and as well as with the making of publications" (56).

I note that both Bernhardt and Sullivan come from the world of technical and professional writing, where teachers tend to speak of "documents" that are almost inherently public and in which the personal is buried deep. And yet what both said about desktop publishing in those early days applies to us now, as we teach in our first-year writing courses. Students now have much greater access to desktop publishing software, if not in a computer-equipped classroom then in their dormitory rooms or in institutional computer labs. So publication of student writing becomes easier, more "natural," and perhaps an implicit expectation in our classrooms. When all is published, there is less space for the private and personal.

E-mail and On-line Chat Programs

Electronic mail (e-mail) has also moved us toward publication—not paper-based publication, but the electronic publication of student writing on lists to audiences beyond the classroom (e.g., Eldred 1991; Harris and Wambeam 1996). It has become a commonplace that on-line communication, whether on a chat program or on e-mail, creates an illusion of intimacy, a space where writers often censor themselves less than they would in a face-to-face meeting (e.g., Hawisher and Moran 1997, 88–90). It is also clear, however, that on-line discourse only seems to be private and personal, perhaps because of the rapid rhythms of response (Hawisher and Moran 1997). On-line discourse is, in a sense, always already published. Once our discourse is digitized, it can be

copied any number of times without cost and sent to people we have no intent to address. As Gail Hawisher and I have noted, "E-mail is not at all like the envelope-wrapped letter. It is even more open to others' scrutiny than the p-mail postcard. The postcard can be read by anyone in the send-and-deliver process, and it can be read by anyone in the household of the recipient. But that is still a relatively small potential audience. The audience for e-mail is, potentially, the world" (84–85). And on-line discussions that are now an important part of our teaching are speech-made-text. Once a discussion is digitized, it can be copied, distributed, and read by anyone who has access to it. There is no on-line space that is really, absolutely private.

The World Wide Web

HTML-authoring programs have made Web publication so easy that I have made this activity a part of my writing curriculum. Again, I am not alone. In the literature of our field, there is substantial interest in Web publication in the work of our first-year writing classrooms. Advocates of the inclusion of Web work in our courses often borrow, to their rather different ends, the vocabulary of Macrorie, Moffett, and others as they argue that writing for the Web is likely to produce "authentic writing" (e.g., Watkins 1996, 225). Tharon Howard (1997) has argued that "with a $2,000–$3,000 investment in the electronic equivalent of the printing press, private citizens can produce and distribute World Wide Web publications on any topic or topics they consider important, and have the ability to reach a potential audience as large as their local newspaper or television station" (48).

After my experience with Web publication last semester, the possibilities excite. And yet, given what I have written here so far, any publication opens up risks, and the risks of Web publication are well known. Locally, parents and teachers tell young children not to give out their addresses, telephone numbers, or e-mail addresses to persons or sites that request them, because there are pedophiles out there who are trolling for victims. At Ohio State–Marion, Scott DeWitt (1997) has come to question the value of the Web for "gay, lesbian, and bisexual students who may be using the writing classroom as a safe space to facilitate their coming out process" (229). Gail Hawisher and Patricia Sullivan (1998) have documented the dangers that women face on-line—stalking and harassment (174–175)—and quote one woman who concluded, "Although I think this is a wonderful medium, it's a dangerous one, and it poses more danger to women than men" (175). And this is the space in which I want my students to publish? No wonder they begin to write carefully. They are adjusting their writing to their audience.

From my students' Web-publishing experience I have learned valuable lessons. As Robert Frankston (1990) has written, "The real impact in computers is not the silicon. It's not even the software. It's the re-thinking" (271). And

I have substantially re-thought. I am now much more aware than I was of the risks we ask our students to take in the name of "honesty" and "authenticity." As I read the work of such theorists as Lisa Delpit (1995) and Harriet Malinowitz (1992), I understand more fully than I did their resistance to an emphasis on personal writing. Personal writing is risky, as Macrorie, Elbow, and Moffett fully understand. But risk is not equally distributed in our society. In America, women are much more likely to be the victims of violent crime than are men. In America, gay men can be pistol-whipped and murdered because of their sexual preference. In America, black men can be beaten and dragged behind a truck to their death. As a white male teacher, I need to keep this constantly in mind: that the world that seems so risk-free to me does not seem that way to most of my students.

Perhaps paradoxically, I am also much more aware of the value of personal writing in the classroom. Based on the writing I see my students performing, I am daily reminded of the power of personal writing. I see students composing their lives; when they write authentically, I learn from them. I do not want the first-year writers in my course to hunker down, to write safe, dead, academic prose. I do not want a return to Engfish. I will, therefore, continue to try to discover safe places for my students to take risks with their writing. I am not certain how I will do this, but I'm guessing that these spaces will not be on-line spaces, which, as I've indicated, are always already public.

Finally, I will not, as I did last spring, so privilege publication that I discourage students from writing just for themselves, or just for me, the teacher. I do not want my writing classroom to become simply a document-processing office. I do not want my students to write, nor do I want to read, what Macrorie called "Engfish." I do want the writing classroom to be a place where first-year writing students can learn to go public and where they can, as needed, compose their lives. I will need to balance these two objectives carefully, and not let my love of emerging technologies draw me so deeply into publication that private writing loses the space it has earned in my writing classes.

Note

1. For a more detailed history of the Writing Program at the University of Massachusetts, see my article, "How the Writing Process Came to UMass/Amherst: Roger Garrison, Donald Murray, and Institutional Change," in *Taking Stock: The Writing Process Movement in the '90's,* edited by Lad Tobin and Tom Newkirk.

6

"Can't We Just Xerox This?"

The Ethical Dilemma of Writing for the World Wide Web

Nicholas Mauriello and Gian S. Pagnucci

> While the politicians struggle with the baggage of history, a new
> generation is emerging from the digital landscape free of many of
> the old prejudices. These kids are released from the limitation of
> geographic proximity as the sole basis of friendship, collaboration,
> play, and neighborhood. Digital technology can be a natural force
> drawing people into greater world harmony. (Negroponte 1995, 230)

At first, Nicholas Negroponte's ideas seem a bit too optimistic when viewed
from the contexts of the classrooms in which most of us currently teach. The
introduction of technology into the classroom has been slow, costly, and ineq-
uitable and, in general, has been littered with failures and dead ends.

While experience belies Negroponte's utopian vision for the digital age,
his vision is still one that marks a shift in social ideology from guarded and
individual to communal and global. It is this shift with which teachers must
struggle if they wish to move their classrooms into the public realm of
cyberspace.

Over the last four years, as we have incorporated Internet technology into
our writing classrooms, at our university we have been struggling to understand the type of community in which we now teach. With our first attempt at
an on-line writing course, we found that the biggest struggle was to expand the
definition of *classroom community*. Some of our students wanted to maintain
what LeFevre (1987) terms "a Platonic view of invention, one which assumes
that the individual possesses innate knowledge or mental structures that are the
chief source of invention" (11). Yet what we found was that on-line communities run counter to this belief. An on-line society can exist only through pub-

44

lic participation. Where our students hoped to create knowledge in isolation, they instead found themselves in a heteroglossia of voices (Bakhtin 1981), a public, dialogic community where writers were actively engaged and challenged by readers. In fact, to some students, this new public classroom community felt so threatening that one person even threw up her hands and said, "Can't we just Xerox this?"

This student's statement raised serious ethical concerns about teaching in an on-line public community. When we talked with this student, we found that her resistance to our proposed public display of writing was much more complicated than we might have anticipated. In fact, her views startled us. She was willing to share her writing with a small, familiar classroom community. But, to her, the Internet represented a public community, which was unknown, uncontrolled, and even potentially dangerous. What she feared most was going public, exposing not only her writing, but herself to potential embarrassment, criticism, ridicule, reprisal, and all the other risks that follow venturing into the open. In response to our student's concern, we began to consider the following questions:

Does the public nature of the Internet community compromise students' safety?

Does on-line public writing force students to mask their identities and, if so, with what consequences?

Does the fear of public writing impact the development of student writers?

How does this shift in community change our conception of teaching writing?

Is this diverse public community an appropriate space for developing writers?

Our student challenged our new pedagogy on ethical grounds, and this challenge forced us to consider not only the ethics of our teaching, but also the beliefs from which those ethics stemmed. The ethical dilemmas our student uncovered were linked to a specific understanding of community, in our case the writing classroom community, one that is normally seen as safe, small, and nurturing. As we considered these issues, we began to wonder if this was how an on-line classroom community should be constructed. In fact, we reflected that teachers were perhaps making a mistake by assuming that any writing classroom, on-line or traditional, should always be safe, small, and nurturing. What we began to uncover was a new set of values, values somewhat counter to the established model of teaching writing, but values that may be necessary for teaching in the public realm of cyberspace.

Does the public nature of the Internet community compromise students' safety? When we first asked students to post their papers on-line, one of the ethical concerns they raised was whether this activity compromised their safety. Some of our students feared that if they posted their writing on-line,

they might be ridiculed or, worse, harassed for their beliefs. Others worried that releasing sensitive information might jeopardize their personal relationships. What these students told us was that they consciously censored their writing, sometimes going so far as to switch from their preferred topic to one that was public-friendly. In this way, they avoided what they perceived as the conflicts and dangers inherent in making writing public.

Having been alerted to our students' initial concerns about on-line writing, we began to conduct surveys and interviews with them to solicit their input as we continued to refine our new on-line composition courses. To make concrete our students' feedback, we established the College Writing Peer Response Project (CWPRP), an Internet-based writing collaborative that links composition students in such geographically diverse areas as Alaska, Florida, Kansas, New York City, and Pennsylvania (Mauriello 1997). As writing instructors, our curricular goal was to have students write for and peer-respond to a culturally diverse Internet audience; however, as reflective practitioners, we knew the success of the CWPRP was based on a "bottom-up" approach. This approach is grounded in the simple notion that if we ask students to participate in on-line writing activities, then they should be instrumental in the creation and implementation of this new writing environment.

Protecting Students from the Internet Public

We explained to our students that the CWPRP was an open environment where anyone using the Web, even those not registered for the course, could respond to any of the essays posted on the site. At the bottom of every student essay was an embedded hypertext link to an e-mail–based response form. As we discussed the public nature of the CWPRP, our students suggested a range of methods to ensure their personal safety when posting their essays. We followed the students' suggestions, giving students the option not to post their essays, allowing them to conceal their identities through the use of pseudonyms, and, finally, protecting the class Web site via a password so that only a limited audience would have access to the students' writing.

To further separate our students from any potential Internet danger, we gave students free topic choice so that they would not be forced to post essays that they deemed too personal. We also filtered the electronic responses sent to our students from outside readers by reading each message before sending it on to the student writer. In this way, we knew we could intercept any messages that were derogatory or threatening.

While we wanted students to share their writing with a public audience, all of these safety measures constrained this objective. Student safety should always be a teaching priority, but because these safety measures often limited or altered the audience for our students' writings—one of the major objectives in any composition class—over time we came to question the definition of *safety* and to examine its implications for our classrooms and our students' writing development.

In the first year of the CWPRP, only three or four students in our class posted their essays. While this was an initial setback for the project, those students who did post their essays reaped the benefits of on-line interaction. These students commented about the usefulness of the on-line peer responses they received and how they directly impacted their revision processes. The early success of these few students became the catalyst for other students' eventual acceptance of this new pedagogy.

Pseudonyms

The use of pseudonyms became an option in our second semester for those students who wanted to participate in the CWPRP but didn't want to reveal their identities. This seemed to make sense. After all, if students weren't comfortable putting their real names on their Internet posting, why not just let them pick an alternative name for the post? They weren't changing their essays, they were just changing their identities.

Sherry Turkle (1997) explores the question of Internet identity changing at length in her book, *Life on the Screen:* "When people adopt an online persona they cross a boundary into highly charged territory. Some feel an uncomfortable sense of fragmentation, some a sense of relief. Some sense the possibilities of self-discovery, even self-transformation" (260).

We hoped that by using pseudonyms our students would gain "the possibilities of self-discovery" Turkle discusses. But that semester and in our subsequent classroom research into Internet identity construction (Pagnucci and Mauriello 1999, 141), we found that pseudonym use by student writers often has highly detrimental consequences for female students. When female students in our classes deliberately chose sexually provocative pseudonyms (e.g., "Pamela Anderson") to attract high numbers of responses from the public Internet audience, they too often found that they received responses that focused only on their pseudonym choice, objectified them, and provided no useful suggestions for revision.

Because pseudonyms proved to be so problematic, we eventually discouraged their use. In addition to skewing readership, our research showed that the use of pseudonyms allowed students to hide behind a disembodied self. When there is no true identity attached to an on-line essay, students "avoid a necessary but often unpleasant aspect of peer revision: telling someone that their paper isn't any good. For peer response to really work, it takes an investment that does not shy away from emotional conflict. Emotional conflicts are real, essential to the revision process, and demand resolution. This conflict becomes the heart of the next draft" (Pagnucci and Mauriello 1999, 148).

Although, on rare occasions, we do allow students who are highly uncomfortable with Web-posting the option of using pseudonyms, we now require that those pseudonyms be ordinary names, such as Maria or Joe. This makes it difficult for the readers to determine whether the student's name is a pseudonym, and it also prevents students from choosing pseudonyms like "Hey Beer

Man!" or "Pamela Anderson," which, as mentioned earlier, were identities that students experimented with in the early days of the CWPRP but found to carry highly troubling cultural baggage.

Password Protection

As Internet use has become more mainstream in U.S. culture, we've moved closer and closer to a free and open CWPRP. We are, however, still using password protection for our Usenet discussion groups. Password-protection technology limits the public display of these on-line discussions only to students enrolled in the course. The general public cannot view or access them.

Recently, though, our students have urged us to abandon even this limited amount of sheltering. We've come to learn that students clearly value having a large potential readership for the project, something that is lost when the site is closed to the public. Even those students who thought that it might be useful to protect the site through passwords generally found that they liked receiving responses from others outside of the project. One student pointed out that having the CWPRP Web site open to the public was actually an incentive for the students to put more effort into writing their essays, while another student even indicated taking great personal pride in writing an essay that was available to a large potential readership.

Open Access

From optional Internet posting to pseudonyms to password protection, we kept developing safety measures for the public display of writing. Looking back now, these measures and our efforts to ensure our students' safety may seem too extreme and even detrimental to our goal of promoting public writing. Yet some students in our first Internet-based course had been so paralyzed by the unknown nature of public writing, we could never forget the echoes of their fears.

We would never want any harm to befall our students, and we can never discount the potential risk that writing for the Web may create. To ensure a level of security, we still filter all electronic responses before forwarding them on to the student authors. We may, however, soon abandon this action in favor of an open-access Web site. Central to this decision are the data we have collected over the past three years of the CWPRP, leading us to question whether there is truly an ethical dilemma in asking students to publicly display their writing on the Internet.

Since the CWPRP began, we have posted more than one thousand essays, accumulated nearly thirty thousand electronic responses, and conducted seventy-five hours' worth of student interviews. We were quite relieved that in all of these data, not one threat of any kind arrived from the Internet public. In fact, of the thirty thousand responses sent to the CWPRP, we deemed fewer than ten unsuitable for circulation to the student authors. None of these ex-

cluded responses were threatening in any way; they were problematic only because they were totally off-task.

Over time, it appeared that our students faced a negligible physical risk when posting their writing on-line. Reflecting this trend, we also found that where, initially, only a few students were willing to post their essays, now almost all of our students want to post their work on-line. We might have two students out of one hundred who opt to keep their work off-line. This probably reflects both the growing popularity of the Internet and the medium's expanding use in a variety of academic disciplines. In fact, our students now tell us that it may be naive of us to worry about posting essays on-line.

Weighing the Fear of Public Writing Versus the Benefits to Our Students' Development as Writers

While it would be unwise to totally dismiss the possibility of encountering hostility when using the Web, we believe this risk is worth the benefits it brings. Fear of the uncontrolled Web readership, either real or imagined, can become a powerful tool in the teaching of writing. We've slowly come to understand that when students are confronted with the uncertainties of the public Web audience, they must develop new rhetorical strategies for addressing this audience, ones they never encountered in the limited space of the traditional classroom.

Rhetorical Problematizing

The rhetorical dilemma of constructing a work for the Internet means balancing readers' interests with the potential fear of the unknown. Our students found that they had to engage their readers in a personal way, but also that they had to hide certain information about themselves.

Writing teachers have always had the difficulty of helping students learn to accurately define their rhetorical problem. Recall Flower and Hayes' (1981) early discussion on the subject:

> At the beginning of composing, the most important element is obviously the rhetorical problem itself. A school assignment is a simplified version of such a problem, describing the writer's topic, audience, *and (implicitly) her role as student to teacher.* Insofar as writing is a rhetorical act, not a mere artifact, writers attempt to "solve" or respond to this rhetorical problem by writing something.
>
> In theory this problem is a very complex thing: it includes not only the rhetorical situation and audience which prompts one to write, it also includes the writer's own goals in writing. A good writer is a person who can juggle all of these demands. But in practice we have observed, as did Britton, that writers frequently reduce this large set of constraints to a radically simplified problem, such as "write another theme for English class." (257, emphasis mine)

We believe it is the "safe" environment of traditional writing classrooms that creates the problematic situation Flower and Hayes described. When the reader is always the same (i.e., always another English teacher), the writing does not have to change. The rhetorical situation becomes comfortable and safe. Students write their next essay just as they wrote the last one, for an audience that will read and grade it. Nelson (1990) tells us that student writers simply decide what their teachers are looking for and duplicate it time and time again. In the public space of the Internet, however, this is simply not possible. Because in cyberspace there is no predefined reader, students must struggle to test for themselves the boundaries of public writing in order to write something meaningful for readers who care. Our students told us that this uncertainty of readership engaged them in new composing strategies: As they wrote, they wrestled with difficult choices about how and what to write for an audience much larger than a single teacher.

When students write for an on-line audience, they may reclaim the sense of authority invested in their texts. They become accountable for their words and the emotional impact those words may stir within the reader. Because there is always the potential that an Internet reader will be an expert on a subject, will think the subject is unimportant, or will be offended by word choices, students successfully writing for cyberspace quickly learn to move from a writerly to a readerly perspective. One student writer, a self-proclaimed political expert, decided against checking sources for an essay on U.S. military tactics in the Middle East. To this writer's surprise, peer responses citing lack of accurate information flooded in from Gulf War veterans and from several students with Middle Eastern heritage. This student writer revised the second draft to include citations, Internet references, and a greater attention to accuracy and detail.

In the last three years of the CWPRP, we have generally found that when a student's authority is questioned in the first draft, the revisions usually reflect a detailed sense of accountability. We believe this accountability is due to a newly formed understanding of the relationship between writer and audience. Because students are both writers and readers within the CWPRP, they come to understand the active dynamics of both roles. Many students have commented on the value of receiving a personal response, and that this causes them to invest much time in revising their own work and in writing detailed peer responses for other students' work. In this environment, students become actively engaged as reader, writer, and person. When students believe that their writing matters, they seem more likely to invest in its development, especially when posting to the diverse audience of the Internet.

Weighing the Paths to a Diverse Audience Versus the Benefits to Our Students' Development as Individuals

At our own institution, Indiana University of Pennsylvania, at least eighty percent of the student body is recruited from within a two-hour radius of the

university. This means the bulk of our students come from small rural communities where white, Eurocentric, hegemonic values are prevalent. We have, then, what we deem to be a consistent difficulty, a general lack of racial and ethnic diversity in our classrooms.

To counteract this lack of diversity, we can, of course, ask students to read about other cultures, to discuss the value systems they hold, and to consider their place within a racially unequal country. But how effectively can we teach students about diversity when they are educated in fairly homogenous classrooms?

In designing the CWPRP, we sought a way to connect our western Pennsylvania students with a truer sense of diversity, with people whose cultures, values, and stories would be radically different from their own. We wanted our students to write themselves into the lives of others, to engage in dialogues that stemmed from lived experience, and to confront the differences and similarities of living in a complicated world. In his book *Eating on the Street: Teaching Literacy in a Multicultural Society,* David Schaafsma (1993) tells a story of his experiences teaching in the Dewey Center Community Writing Program, an inner-city Detroit summer program that was richly diverse in the composition of both its students and its teachers. Schaafsma sees the multiple perspectives of those involved with the project as crucial to its success, and so his account preserves the voices of six different teachers in the program, teachers who were diverse in their races, genders, and views about pedagogy. For Schaafsma, one of the values of working among such diversity is the opportunity it brings to directly confront our myths about other cultures: "People working in a multicultural setting—such as we were in our summer program—people intent on not silencing each other's voices and working together on common goals of learning and teaching, both transform and are transformed to some extent in the act of sharing stories. This is a view of myth making . . . that makes use of differences for growth" (198). We hoped that the CWPRP would open the door to this multiple perspective of culture, and engage our students in the lived realities of difference.

In planning the CWPRP, we knew that the Internet offered the potential to unite diverse populations, but we were unsure of what this diversity would do to our classroom community or the impact it would have on how our students developed as writers. What we discovered was that, like Schaafsma's community, when we created a diverse public community, we enabled our students and ourselves to confront stereotypes, to expand knowledge of other cultures, and to engage in constructive discussions of difference. Our students told us that it's not just reading about other cultures that promotes diversity, it's also the presence of others. For meaningful dialogue to take place in a public realm like the Internet, people must move beyond cultural roadblocks like language differences. When this happens, the public classroom of the Internet becomes the first step toward building a truly multicultural community.

After four years researching the CWPRP, we can now answer our original student's question, "Can't we just Xerox this?" Our answer is a resounding

"No." Our students have shown us that writing for the public audience of the Internet can build community, foster rhetorical problematizing, and encourage understanding of difference. What started as one student's ethical concern about the nature of public writing led us to reflect on our teaching and to search for ways to bring students into our curriculum design. Going public is risky business. If we are going to ask students to make their writing public, on the Internet or anywhere else, then, as teachers, we should be willing to take the same risks. By making our pedagogies public, we invite our students into the process of knowledge creation.

7

"Some People Just Want Their Stories to Die with Them"

Derek Owens

The title of this essay comes from something a student said to me the first semester I started inviting my students to publish their oral histories on a Web site I had built to archive student writing. His comment caught me off guard, and as he, along with another Chinese American student, explained to me their reasons for refusing to make their work public, I realized how presumptuous and insulting my invitation must have seemed to them. His insight helped me differentiate between the kinds of student texts that (at least in the context of my own classroom) will often be better off left private and unpublished, and those that, because of their social value, really do belong in a public space such as the World Wide Web. This essay explores my rationale for encouraging writing in both "local" and "global" contexts, focusing particularly on why I now tend to associate the writing of oral histories with the former, and the writing of "place histories" or neighborhood narratives in the latter. I also address how my student's reference to "dying stories" has larger implications for teaching at this particular historical moment.

Several years ago I started building a Web site—originally on my own AOL account, but now housed on an "unofficial faculty Web site" provided by my institution—to house my syllabi and archive my students' writings. In each of my composition courses I make students aware of this site and encourage them to submit their revised essays in HTML so that I might post their work on the site. Originally, I had three objectives in designing the Web site: to facilitate a greater sense of community among students, to encourage revision, and to promote what I call "sustainable thinking."

Because most of the eighteen thousand students at the university where I teach commute, and most of them work over twenty hours a week while taking a full course load, a common complaint among my freshmen is that they have few opportunities to get to know one another. This is particularly frustrating at an institution like ours, which enjoys an unusually strong

53

multicultural population. (St. John's University is located in Queens, which has the most ethnically diverse population in the United States, if not literally in the entire Western Hemisphere.) With a population as diverse as ours, such familiarity could go far in promoting cross-cultural awareness. Because, in my writing classes, students write memoirs, essays, interviews, and narratives about their neighborhoods, families, cultures, jobs, educational experiences, and fears and hopes for the future, I feel that such a collection of work, made accessible to the rest of the student body, could, over time, develop into the student body's evolving autobiography, a tool by which students might come to better know their peers and themselves.

Another purpose for the Web site was to create a catalyst for revision. Any of my students can post their work on this Web site—which is why I call it an "archive" as opposed to a "journal"—so long as they discuss their writing with me and some of their classmates first, as well as pay at least one visit to our Writing Center to discuss possibilities for revising their work (I direct our Writing Center, so our counselors are aware of my on-line archive). Like many writing instructors who have used the World Wide Web as a heuristic, I believe that if students know their writing might be read by a larger portion of the student body (and faculty), as opposed to writing solely for me and a few classmates, this might give them more incentive to further revise and think more carefully about their work.

My third objective was more idiosyncratic. I need to back up here and explain briefly my commitment to designing courses and curricula that promote "sustainable education": that is, cross-disciplinary environments that foster an ongoing exploration of the problems and possibilities associated with living in a sustainable culture. By *sustainability* I mean, to use a common but generic definition, meeting the needs of the current generation without jeopardizing the needs of future generations. I try to choreograph composition assignments that might lead students to reflect on the interrelatedness of mind and place, individual and community, present habits and future implications. If nothing else, I hope to instill within them a desire to become more aware of the complexities inherent in the goal of sustainability. I also try to promote a "preservational ethic"—a desire to identify those qualities within one's family, culture, and community that are worth saving and salvaging. Certainly this motive is shared by other "ecocompositionists" who use green and cross-cultural readers in their courses, or have their students explore forms of "nature writing." But because almost all of my students live in New York City or on Long Island, conventional interpretations of *nature* can easily seem distant if not irrelevant. Instead of discussing essays about rain forests, collected in the typical ecoreader, I choose to cultivate a preservational ethic by asking students to investigate and testify about their neighborhoods, their cultures, their families—the social and geographic landscapes they know firsthand—with an emphasis on preserving those sites and communities through their words and photographs, their memories and observations. And so, one of my assignment

options is an oral history project for which students spend three to four weeks interviewing a family member, neighbor, or close friend, during which they record and later edit their findings, thereby fashioning a small portrait of that person's life.

Although it is now an optional assignment, the first time I incorporated this "oral history preservation project," as I call it, into my classroom, I made it a requirement. Even so, it turned out to be the most popular assignment in the course. Students interviewed mothers and fathers, aunts and uncles, cousins and grandparents, gathering stories and learning things that had never before been revealed to them. After completing this project, many of the students were eager to read their interviews and share their tributes to family members and friends. More than a few of these testimonies were emotionally captivating, and many were transfixed when reading or listening to these accounts. The finished pieces were moving, inspiring, and honest. Stories about mothers studying to become RNs while working full-time and raising a family. A mother's correspondence with dozens of young men in Vietnam, most all of whom would die. A father's war stories. A cousin coming to terms with his brother's suicide. One mother's account of how, as a single working mother, she forfeited a career as a model in order to raise her daughter. I realized all over again how the conversational space of the composition classroom, when grounded in the lives and histories of the students, can be one of the richest in the university curriculum.

The first time I presented this assignment I was so impressed with the results that I encouraged any interested students to get permission from their family members and place these accounts on the Web site I had just created. Even though I had made it clear that no one was required to post this work—they didn't even have to share these accounts with their classmates if they didn't want to—in retrospect, I know I must have come on too strong in goading them to go on-line with their work: "Of course, you don't *have* to put this on the Web site if you don't want to . . . but it's such a wonderful account, don't you think others would benefit from reading it?" Most of the students responded eagerly, assuring me that the relatives they interviewed were pleased and proud to have their work presented in such a context.

But there were two students in this particular course—both Chinese American—who informed me that they were not about to let anyone else in the class read the interviews they had conducted with their elderly relatives, let alone give me permission to put them on my Web site. Again, this was, of course, their choice, and a few others in the course had also come to this decision. But these two students were so adamant, I spent some time with them to better understand their reaction. We spoke at length after class, and continued an e-mail correspondence sometime afterward, during which I asked them a number of questions in order to better understand their reservations about my assignment. Among other things, what they taught me was that, as Chinese students, if they had publicly told stories about themselves or their family

members, it would have been regarded by their families as privileging the individual over the community. An individual's history dies with that person, they explained to me; consequently, only the broader Chinese culture should be preserved. And while they considered it taboo within their families to make such blatant displays of individualism, conversely, the family unit was strengthened through secrecy: The more one keeps one's family accounts private, the stronger the family group. Finally, at one point in the conversation, one student blurted out, "Some people just want their stories to die with them."

All of this made me uncomfortable for a number of reasons. For one thing, their oral histories were absolutely fascinating and splendidly composed, revealing so much about their elderly relatives' lives in Chinese villages and growing up in Hong Kong, that I selfishly wanted to show them off on this Web site so other students and faculty could read them. After years of hearing several colleagues express frustration at having to deal with "all those Oriental students" in freshman writing courses, I was looking forward to creating a space where Asian American students could testify about themselves on their own terms, something I considered important, given the exceptionally large Korean and Chinese American population at our university (today there are more Chinese people in Flushing, Queens, just a few miles from campus, than in Chinatown in Manhattan).

I was also chagrined at realizing that in my desire to create a cross-cultural discursive space on "my" Web site, I might have been exerting too much control over my students. At one point in her study of the secret literacies of junior high school girls, Margaret J. Finders (1997) examines the ritual of yearbook signing, and the hierarchies of acceptance and exclusion that inform the politics governing who does and does not get to participate in such discourse communities. As might be expected, the groups with more social clout and esteem have more control in determining who can and cannot sign their yearbooks: "Those who had the right to write was clearly an issue of entitlement" (42). Likewise, I could not have helped but used my influence as the professor to coerce my students into signing my own Web book—and not only with their own signatures, but also with those of their relatives. I had been culturally myopic in assuming a common need to share and preserve one's stories. Even though I had chosen to use my Web site as a space for their work, knowing full well that many of my students hadn't the time to create their own Web sites, I came to understand that I had to be particularly cautious in posting their oral histories.

Even more embarrassing was coming to realize that I had run roughshod over the cultural beliefs of not just these two students, but also any students who might regard subjective testimonials as inappropriately intimate. For all my talk of wanting to promote community, my Western perspective still operated according to a very individual-centric bias. My ideal concept of the classroom space was one of a commons, where people gathered to investigate shared texts. It started to dawn on me how much of what I have introduced in

past composition and literature courses has been, if not directly in sync with what Mary Louise Pratt (1996) has in mind when in describing the genre of the testimonio, at least somewhat related in spirit. For Pratt, the testimonio

> emerges in the context of an imperative to renegotiate relations between intellectuals and grassroots constituencies in the domain of print culture. From this perspective, perhaps its most salient feature is its collaborative mode of production. Testimonios are produced through voluntary collaboration between a metropolitan intellectual and a subaltern or grassroots individual. The two subjects are linked by shared commitments to social justice and the radical transformation of capitalist society. Despite their solidarity, their collaboration is nearly always an exercise in cross-class, cross-cultural, and often cross-race interaction involving mutual dependency, accountability, and risk. (65)

Much of the writing I have featured in composition courses through the years has had some of the qualities of the testimonio: autobiographical or biographical works by Maxine Hong Kingston, Akemi Kikumura, Michelle Cliff, Sun Chief, Lame Deer, and Black Elk. Each of these texts could be considered "coming out" tales of willful disclosure. And what I had not yet considered, until speaking with these two students, was how this bias had prevented me from creating a space for collective or tribal, as opposed to individual, testimony. As much as I wanted a map to emerge via my Web site, I was still approaching it individualistically. Even the term *homepage* reveals a distinctly Western bias, a certain comfort level with the prospect of letting outside voyeurs get a glimpse of one's private virtual domicile; had this technology grown out of Chinese culture, one wonders if we would have "villagepages" instead. Ultimately my students' observations led me to make some changes: Writing oral histories, whether of family members or anyone else, had to be an option, not a requirement. Nor was I going to publish any of these oral histories on my Web site unless the students expressed considerable interest in doing so, and even then only if they received written permission from the person interviewed.

But even after this, I still couldn't get that observation out of my head: that some people just want their stories to die with them. How could one promote a preservational pedagogy when some students need to let their own family histories remain secret, and eventually disappear? What would there be left worth preserving if not one's own family memories? Eventually, I realized that what bothers me most about this statement is that all of us are implicated within a multilayered network of "dying stories," stories that, as educators, we ignore at our own peril.

All of us, students and educators alike, are connected by a constellation of death narratives. First, there are the deaths our students bring to the classroom. It is not just that many college students first encounter the death of a family member sometime around their freshman year. With few exceptions, in every freshman course I've taught, there has been at least one student who has recently lost a parent, grandparent, or sibling. Many times, a student has had

to withdraw from a course to take care of an ailing parent or grandparent, something not uncommon among the students I teach, so many of whom lack sufficient health benefits (almost half of our incoming freshmen class comes from families living below poverty level) and often have cultural obligations to assume family responsibilities when a parent falls ill. Then there are the various near-death encounters—friends attempting suicide, assaults by stalkers/boyfriends, domestic abuse, drive-by shootings (the freshman student I had one year who apologized for missing classes because she had to take care of a seven-year-old niece, shot down in neighborhood crossfire). Violence and death are ever in the background, and increasingly in the foreground, of our students' lives. As Michael Blitz and C. Mark Hurlbert (1998) write in the opening of *Letters for the Living: Teaching Writing in a Violent Age,*

> Ours is a society that tolerates violence more and more as a natural part of life and sees peace more and more as an abstraction. The teaching of writing is connected to living. Not living in the abstract, but living—and dying . . .
>
> What do we find out about living when we read and discuss our students' compositions or when we examine our own? What do we find out about dying? We find that our students face deaths of all kinds—every day—of the body, of spirit, of hope, of desire, of the ability to care. When we address some of the struggles just to live that our students face, we also address the tensions that tear at the health of the world. It is time to ask ourselves: as teachers of composition, are we prepared for the truly powerful stories our students are ready to tell?
>
> We are going to have to be willing to face the truth that our students are not only among the living but also among the dying, and, like it or not, we are fully in the presence of both. (1)

We find death in our neighborhoods, too. Good neighborhoods—that is, mixed-use, walkable communities designed more for pedestrians than cars, with ample and affordable public transportation, where residential, business, and educational sectors converge—are dying out. When my students write about their immediate neighborhoods, the overwhelming majority of them paint portraits of places that have gotten worse: more traffic, more graffiti, more garbage, more isolation and anonymity; less sense of community, less respect and tolerance among neighbors, fewer kids playing outside. A few years ago, New York City's Regional Plan Association, the oldest planning association in the country, released *A Region at Risk* (Yaro and Hiss 1996), a study of the changes to come for the New York–New Jersey–Connecticut metropolitan area. Their conclusion: In roughly two decades, this region where my students and I live will, unless massive and expensive changes take place immediately, slip into a period of *irreversible* decline (239–241).

As I think about the ways in which my students, as Blitz and Hurlbert put it, are at once living and dying—indeed how all of us are—and as I think about how to use the landscape of the Internet in response to our shared autobiogra-

phy of linked deaths, I find myself recalling the insights of multicultural planners along with those of Australian aborigines.

In a work on urban multicultural planning, Leonie Sandercock (1998) envisions an urban map where traditionally underrepresented ethnic people experience "a thousand tiny empowerments" within "the interstices of power" that overlays any urban grid (129). But for Sandercock, if people are to endure, they must first have at least partial dominion over local spaces within that urban map (129). While we might not be able to help our students physically redesign their immediate neighborhoods within a semester, we can help them approach the World Wide Web as surveyors and cartographers, using that virtual space to testify not about their private lives but about the places they live in, letting everyone else know what's good about them and ought to be preserved, and what's awful about them and must be changed. An evolving, psychotopological map could emerge, providing a potentially valuable source of information for students and professionals in urban studies, environmental studies, and planning. Imagine if just ten percent of the nation's freshmen took pictures of their immediate neighborhoods, wrote about the status of those neighborhoods, and then placed all of this information on the Web. What kind of map might surface? What political attention might be drawn to these places over time?

Many indigenous peoples are known for cultivating and intuiting a "sense of place," largely absent and inaccessible in Western cultures. Aboriginal Australians, the oldest of human cultures, dating back perhaps as far as 150,000 years, reveal one of the more intense and complex understandings of mind and place as coalescent realities: "There is no Aboriginal story that does not make reference to places, and land formations are never discussed without reference to their mythological stories" (Lawlor 1991, 237).

> To the Aborigines, place is inseparable from the original activities that gave it form. Reliving those activities in performance makes place inseparable from meaning. All experience of place and country is culturalized. Relating to space in this way enables people to establish a home or camp almost anywhere they may be with no sense of dislocation. The question of identity, of who I am, is resolved in the Aboriginal consciousness by knowing the full implications of where I am. (236)

The Pintupi word for this concept is *ngurra,* which signifies not only "country," "landscape," "campsite," "place," and the like, but also memory and identity—memory as identity made aware through the sustained consciousness of place. How might a public forum for student writing facilitate, to some degree, some partial comprehension of this concept of *ngurra*?

My practice of archiving student writing and photographs continues. The archival section of the Web site features students' stories and photographs of where they live, because I feel it's important that teachers understand what students think about the buildings and communities they go home to when they leave our classes. The archives also contain their thoughts about the next

twenty-five years, their hopes and fears for the immediate future. Because typically more than half of my students seem sure that environmental, economic, technological, medical, or social catastrophes will arise in the next two decades, I think this is important information for educators to reflect on: What does it mean to teach to a student body that, at least in my case, matter of factly (and not illogically) sees things as inevitably getting worse? Finally, I also reserve a space in the archives for their oral histories, although I am more cautious about what goes up there—I don't push my students to contribute here; instead, I make the invitation, and leave it at that. Those who make it clear they want their oral histories shared can have them posted (assuming, of course, the interviewee is also eager).

When we talk about student writing in public places, what interests me is the changing quality of those places and the degree to which they shape our students, and vice versa. To use Gregory Bateson's term, what can we learn of our students'—and our own—*mind/environments,* whether expressed publicly or privately? How might "going public" with one's work literally result in the preservation or revitalization of our local communities? And how might remaining private and "invisible" just as dramatically alter the changing nature of our local environs? How might these conflicting desires—to preserve through testimony, and to disappear through silence—unfold over the next several decades, when so many decisions will be made, for us and by us, that will determine the quality of our public and private spaces? To what extent are too many of our stories dying out, going the way of the Aborigines? And to what degree is it the educator's responsibility to resist the urge to disappear by equating pedagogy with preservation, and survival? Which stories will die with us, and which will remain?

8

Field Trips to Virtual Public Squares?

Purposes, Audiences, Teachers,
and Student-Written Web Pages

Jonathan Benda

The other chapters in this section deal with the ethics of requiring students to transfer their writing to the Internet, thus turning more or less "private" writing into public writing accessible to anyone with an Internet connection. In this chapter, I deal with Web writing of a somewhat different sort—writing meant to be published, from the moment it was assigned, on the Web.[1] A look at the Web sites of university English departments, library science departments, educational technology programs, and information science departments reveals a variety of approaches to the teaching of writing for the Web. There are courses on "writing for the Web," on "on-line publishing," and on "Website design." Also, upper-level or elective courses in other subjects, such as Financial Accounting and even Building Construction, often incorporate Web design projects into their syllabi.

The effects of having students publish their work on the Web, to be made available to readers outside the boundaries of the academy, are complex and manifold. Myron Tuman (1996) addresses the question of how it changes the "notion of publication and hence authorship" (37). In an article entitled, "Literacy Online," he predicted that soon all university students would be able to post their work on the Web, making it published work as opposed to writing practice. Tuman argued that once this happens, "then the value of authorship is liable to migrate (since value requires some notion of scarcity) from being published to being read" (37).

Tuman's prediction has basically already come true in many universities around the world—particularly in the United States, where the Internet seems to have been embraced as an answer (if not *the* answer) to the problem of finding places to publish student writing. Some educators suggest that one of the best uses of the Web for education is to have students compose texts that can

interact with an audience (Woodlief 1997). Compared with "fixed" texts that are composed for a teacher and students, these "fluid" or "dynamic" texts, it is argued, are more responsive to suggestions, comments, and criticisms from a large international audience.

Many educators would argue that the students' ability to publish their work to an international audience gives their writing a *real* audience. Kevin Hunt (1997) goes so far as to suggest that "if the Internet is to become a democratizing force, it will require students to *create* as well as to consume information on the Web" (emphasis in original). The teacher in this kind of classroom becomes something of a coach who facilitates students' interactions with the world.

Web-based educators would also agree with the claim that course-related student Web pages have the additional advantage of allowing the students' learning and textual production (the process) to continue after the course is over. Depending on the location of the pages and the school's rules about student Web pages, they can stay on the university server for as long as the students matriculate. Furthermore, students can download their pages and remount them in another account (a commercial Internet Service Provider [ISP] or Web-space provider like AOL or Geocities, for example). Students may decide to revise, rewrite, reorganize, or completely replace their Web sites in reaction to feedback from teachers, classmates, or the larger Internet audience. Thus, in a very real way, the students can be in control of their writing, which doesn't "disappear" from public view after the end of the semester.

Though all of this is theoretically possible, I will investigate the rhetorical considerations involved in student Web publication that complicate the preceding idealized description. The foregoing paragraphs make three kinds of claims for student writing on the Web: (1) a claim about the affective value of Webbed writing to motivate students; (2) a claim about Webbed writing empowering students to see their writing as interacting with readers and others' writing in the virtual public sphere; and (3) a claim about the value of Webbed writing to enable students to understand writing as process.

I want to concentrate on the second and third claims because I believe that the extent to which they are acted upon can affect the strength of the first claim. I argue that the effort to help students in a Web writing course recognize the roles audiences play in the process of Web-making should not be undercut by teachers' classroom practices. Nor should those practices undermine students' developing notions of writing as a process that doesn't have to end at the end of the semester. Teaching Web writing needs to be a reflective practice in which students are given a writing purpose that both helps them extend themselves beyond their classroom audience and enables them to reach that wider audience.

Student and Teacher Goals for Student Web Pages

The reflections in this chapter come from both my "trips" to other teachers' on-line course materials and my own experiences in Taiwan teaching a univer-

sity EFL (English as a Foreign Language) elective called "The Internet for English Majors." When I asked students why they chose to take my course, which requires a rather heavy amount of on-line reading and writing, almost all of them mentioned that they wanted to learn how to make Web pages. When I asked them why they wanted to do that, many of them answered that they wanted other people to get to know them.

Despite the students' excitement about the possibilities for Web writing, I also have to admit to feeling a degree of frustration in teaching writing for the Web. Since I started teaching my course in 1995, I have experienced mixed results in the quality of students' Web pages. My students have come to the Web development part of the course with the opportunity to use increasingly sophisticated tools to make their sites, but lack background in the principles behind designing a Web site that really communicates something to an audience. Although students want to share something of themselves with others, there is also a strong sense of producing something that is pleasing to the authors themselves. This latter desire, while certainly laudable, often leads to a Web page that might be hard for anyone besides the author to appreciate.

To give myself new ideas for my class, I analyzed Web pages that students created for "Web writing" courses to see how different students and instructors dealt with the issues of assignment types, audience, and Web site contextualization. To find such courses, I used "The World Lecture Hall," located on the University of Texas' Web server (http://www.utexas.edu/world/lecture/). The World Lecture Hall consists of links to a variety of university, college, and community college courses whose materials are delivered on-line via the World Wide Web.

After locating the course descriptions in which the key words *student work* appeared, I analyzed the course Web sites (thirty in all), noting how Web design assignments were described, how students were taught to think of purpose and audience when designing their sites, and how students' sites were linked to the course homepage. I also sent a short e-mail survey to the teachers and students of each course. In it, I asked them about the teachers' goals for requiring students to make Web pages, how successfully these goals were met, how students were taught to conceive of audiences for the Web, and what kind of feedback students received in response to their work.[2]

For some teachers, the goal of having students make Web pages is in the making itself, in the view of the Internet as a new and important "frontier" for students.[3] In response to the survey, Kari B. McBride of the University of Arizona, mentioned that she wanted students to understand that they "are contributing to the common knowledge when they write their assignments. I also want them to learn how to create Web pages—not to be intimidated by the technology. In addition, when assignments are public, students tend to devote more time to their work and to write better." Dr. Yasser Mahgoub, now at Kuwait University, who formerly taught Architectural Engineering at the United Arab Emirates University, replied to the same question with the comment that

writing for the Web "is a helpful tool for thinking and communicating ideas." He felt that students could learn how to organize and present their thoughts through Web page writing.

The students I surveyed mostly agreed with their teachers' conceptions of the goals for making Web pages. A student in one course stated that it was important to their instructor that they make a page about a topic that was not currently on the Web. A student from another course wrote that she felt it was her teacher's goal to reduce novices' fear of the Internet. In addition, the student felt that it provided a way for classmates and other people outside the class to read students' essays. Generally speaking, students who responded felt excited about the opportunity to make a Web page that could reach a worldwide audience.

Some of the instructors gave explanations of specific goals for having students write Web pages. Gretchen Whitney, of the University of Tennessee–Knoxville's School of Information Sciences, teaches a course in "Information Network Applications," in which students "create [Web] pages for social service organizations." Because the primary objective of this course is to enable the students to function in a heavily networked environment, the goals of the project are also more specific, enabling them "to apply the skills and knowledge that they have gained in other courses (needs assessment, working with users, collection development) in a practical and real setting," and facilitating a better appreciation of "the ethics and customs of the Web/Internet."

In another survey response, Heiko Haubitz, instructor at the Graduate School of Library and Information Science at the University of Texas at Austin, emphasized the necessity of giving students a real purpose for making a Web page: "These are Internet/Web Design classes and students can only learn by doing. The specialty in my classes is that they have to do these pages for real clients who are in a need of a Web presence. This motivates most of the students obviously much more than just doing pages as a requirement for the class only."

These responses already go beyond a concept of the Web as a medium on which students can publish in order to get a taste of putting their product out in public and to take pride in their work—to courses where students are responsible for designing and providing a client's content to the Web's audience. Between these two kinds of activities, however, is a whole range of possible Web-making assignments, including annotated "Webliographies" of useful Web sites, Web pages that inform others about a particular subject, and Web sites that provide some sort of service to users.

As public writing, a student-created Web site should be designed so that the surfer approaches it on its own terms as a site with a clear purpose. Whether that purpose is to provide information, provide a service, or attempt to persuade the reader to believe in a certain way, the site should have a reason for existing besides being a student's site. Moreover, if attention is not given to developing an understanding of Web audiences, then Web assignments will function similarly to writing assignments in traditional classrooms

where students write for classmates and for the teacher. The connection that needs to be made between the writer and the audience is the link between the purposes of the writer and of the audience.

Web Audiences and Public Writing

In teaching audience, some teachers have followed the same line of thought as one teacher who argued that writing for the Web "means PUBLICation," which involves "both the opportunity to excel in that public space, as well as the danger of public failure" (McBride). On some teachers' course Webs, instructions to students also revealed something of the teachers' approaches to audience. On one course Web site were listed "Criteria for Evaluating Websites," including items such as layout ("It should be easy to move about and find what you are looking for"), design ("The graphics should be attractive and the relationship between graphics, text, tables and frames, if you use them, should be visually pleasing"), and creativity ("This is harder to define but I recognize it. New ideas for content, innovation in design, surprises in the lay-out and text are what we are always aiming for.") (Beard 1998). These criteria are clear enough if the students consider their audience to be one person—the teacher; but if the students' assignment is to write to a worldwide audience, they will find that the concepts of easy movement, attractiveness, and creativity are nowhere near as intuitive as the "criteria" make them sound.

Other teachers emphasized the role of peers as audience. Brad Cox, formerly a George Mason University professor with the Program on Social and Organizational Learning, stresses the notion of classmates as audience, suggesting that his students "[r]ead each other's bios" to become more aware of their audience. From the students' responses to my survey, most teachers use some form of peer feedback at some stage in the process, and most of the students make changes in response to that feedback. However, after their courses were over, the students I surveyed, with a few exceptions, had stopped receiving feedback on their pages—a student in one course even lamented that he didn't think anyone had been to his site after the end of the semester.

If, as in the preceding cases, the same kinds of conceptualizing about audience is going on for Web writing as usually happens in traditional writing classes (teacher as audience, peers as audience), then one of the major advantages of having students design Web sites—writing for readers outside of the classroom—is left unexplored. Whether students are designing sites for clients or based on their own interests, they need to try to reach readers outside of the classroom—the question is how to do it. Moreover, the very fact that the Web *is* so public—that a Web page can be read by people all over the world—would make it even more difficult for students to imagine who their audience might be.

Catherine F. Smith (2000) calls the traditional methods of audience analysis incompatible with the needs of people who wish to address the Web audi-

ence. She argues that the Web "supports inclusion, not exclusion" (248)—that because readers might come to a particular Web site by any number of paths, students need to be taught to write for a general audience. Anything that is published on the Web is public writing, in that it can be read by "anybody." In this sense, "anybody" is the audience (248).

How well this conception of audience works in practice depends in part on the kind of Web writing assignment students are doing. Many of the students I surveyed commented that they didn't think anyone had been to their Web sites after the end of the semester. The problem for many students seems to be more of finding any audience rather than how to write for an audience of anybody. As Smith mentions, her students found they needed to design their Web sites "to attract outsiders while speaking to insiders" (243). If nobody is listening, it might be best to target particular people or groups. Even in writing for the Web, it is necessary, if not to address an audience, then to invoke one.

Invoking/Directing Audiences

In order to invoke an audience, it is necessary to have a general understanding of how these audiences might arrive at one's Web site. There are, of course, many paths a person might take to get to a particular site—including through search engines, external links from almost any kind of site, and even e-mail signatures. But there are approaches that Web writing students can take to increase the chances that a Web site will be approached in a certain way.

To direct an audience to their pages, Web authors can register their pages with various search engines or directories under the subject matter, keywords, and so on, or they can link to, or ask to be linked to from, related professional sites. Students can be encouraged to use various means to contextualize their work, including submitting their URLs to a search engine, adding appropriate and meaningful <META> tags to their pages (<META> tags can be used to identify content or keywords—they do not show up on the Web page itself, but are read by many search engines), linking to other related sites, joining a "link-sharing" group (for example, CREW—The Compact for Responsive Electronic Writing) or a Web-ring, and simply giving readers of their Web pages "very explicit information about why the site was written and what purpose it serves" (Bauman 1997). Writing <META> tag descriptions and joining link-sharing groups can also help students think about categories that their content might fit into and about how they can describe their content in such a way that someone would be interested in going to their page. These methods can help give a context to students' pages by increasing the (admittedly tenuous) control that writers have over the paths by which their pages are accessed. While "a [W]eb's meanings and contexts are always more controlled by readers than by writers" (Smith 2000, 239), student Web-makers still have some ways to target, or "invoke," their audiences.

Web Page Access and Ownership

We have already seen how difficult it might be for students' Web pages to find an audience. The fact is that the most common kind of connection to students' Web pages is established by Web-using teachers in the form of a page of links to what are often labeled "student" Web pages, "student" projects, or even "sample student projects," a rhetorical act that foregrounds the student's role *as* student, and thus the teacher's role in the students' textual production. In the case of most "student" projects lists, when Web surfers approach the students' Web pages, they are looking at the students through the eyes of the teacher. The context of the page is the context of a class, as opposed to what might be called the "virtual public square."

It may sound odd to suggest that teachers should not link to students' Web pages; after all, if people come to a teacher's course Web page and don't see any links to the Web projects, they would certainly wonder if the teacher had no student Web pages of which to be proud, no examples to show other students who are interested in taking the course. But teachers also need to be aware of the rhetoric of Web links—what does a link to an informative Web site, client Web site, or service-providing Web site say about the authority of the student's site? A link from a teacher's site that classifies a Web site as a class project might discourage the audience from viewing that site as a serious provider of content. While it is not necessary for students to be ashamed of the fact that they are students, if we want to enable our students to be writing for a real audience of people who are not merely interested in visiting "student Web pages," we need to release our grip on the paths that visitors might use to access those pages.[4]

Not only are many students' Web pages (or the links to them) buried in teachers' or course Web sites where they are rarely accessed by the kinds of audience they are supposed to invoke, but also many of the students whose pages I visited lacked editorial access to their own pages after the course was over. A student in one class complained that the professor moved the students' sites to a commercial ISP after the end of the course, making it impossible for students to access their sites. The issue of ownership of a student's Web page is complicated by the page's roles as an "educational product" for a particular class at a particular university (see Smith 2000, 245). Universities are only now beginning to develop policies governing ownership of the files that are located on their equipment, but it already seems to be common practice for schools to delete the accounts of students after they have graduated. Alternatives exist to having students' pages placed on university servers; for instance, commercial sites exist where students can mount a Web site for free or for a small fee. Some of my students, for example, have mounted sites at free Web services. Again, it is important to look carefully at the service's ownership policy. It remains to be seen how universities will resolve the question of own-

ership over students' on-line intellectual products, but it is an issue that teachers of on-line writing need to watch, even as they think of practical ways to give former students editorial access to their Web pages.

As Selfe and Selfe (1994) have noted, one of the problems associated with a "rhetoric of technology" is the tendency to make, unexamined, the claim that in computer-mediated communication, students can feel safe to "speak without interruption[,] and marginalized individuals can acquire more central voices" (483). Writing for the Web *can* help students "acquire more central voices," but if student-written Web pages are to be seen as anything other than the kind of "preliminary" writing that Tuman describes—in other words, as "field trips" to virtual public squares—then they need to be held to similar standards of content, purpose, and audience awareness as are those of more experienced Web content providers. The instructor's job can be to assist in this task of making the course-related Web pages *less* course-related. Having students consider and write for particular audiences as they write, encouraging them to register their pages with search engines or with link-sharing groups, and freeing them to do what they want with their Web sites after the course ends can contribute to the goals teachers envision for Web writing classes. Those Web pages can then overcome the limitations imposed on them by their role as student-written pages and can continue to grow and develop well after the course has ended.

Notes

1. Portions of this chapter were presented at the 1998 Rhetoric Society of America conference in Pittsburgh, Pennsylvania. The presentation was supported by a Republic of China (Taiwan) National Science Council travel grant.

2. In total, I sent e-mail messages to the thirty instructors and 287 students of about twenty-eight courses, ranging in subject from "Women and Western Culture" to "Building Construction II." Only one course was from outside of the United States. As of June 2, 1998, I had received replies from twelve teachers and twenty-four students; seventy-four of my messages to students had been "bounced back" as undeliverable. I want to thank the teachers and students who responded to my e-mailed survey. I especially want to thank the teachers quoted in this essay.

3. Nedra Reynolds (1998) cites various uses of the "frontier metaphor" that is used in reference to the Internet, including one course—"Taming the Electronic Frontier"—the homepage of which features an image of wagons and Old West–style language (27). (The author of that page has since removed the "Wagons Ho" theme, though he has retained the Electronic Frontier metaphor.)

4. That is not to say that teachers should not consider *any* links to their students' Web pages. They could, for example, link to them in the context of the bookmark pages or "Links of Interest" pages that most people with Web pages seem to have. If their links are annotated, they might even mention that the student being linked to is, or was, a student.

9

Completing the Circuit

Why (Student) Writers Should Share Products

Wendy Bishop

[W]hile many of us advocate student-centered pedagogy, we are
still struggling to see how to get the student into that center.
(Yancey 1998, 20).

The question may not be has the new pedagogy changed students,
but has it changed us? (O'Reilley 1993, 71)

It's funny. I have never heard the term *postcognitive* or *postquantitative,* but I
have started to hear the term *postprocess.* Make that, funny-odd not funny ha-
ha. Certainly times change, understandings shift or deepen, what was advanced at one point as the new best thing gives way at another time to a
different improved version. For instance, cognitive theories of composing have
been enhanced by contextualization, and social theories of discourse complicate our understandings of the politics of composing. Yet those who claim
we're in a state of postprocess seem to me to be too eagerly encasing process
in amber, putting it behind us, setting it aside before it has been fully explored,
understood, and utilized. *Post,* then, seems like a theoretical power-play, intended as part of an intellectual skirmish to deactivate a constellation of still
useful—since still evolving—pedagogies that, more often than not, remain
beneficial for those who are being taught—writing students.

Let's be less eager to gallop away from or gallop beyond process—emphasizing workshop-oriented writing instruction where student work is shared
in a public forum—whether one-to-one, in small groups, in workshops, and/
or in class books. I suggest instead that we complete the circuit and live with
these pedagogies more fully and then let them evolve into something new and

better once we've grown or found that new or better set of practices (something I'm not yet convinced we have done). I believe the critique implicit in the move to cultural studies and explicit in the discussions of academic discourse proponents (see Bartholomae 1995) is threatening to label those interested in further exploring this often misunderstood set of teaching practices as unreflective and downright unthoughtful. Meanwhile, other scholars, myself included, have been struggling to provide better definitions and terms (Rhodes 1994; Gradin 1995; Jones 1997; Bishop 1999). In effect, this collection, devoted to examining public sharing of student texts, is clearly in service of examining similar issues.

To live more fully with process—to see what it still promises and provides for our teaching lives—to come full circle, to complete the circuit, we need to consider how students' writings—the products of our processes—are a largely unappreciated part of the writing classroom. In fact, student writing has been most often discussed as a problem, as something we don't know how to deal with, what to say about, or how to share comfortably or productively. In our professional writings, we discuss ways of managing student writing: reducing the paper load, evaluating it, grading it, developing it for portfolio assessment, and understanding where it went wrong (by error-based definitions). We explore why we're tired of certain forms of it:

> At our annual "Papers From Hell" staff meeting—I invite faculty to bring in the kind of essays that they least like to read—there is always a wide range of dreaded genres represented, including the author-vacated research paper, the politically incorrect persuasive essay, and the plot summary response to a literary text, but each year the conventional male narrative is right up—or down—there with the worst of them. (Tobin 1996, 161)

In categorizing genres of student writing, Lad Tobin speaks to the experiences of any college writing teacher who—no matter what pedagogical orientation—has seen these predictable types of essays arrive on his desk. Still, this is primarily understanding student writing from the writing teachers' point of view. In this chapter, I look at student writing as a genre in which writers are intentionally making decisions that are not always obvious unless we create a classroom environment that allows them to explore those choices, often, by sharing their writing in a public forum of peers who are trained to respond to their writings.

In one of my advanced writing workshops, the first paper assignment centered on the theme of nature; the second paper asked writers to begin with the idea of language communities and work out to a paper on a topic of interest to them; and for the third paper, writers read a popular magazine rhetorically and proposed an essay they would like to write for that analyzed readership.

The writer of the following excerpts, Millie, chose to write for a general readership like that of *Reader's Digest,* but the paper she produced has some classic hallmarks of the visit-to-Mexico-turned-nightmare essay in which readers quickly get a glimpse of ugly-American-thinking on the part of the

twenty-plus-year-old narrator and her friends. Some would point to these selections from a road-trip essay as problematic examples of my personal-writing–based workshop pedagogy, but I would suggest instead that this writing is more simply the result of a writer learning to write. She is someone who needs to go public with her text in order to understand what she composed, why she composed it that way, and how it is read by others.

> As we entered the airport we were faced with a row of Mexican customs officials in uniform.
>
> "Is it me or do they all look like Manuel Noriega?" I joked as we took our place in line.
>
> "Manuel who?" Suzanne said a little distracted by all of the going on.
>
> "No one," I muttered, "Now turn around and give the man your passport."

> "The Mayan Palace," was painted in vibrant pink on a ramshackle old school bus, the short kind, over a baby blue background. Not what I had in mind if you know what I mean. This was the first realization that I had about second world countries. If I was to have fun on this trip, it began to become apparent that I would clearly not be able to judge Mexico against my increasing cherished United States.

These excerpts lead me to critique the critique of expressivist pedagogies. Scholars like David Bartholomae, Patricia Bizzell, James Berlin, and John Trimbur critique a pedagogy such as the one I'm describing as one that keeps students in a state of naiveté, doesn't prepare them for the discourses of the academy, and—most applicable, perhaps, to Millie's essay—abandons them to the forces of politics and culture "that emphasize a type of self-actualization which the outside world would indict as sentimental and dangerous" (Fishman and McCarthy 1992, 648). However, when critics assume that expressivist pedagogy is solely or primarily responsible for the generation of such a paper, they are straying far from the complicated realities of writing classrooms and grossly simplifying cause and effect. In this case, the writer, Millie, has brought many assumptions about genres of writing with her. The course structure didn't encourage her tell-all about her trip to Mexico—her reading of writing she likes to read did; and/or her life experiences led her to shape a dramatic moment from that life into expected—often too expected—patterns.

It is egotistical (and wrong) to assume that our writing course is the galvanizing force behind all the strong and weak writers' choices made by students in our courses. Instead, we need to realize that many forces are at work. Our curriculums, as Kathleen Blake Yancey (1998), explains it, are multiple:

> We tend to assume that we offer a single curriculum. . . . By my count, we have at least three curricula that operate simultaneously. The students bring with them their lived curriculum, that is, the product of all their learning to date. In the classroom, they engage in the delivered curriculum, which is the planned curriculum, outlined by syllabi, supported by materials and

activities, and so on. The delivered curriculum however, is experienced quite differently by different students: it is the experienced curriculum. The intersection among these three curricula provides the optimal place for learning; reflection is one means of establishing the location of that place. (18)

And, in fact, it is the workshop discussion that followed the sharing of her paper that encouraged Millie to rewrite that paper with greater cultural sensitivity, an encouragement that proponents of social constructionist and postprocess classrooms are quick to assure us are results solely of their own pedagogical approaches. Sherri Gradin (1995) argues that such is not the case, and, in fact, that a relentlessly social approach can be as alienating as a relentlessly unstructured approach. For the critics of process instruction, *unexamined, naive,* and *unstructured* appear to be the opposite of academic discourse's disciplinary organizing structures of *comparison and contrast, problem–solution,* and *argumentation.* Implied in this valorization of linear, often argument-based writing is the assumption that in a process-oriented classroom, only generation—and never reflection and production—takes place. In short, they worry that in such classrooms, students write and then move on, unchanged, uninstructed, and unreflective about what has been too freely shared.

As a practicing writer—both within my classes as a class participant and on my own time as a writer who aims to publish most of what she writes—I find our field's perplexity about student texts—well, perplexing. In this chapter, I'd like to argue we would be doing our writing students a disservice *not* to celebrate them as writers by sharing their texts in our classrooms, publicly, in whatever ways are most appropriate for supporting their growth as writers and for enacting our best pedagogy. As Kathleen Yancey argues, we need to teach reflection, for by doing so "we learn to understand ourselves through explaining ourselves to others. To do this, we rely on a reflection that involves a checking against, a confirming, and a balancing of self with others" (11).

Students can theorize about their own writing in powerful ways. Through reflection they can assign causality, they can see multiple perspectives, they can invoke multiple contexts. Such theorizing doesn't occur "naturally": As a reflective social process, it requires structure, situatedness, reply, engagement. When treated as a rhetorical act, when practiced, it becomes a discipline, a habit of mind. When treated as a rhetorical act, it has ethical implications (Yancey 1998, 17).

And it is in such a classroom setting that I want attention to be paid to the student essay that I quoted earlier. I want Millie's work to receive a hearing from her peers (as it did, and many found her attitude as portrayed on her Mexico visit quite problematic). I want her to mature as a writer because she is making a writer's choices, not the teacher's choices. Here is our opportunity to see "student writing as a 'metagenre,' a kind of experimental, knowledge-building writing which contains many other kinds of writing" on its way to becoming more academic (Mirtz 1997, 194).

A writing class is a public forum, and within it, writer/citizens seek freedom and accept responsibility; they share their work and they receive responses. There are many ways to accomplish this, but overall, process-oriented composition teachers have worked to allow students to complete the circuit by training them to respond to each other's texts in productive ways, by allowing for real readers in the interactive computer classroom, for example, and through portfolio production—and finally, and maybe most difficult and important, by allowing them room to make their own revision decisions, which sometimes will result in a text that does not do what the teacher thinks it should do, because an effective process workshop is an examined process workshop, is the process in the context of a writing community, is the result of a writer taking her or his position within her or his culture.

Let's look for a moment again at Millie's paper. Millie opened in familiar *Reader's Digest* (and heroic narrative) style:

> About a year ago, I had an experience that changed my life. Two friends of mine, Suzanne and Anna, invited me on a once-in-a-lifetime trip to Acapulco, Mexico. Suzanne had a time share condo there and I could think of nothing more fun than exploring the famous tourist city. Visions of white, sandy beaches and aqua, blue water floated around in my head as I boarded the red, white, and blue, freshly painted Delta jet. We had a short layover and change of planes in Houston, Texas, where we had to go through customs. It was easy and soon we were 25,000 feet over Mexico City marveling at its immense size. Because this was a vacation, when the flight attendant asked me if I would like a beverage, I immediately ordered a Corona in honor of our destination. She winked and asked if a Bud Light would do, we were in a plane, after all. As we got closer to Acapulco, we could hardly contain our excitement. This was the first trip to Mexico for all of us. We began our decent to the airport and the tiny hotels looked more and more real. I wondered out loud which one was to be our home for the next eight days.

In full-class workshops these days, I ask the author to read a paragraph—and Millie chose to read this, her opening paragraph—and then remain quiet during the discussion. Respondents are asked to share their readings of the text and to clarify interpretations with each other. Speaking of the writer/author as he/she and referring to the text instead of directing remarks directly to the writer, they poll the class for agreement or disagreement. Within this response structure, the author has the rare chance to listen and I transcribe the discussion as shown below. At the end of the discussion, as we're returning papers, the author is invited to join us and is encouraged to clarify, question, comment, and respond, but briefly.

In this workshop, Millie's classmates, who had taken the essay home, read it, and prepared written responses before discussions took place, noted that the opening set up the reader for one type of essay (quotes beginning with dashes come from my handwritten workshop manuscript; each dash represents a different speaker):

—It starts off with an experience that changes the writer's life but we don't get that until page six.

On page six of Millie's essay, one of several Canadian men the vacationing women have befriended is taken ill and to the hospital, and they try to find the hospital in a midnight comedy of errors and language confusions. The paper we had in hand, however, ends before arrival at the Canadian man's bedside, with the women being dumped by taxi on the hospital steps.

Millie notes this problem herself in a statement to her classmates, typed on the ninth and final page of her draft, warning us before we arrive at class the next week to discuss the essay: "SORRY, I have decided to change the ending—I am not quite through."

During workshop, another peer says,

—I thought something horrible was going to happen in customs [page 1].

By the time the fifth class respondent speaks, we are discussing Millie's portrayal of Mexico and Mexicans and she is questioned by a classmate of Cuban American heritage:

—When I was looking at it, one of the problems was barriers in language. I thought the writer was unsympathetic to the country. Mexico bashing . . . looking like Manuel Noriega.

This comment unleashes a discussion that includes one classmate arguing that taking out the Manuel Noriega remark would make the paper politically correct and she (that reader) was against urging political correctness. The following is a portion of my transcript notes; each dash again indicating a new speaker:

—I agree about the Mexico bashing. I was sympathetic—so something's gonna happen. Difficulty of getting to hospital, some of the feelings about Mexico were needed for hospital worry. Her opinions are so blatantly out there. She was so pissed about so many things. I was sympathetic to a degree. Maybe a little less anger—or more insight?
—I kind of disagree to the Manuel Noriega. Take it out, you're politically correct.
—I agree with both. I'd like to see a transition—the ending is going to be learning to cope with problems. Tourist aspect and reality—expectations and downfall of those expectations—what was learned?
—That was my biggest question—how this experience—her being naive—how did it change her feeling about Mexico?

At the end of the fifteen-minute discussion, Millie responded by thanking us for our response and then said: "I like Mexico. I didn't realize it would sound like bashing."

Reviewing the discussion, we see that Millie has received reasonable requests to show her insights, provide transitions, and explore what she learned

and how she felt about what was learned. In Millie's executive summary—a response to the workshop, a tabulating of suggested revision directions, and her statement of her own revision plan—we find that she has taken the critique about Mexico to heart, but less on the basis of politics than on the basis of her intentions and decisions about what constitutes a more effective storytelling strategy. Realizing it had taken her six of her nine pages to get to the life-changing event promised in her opening sentence—the midnight trip to the hospital—Millie decides she will have to shift, condense, and rearrange. She writes,

> I will introduce the characters Adrian, Ty and Ryan much earlier in the paper so that the reader will feel closer to the boys. . . . I am going to cut most from the part about the trip from home to the hotel. . . . I am going to rewrite the ending giving the reader more closure. . . . Lastly, I will remove the comment about Noriega because even though it's true, it might make the reader mad and I don't want that.

Although this might seem like Millie is giving in to peer pressure (even if reasonable peer pressure), it appears from her final comments in the workshop (surprise that she appeared to be Mexico-bashing) that her intention all along was to relate the hospital story. In this way, the class workshop functions much like the one-to-one teacher–student conference advocated by teachers like Donald Murray and Thomas Newkirk.

Now certainly the workshop could have played out in different ways. I have learned to trust, though, that in a given response community, when the respondents have been trained, any critique I might have made will be made, and made perhaps more effectively, by other class respondents (and nine out of ten times, this proves true). And responses evolve because they are made from the position of a reader's interested perplexity rather than from the position of my teacher's authority. Ironically, this is the teacher-less classroom of Peter Elbow's well-known book, *Writing Without Teachers;* but, as in most expressivist classrooms, the teacher is very much here, to the side and not at the center, orchestrating and encouraging, not dominating, letting student writers make and articulate discoveries about their own work—discoveries that can best be made in the public forum of a well-run workshop.

Through public sharing of her student text, Millie was able to hear various points of view—readings—of her work and see that she was both understood (the person who wanted her to tell it how it was) and misunderstood (the readers who thought she was slamming Mexico when she was trying, she felt, to dramatize the night taxi ride). Without this public sharing, I could have quietly conferenced Millie into politically correct views on presenting her Mexico trip as "more acceptable" to the white, middle-aged, middle-class teacher who I am; or I could have encouraged her to adopt fictional techniques as rules (always start midway in the action, don't introduce more than two characters into a short piece) without her understanding the way those useful rules-of-thumb played out, given her target audience (*Reader's Digest*) and the genre expec-

tations she brought with her to the writing classroom. By sharing her public text, she developed a wider sense of possibility; she disclosed, reflected, examined, and learned better to judge her own work.

One commonly voiced concern about the practice of sharing students' texts in public forums centers on whether or not personal pedagogies, pedagogies of process and disclosure, reflection and response, ask a writer— especially a novice writer—to reveal more than he or she wants to reveal. I've argued elsewhere that it can be just as problematic for a student who has been raped or who has survived an economically deprived childhood or who has a visible cultural difference (race) or an invisible one (sexual orientation) to feel silenced by discussions based on multicultural reading and taking place in less than perfectly moderated classroom forums. Equally, this concern implies that other classrooms are risk-free. One has to wonder if it is any less confusing or upsetting to a class member to sit silent through a clumsy class discussion on a published account of being gay in America than it is to do so during a discussion of one's own or a peer's written account?

To a degree, class members may be more reflective if they know the author of the piece in question is in the classroom, when they go public in a well-moderated and supportive forum. Equally, it has been my experience that students' lived curriculums (I'm recalling here Kathleen Blake Yancey's three types of curriculum) are often resistant to the delivered curriculum, so that their experienced curriculum may be like Millie's—an editing of intention in light of class responses.

Some End Thoughts

When public sharing of student texts works, it works at least as well as in the workshop excerpts I've shared here. When such sharing doesn't work, why doesn't it and what does this pro–public text advocate think needs to happen next?

Well, I think that there is a dangerous movement afoot to throw out process and that we do so at our own—and even more, at our students'—risk. I sense that although we've ushered in an era of teacher–researchers, I don't often enough see teachers research in ways that attempt to describe the rich complexity of the process-oriented pedagogies I've been discussing (see Bishop 1999). I take some consolation that David Bleich (1998) and Kathleen Yancey have presented formulations of their evolving pedagogies which ask us to consider again the worth of this sort of classroom. I would urge more of us to do so—in depth and at some length.

If nothing else, I believe we teachers need to ask students to share more, not fewer, public texts: to offer public readings of texts—their own and professional ones—to pursue public examinations of drafting decisions, of processes (those they undertake at our suggestion and those they actually undertake, including the full range of writings—from procrastinated, late-night, never-quite-invested-in-or-finished papers to passionately engaged pa-

pers). We need, also, similar detailed accounts of postprocess classrooms and continual definition, redefinition, calibration, and recalibration of the language(s) we use to talk about pedagogies.

As much, we need to listen to and hear the language our student writers use. We need to invite ourselves into their worlds and hope we can inhabit those spaces with as much grace and patience as I've seen writing students inhabit the complicated space called the college writing classroom.

I would question the ethics of dismissing an influential constellation of pedagogical approaches out of hand, and I would question introducing new approaches without research, discussions, and examinations that are at least as rigorous as the critiques those pedagogists raise against the classrooms they purport to change. And I remain certain that the best first way for us all to begin is to listen to, reflect upon, and disclose to each other the learnings we gain by examining our own classrooms—processes and products. The twain always meet. And where they meet, we learn how to learn.

10

Fending for Themselves

A Student-Directed Model of Peer Response Writing Groups

Jason Palmeri and Sara Daum

In the past few decades, writing groups have gained popularity as a response to the traditional writing classroom's presentation of writing as a private communication between the novice student-writer and the knowledgeable teacher-reader. Challenging this private conception of writing, writing group theorist Kenneth Bruffee (1985) asserts that for students to view writing as a "social, collaborative act, student writers must learn to converse about writing in a profitable way with people who are their equals with regard to learning to write" (4). However, while much work on writing groups has opened up student texts to audiences beyond the professor, most writing-group theorists have centered their attention on the use of writing groups within college composition or K–12 English classes.[1]

While we welcome writing groups in the classroom context, we contend that the professor's evaluative authority, expressed through comments and grades, keeps student writers from truly claiming the empowering position of writing-group members who can choose to accept or reject critiques of their work offered by their peers. In the classroom context, students still tend to see the professor, the one with the power of the grade, as the true audience for their work. The challenge, then, is to establish opportunities for students to participate in writing groups that function outside of the hierarchical and evaluative context of the classroom.

We arrived at this critique of writing groups as a result of our experience with a teacherless, student-directed, peer writing group at New College. In January 1998, with the assistance of a faculty sponsor, Jason developed the student-directed writing group as a group independent-study project (ISP) with minimal attendance and participation guidelines. The faculty sponsor evaluated the group members on the basis of their attendance, participation, and completion of a self-evaluation detailing how the group did or did not meet their indi-

vidual needs as writers. The faculty sponsor did not necessarily read, much less evaluate, students' writing. This student-directed model contrasts with the use of peer critique groups in classrooms in which the professor evaluates the students' writing products after they have been through the critique process.

We were able to explore this model of student-directed writing groups because we are undergraduates ourselves. Sara's position within the group was as participant–observer studying small-group dynamics. Sara took unobtrusive notes about the daily activities of the group and reflected on the nature of the group's formation and cohesion. As a participant–observer, Sara sought to become a "member" of the group by actively participating in meetings and completing the same activities as everyone else.[2] Jason was drawn to the project because of his experience in peer tutoring and interest in composition theory.

Privacy and Authority in the Composition Classroom

Although public writing in the form of peer response groups has been widely accepted in the field of composition, our experience in other classes suggests that the private writing model is still dominant in the wider college curriculum. In the traditional classroom, students view writing as a private communication between themselves and the teacher. The final word on students' papers comes from the professor who reads them and responds privately with evaluative comments and grades. Thus, the privacy of the paper-writing process creates and maintains the professor's authority over the student.

Many professors have sought to subvert the authority embedded in the private teacher–student relationship by utilizing peer response groups in their classes. Rather than just turning their writing in to the professor, students in the peer response–based classroom share their papers with a group of peers, revise their work based on peer feedback, and then submit their "final" products to the professor. In this situation, the professor tries to place authority in the peers' evaluation by hanging back from controlling students' writing, but in the end reasserts his or her authority by grading both the final products and the process of peer critique itself. Furthermore, a writer may blame the other students if he or she does not come up with "what the professor wants." By investing evaluative authority in the largely absent professor, the student writer deemphasizes the feedback of his or her peers. While professorial evaluation does play an important part in developing students as writers, a professor's evaluation of the writing group process inhibits the students' ability to view the other members of the group as a valid critical audience.

The Student-Directed Writing Group

For a peer writing group to succeed, the writing group must first remove itself from a hierarchical, evaluative context of the classroom. Second, the group must establish trust so that writers can share their writing and accept criticism

without feeling personally attacked. Third, in order to break out of the habit of writing for a monolithic professorial audience and develop the ability to write for public audiences, students must come to view the group as an audience for whom they can write. Finally, the group must be recognized as a diffuse collective authority in which no one person has all of the authority, but each member has some.

When all of these conditions are met, the student-directed group has the potential to enable writers to develop new writing processes and techniques and to learn to revise based on the constructive criticism of others. Furthermore, the student-directed writing group can teach students how to present their writing in a way that is effective for a public audience.

Student-Directed Writing Groups in Practice: A Case Study

In the fall of 1997, Jason enrolled in a tutorial on the theory and practice of teaching writing and became interested in facilitating a writing group. Influenced by Peter Elbow's *Writing Without Teachers* (1973), Jason aimed to establish a peer writing group organized according to the needs of its members, and without a teacher or other authority figure. Although the evaluative structure Jason designed, and his faculty sponsor agreed to, deemphasized final products, it did mandate that students participate in the processes of writing, peer critique, and self-evaluation. By making self-evaluation one of the main criteria for satisfactory completion of the ISP, Jason and the sponsor hoped that students would realize that the aim of the group was for writers to create and meet their own writing goals. The importance of the mandatory requirements and incentives became evident when the group attempted to continue meeting on a completely voluntary basis after the January interterm. Despite the participants' good intentions, the group fizzled when they prioritized other activities.

Jason recruited five students for the group by contacting students he had previously peer-tutored and by placing flyers in students' boxes. The participants came from varying academic disciplines and number of years in school, though all of them joined the group to improve their academic and/or personal writing. Two students, Sara and Elliot, exemplify the diverse writing concerns that participants brought to the group. Sara joined the group with some apprehension because she was fairly self-conscious about her writing. She seldom shared her work with peers and tended to write her papers in one sitting without revision so that, as Sara explained, she "wouldn't have to reread them and see how bad they were." Sara's actions stemmed from an intense fear of criticism, and led her to make excuses for her work. Elliot,[3] who joined the group after some positive experiences with a peer writing tutor, wrote in a grand, exaggerated style and ignored suggestions that he tame his flowery language and the often lurid examples he used. When comments were made about his writing style, Elliot usually replied that he wrote for his own pleasure and

readers could "take it or leave it." However, he recognized that professors' displeasure with his writing could affect his success at college, and so he joined the group, looking for a way to improve their evaluations.

The group met three times a week, for about an hour, in the student center on campus to present and discuss each person's writing. For each meeting, everyone brought two to four pages of new writing to share. Group members presented their writing for the day by reading it aloud or distributing copies. After a piece of writing had been presented, members of the group verbally offered their personal comments and reactions, which ranged from suggestions for revision, to praise, to personal anecdotes about how the piece affected them. Although students were often offered suggestions for revisions of the written work, revision requirements were limited to revision of one previously written academic paper and one essay written during interterm.

Although Jason had originally conceived of a focus on persuasive writing, and the group had agreed to write only nonfiction, participants generally centered their attention on personal essay writing. Participants tended to feel that they did not have enough knowledge of the formal conventions in others' disciplines to respond adequately as part of an audience of peers. Notably, in order to function as a *peer* audience, participants believed they had to share knowledge and interest in the topic of the writing brought to the group.

Furthermore, some personal revelation in the writing allowed the students to get to know each other indirectly, facilitating the development of group cohesion and trust. For example, the most reserved group member, Michael, wrote an essay that compared and contrasted three different cartoons: *Josie and the Pussycats, Captain Caveman,* and *Scooby Doo.* The rest of the group was delighted with the essay, on a personal level. The usual structure of critique broke down, because the essay sparked a conversation about shared childhood experiences. The sharing of this paper positively affected participants' sense of membership and cohesion through shared experiences.

At the first meeting, Jason gave the participants chapters from Elbow's *Writing Without Teachers,* focusing on freewriting and peer response in the teacherless writing class, and talked about his experience with peer tutoring and writing-group theory. Jason outlined the basic requirements of attendance and required writing, but then made clear that the rest of the structure was up to the group to determine. At Jason's suggestion, students discussed their goals for the group, which included gaining confidence about writing, experimenting with different styles and genres, and improving professors' evaluations of their writing. Students were less comfortable, however, discussing what form they wanted the group to take, apparently preferring to defer to Jason as a knowledgeable guide. Seeking to resist the role of group leader, Jason suggested that they wait until after reading Elbow and participating in the first peer critique session to decide on the group's final structure. Ironically, in order to facilitate the group's ability to take charge of itself, Jason had to take on a teacherly role. However, in taking on this role, Jason reinforced the students'

image of him as a knowledgeable guide, ensuring that he could never be just like the other members of the group.

At the second meeting, with Jason's encouragement, group members discussed how they liked Elbow's emphasis on the subjectivity of peer critique and the need for the writer to decide which critiques are most helpful. While the group members liked Elbow's suggestion that each person both share his or her writing and offer critiques of everyone else's writing, they did not like many of Elbow's suggested exercises for generating peer critique. Participants particularly enjoyed poking fun at Elbow's suggestion that students make animal noises or drawings to express how the writing made them feel. Elbow was useful, however, for providing a basic guideline for giving and accepting criticism while still maintaining each writer's ownership of his or her work. His suggestions that struck group members as outlandish were also helpful in this group, because they allowed students to utilize his model critically rather than turning his text into the new authority for the group.

In addition to introducing the Elbow selections, Jason guided the group through its first experience with peer criticism by establishing that members of the group should share their work and comment on the work of others. The group then began to discuss process. Jason suggested that writers read their work out loud, but some students expressed discomfort at this and suggested distributing copies of their work as an alternate option. Having a choice of how to present their work allowed all members of the group to feel that they had some control over the reception of it. Though some students felt uncomfortable reading their work aloud, everyone seemed to take it for granted that feedback would be given verbally.

Before the third meeting, Jason came down with mononucleosis. He was unable to attend any of the next six meetings, which left him only the last four to try to rejoin the group. In the meantime, the group was left to fend for itself, with minimal direction from Jason, which turned out to be a fortuitous event for the group's development. While the group had needed the initiative, structure, and basic training provided by Jason and the faculty sponsor to get started, Jason's presence prevented the group from reaching its full self-directed potential. Jason had intended to participate as no more than a common member, but his initial leadership had led participants to expect that he would continue to lead. Participants needed to take responsibility for the group. In this way, they began to develop a diffuse collective authority, enabling writers to balance properly their ownership of their work and their responsibilities to each other.

Jason had originally suggested that the group rotate the position of facilitator, but the group, now operating without Jason, agreed to try meeting without an acting facilitator. Instead, the writing and comments proceeded on a voluntary basis. There were some initial awkward moments as the group negotiated the order in which people would give comments. Once, Sara asked Michael if he would speak first about Elliot's writing for the day. Michael calmly said "No," and sat waiting for someone else to speak. No one asked this

type of question again. Instead, everyone gradually become comfortable speaking without the impetus of a facilitator. When decisions needed to be made, someone would bring up the issue for discussion. The discussion would then be followed by a suggested solution, which was generally agreed upon by consensus. The students' decision not to have an acting facilitator demonstrates their implicit investment in developing a diffuse collective authority.

Although Jason's direct influence on the group had largely disappeared, participants completed one last activity that he had suggested: brainstorming at least ten possible topics for future writing. Everyone did this brainstorming and shared their results at the next meeting. One student, Elliot, suggested writing a "war diary" of a date—an idea that the rest of the group considered totally inappropriate and distasteful. Because the group was vocally opposed to his suggested writing topic, Elliot trailed off in his explanation of the proposed topic and, in the end, never used it. This event demonstrated the group's exercise of collective authority and also began to teach Elliot about the importance of writing for an audience.

As the group continued to bring in daily writing assignments and critique them, its members' trust in each other increased. The participants began to spend time together before and after group meetings, and continued to become more comfortable critiquing each other. Building trust further, participants occasionally shared more personal experiences through their writing. For example, Michael shared a piece about his experience dealing with Tourette's syndrome, showing a willingness to take risks, which the group supported by responding with sensitivity. Michael's risk-taking in revealing personal experience generally encouraged group members to take risks in other areas, such as experimenting with new styles of writing and giving more honest criticism.

At the beginning of the group, several people identified expanding their stylistic repertoire as a personal goal. In giving comments, the group helped people to reach this goal by validating their work in one style while also challenging them to experiment further. For example, at one meeting, Elliot read a piece that was in the same style as his previous two pieces. Rebecca in particular praised his style, and then suggested that he try a new style for the next meeting. Responding to Rebecca's positive encouragement, Elliot could view this criticism as an exciting challenge rather than as a restrictive requirement, enabling him to overcome his tendency to keep the same style regardless of audience. This advance in Elliot's conception of writing developed because he was sharing his writing publicly with a group of people that he had learned to trust. We do not think that Rebecca's challenge could have had the same effect had she responded to Elliot's writing with a written comment, outside of the group situation.

The students eventually became so secure in their group authority that when Jason returned, they challenged *him* to try a different writing style. At his first meeting back, Jason shared an editorial about the possibility of war in Iraq. This composition, his second for the group, was also his second editorial. The

group made an attempt to simply critique the writing, and then some students commented that Jason should have made the letter more personal; eventually, the group stated forthrightly that he should try a more personal essay form, displaying the collective authority that had developed in Jason's absence. By the time Jason returned to the group, the group had not only assumed a collective authority but was comfortable enough with that position to attempt to direct Jason's writing. Furthermore, the group was willing to assert itself as an audience for whom the others should write, rejecting Jason's desire to write for distant audiences, such as college administrators and politicians.

Interestingly, this conception of the group as the primary audience for written work was not part of Jason's original formulation of the group. Jason had envisioned that the group members would write papers on issues within the campus and community, with the aim of reaching a public audience. However, Jason's intent to create a group that would define its own purpose eventually won out over his more concrete plans. In this development is evidence that the group did come to function as a collective authority distinct from Jason and the faculty sponsor.

The faculty sponsor had not met many of the members of the group until the final meeting, when group members shared a self-evaluation and discussed the previous month's activities. Destabilizing her position of authority, the faculty sponsor focused on what the students said they had learned from the ISP rather than on looking at their written products to ascertain how she judged they had "improved." Thus, the faculty sponsor was able to evaluate the group without diminishing the group's own authority to critique the work of its members.

Students' self-evaluations demonstrated the varied steps that they had taken toward overcoming their previous writing problems.[4] Elliot thanked the group for nudging him to move away from his usual grandiose style and try other styles and genres of writing. By modifying his style to take into account the needs of the group, Elliot came to realize that writing for a specific audience helped him expand his persuasive repertoire. Whereas Elliot's early essays were full of flamboyant language and outrageous claims, the later essays were written in a style that would adapt easily to history, his main academic field.

In her self-evaluation, Sara detailed the ways in which the group helped her deal with her intense fear of sharing writing. She gradually went from distributing copies of her work to reading aloud, which she saw as a big step for someone who previously would not allow even friends to see her writing. Over the course of the group, she came to trust that group members would not think less of her because of the quality of her writing. Once this trust was established, Sara was able to move beyond making excuses for the quality of her work and come to use her peers' criticisms constructively. Her self-evaluation explained that she had learned to respond to her peers' critiques with honest questions or clarifications, rather than listening silently and then offering excuses as to why her work was not her best.

On the whole, the writing-group experience positively affected writers in

a number of ways. The group broke down the traditional private and hierarchical context of writing by providing a safe space outside of professorial authority in which students could feel comfortable sharing their work publicly, learning both to give and to receive peer critique. Ultimately, the formation of a professor-less group authority allowed students both to own their own work and to learn how to write for a particular audience.

Applications for the Composition Classroom

Although our writing group experience occurred outside of the traditional classroom, the methods we used to challenge private writing and destabilize the teacher's authority can be applied to the composition classroom. The particularities of our college's academic structure enabled us to develop a model that may need to be modified to suit a particular course structure. The pass–fail narrative evaluation system at New College allowed the professor to avoid giving a grade to the participants' writing products. However, a writing group could be implemented on a pass–fail basis as a supplement to the rest of the graded coursework in a composition class. The group could be evaluated, for a percentage of the final class grade, based on attendance and participation. Because the writing products that students would complete for the group would not be graded, they would remain distinct from the graded writing that the students would do for the professor.

Emphasizing the student-directed nature of writing groups, groups could meet outside of class time, ideally, in a writing center. To ensure that students participate in a writing group, they could be required to turn in a portfolio of works completed. Having the groups meet in the writing center would also be valuable if peer writing tutors are available to help with specific problems. A writing tutor would also need to facilitate the first meeting of a group in order to familiarize the participants with the process of peer critique. This would recreate our situation in which Jason (the de facto leader) left the group due to illness. Once the writing-group process was complete, the professor could lead an in-class discussion among the different groups about their experiences.

Although we recognize that our model of peer writing groups would have to be modified to fit into the variety of institutional contexts in which composition teachers work, we believe that nongraded, student-directed writing groups have an important role to play in helping students overcome writing problems that develop in the private, hierarchical classroom. It is not enough to ask students to go public with their writing while still retaining the evaluative structure of the traditional classroom. To facilitate students' transition from private to public writing, we must work to create a safe space in which students can truly learn to write for audiences other than the professor, as we have shown with Sara and Elliot. The other students in our group had similarly helpful experiences; thus, we think that this structure warrants further attention and use in the larger field of composition.

Notes

1. For a discussion of writing groups in college classrooms, see Brooke, Mirtz, and Evans (1994). For a discussion of the use of writing groups in the secondary school classroom, see Spear (1993). While most current work on writing groups has focused on the use of writing groups in the traditional graded classroom, voluntary writing groups have existed outside of the academic context for quite a long time. For a discussion of the history of nonacademic writing groups, see Gere (1987).

2. In place of the final revision, Sara wrote a paper about the dynamics of the group.

3. With the exception of our own names, participants' names are pseudonyms.

4. Aside from the two students we discuss, the three other members of the group expressed strong satisfaction with their participation and writing improvement but did not mention any specific changes in their writing strategies.

11

Creating Rhetorical Exigencies

Two Communication Dramas

Chris Benson and Joan Latchaw

> While acknowledging that artificiality cannot be eliminated com-
> pletely from the classroom situation, somehow we must create more
> realistic communication "dramas" in which the student can practice
> being a [speaker and a listener] with better motivation and in a way
> more resembling how he will have to read, write, speak, and listen
> in the "afterlife."
>
> James Moffett, *Teaching the Universe of Discourse*

Hurdling Toward the Finish Line

As two college-level teachers, our combined experience spans several decades
reflecting the triumphs and tribulations associated with composition classrooms. While we have celebrated the triumphs, we have agonized over the
tribulations—despairing that student writing is often automated and bloodless,
a mimicry of academic discourse. Moreover, students' attitudes toward their
writing too often seem indifferent and disengaged. We suspect this view stems
from their attitudes toward education in general. Students often tend to view
education as a linear progression of classes leading to the end of their education. John Dewey's paradoxical definition of *education*—the capacity for further education—would be nonsensical for many students; most are focused on
their career goals, understood as the reward of education. Consequently, students tend to view writing classes as one hurdle in a long series of hurdles that
represents a college education.

This linear view of education, shared by many teachers, shapes attitudes
toward students, informs pedagogies, and ritualizes classroom practices. In

writing classes, the real error here is twofold. First, discrete, hurdle-like tasks fail, by definition, to include real rhetorical situations, which are meaningful and inspiring for students. Second, writing contexts that are narrow and isolated from the "universe of discourse" (i.e., in which the student writes for the teacher's eyes only) reinforce classroom rituals that imply the teacher is the sole authority and arbiter of discourse. This imbalance of power (in favor of the teacher/authority) prevents dialogic interactions, such as Moffett advocates in "communication 'dramas.'"

Creating more realistic communication dramas will necessarily involve broadening the social contexts of writing in the classroom. To do so, teachers can apply Lloyd Bitzer's concept of rhetorical exigency, whereby students participate in the "real world" as part of their education. An exigence is a state of affairs that makes urgent demands. According to Bitzer (1995), an exigence is rhetorical when the state of affairs "requires discourse or can be assisted by discourse" (304). While compositionists, such as Bartholomae (1985), Berlin (1988), Bizzell (1982), Bruffee (1986), and Carter (1990), have acknowledged the social nature of writing, college composition courses only rarely offer ways to construct a full rhetorical situation whereby the "constraints which influence the rhetor [student writer/speaker] . . . can be brought to bear upon [a particular, targeted] audience" (Bitzer 304).

Why Go Public with Student Writing?

Going public with student writing creates a context for learning that encompasses more than an event, a set of skills, strategies, and heuristics, or even a sociocognitive process. Rather, this context for learning occurs within a culture, by which we mean an interconnection of classroom, university, region, society, and individual. In going public (i.e., responding to a rhetorical exigency), students acquire knowledge through active discovery in which writing, reading, and thinking processes lead to "products" valued by a larger community. Publication or dissemination of the knowledge is an important cap on the process because it provides a cultural context that makes the learning purposeful, lasting, and meaningful. In such contexts, students resembling a team of experts bring personal beliefs, skills, knowledge, and problem-solving abilities to share with others, working toward common goals. The culture of the classroom may shift from a hierarchy of learning—with the teacher controlling the assignments and daily activities—to a democracy of learning whereby students develop their own voices, texts, and individual beliefs. The teacher becomes, in new-age corporate terms, a team leader who offers guidance and expertise, but also learns a great deal—about pedagogy, his or her own personality and beliefs, and information spawned by the group.

The cultural reshaping of the world beyond the classroom grows out of the cultural reshaping inside the classroom. The class' "developing text," which is geared for publication, bridges these two domains. For instance, going public

will require the classroom discourse to be extended, modified, and revised for readers outside the classroom, writers of other texts, and people whom students will interview, consult with, collaborate with, and inform. The distinctions between teacher and student, expert and novice, private and public, informer and informed begin to blur. In the projects we describe here, the "developing texts" led to publications, which had an impact on the university/college, the region, and the society. And, in a few cases, the authors themselves were reshaped as learners, citizens, and individuals.

In the first narrative, students in a junior-level technical writing class contracted to write an e-mail manual for their university's computer center. In the second, a basic writing class, responding to a rape on campus, devoted a semester to investigating and writing about rape and related issues. Both stories discuss the successes and problems in establishing collaborative communities, developing rhetorical situations, and shifting power relationships between students and teachers—which eventually changed and shaped individuals, culture, and developing texts.

Creating a Universe of Discourse (Chris Benson)

In the Beginning Was the Word

During the early 1990s, Clemson University, where I taught technical writing, faced cutbacks from the state legislature. This shortage of money forced the university to restructure; the nine colleges were collapsed into four. In the process, the budget centers were relocated further away from the instructors, and the administration implemented something called *block funding*. While this term seemed vague and innocuous, the results were clear-cut and drastic. Infrastructural facilities and services that once generally supported the entire university population were restructured. Staff and faculty were forced to rely more and more on their own departments for equipment and other resources. This downsizing created an us-and-them mentality between departments. Those interested in interdisciplinary collaboration had to develop new ways to work together.

Endeavoring to maintain a collaborative spirit, I introduced my technical writing students to Kathy Wright, Assistant Manager of the Microcomputing Center at Clemson University. At the time I met Kathy, I was a part-time administrator of the University writing across the curriculum (WAC) program, which had been in existence for five years. The WAC program was reputed to be a collaborative gold mine. Because of diminishing resources, Kathy was looking for some way to revise her e-mail manual without incurring costs. Having heard through the WAC program that I designed real publishing projects for other courses, she contacted me.

Kathy asked if my students could write a user's manual for the university's electronic mail system and receive course credit for the work. After some thought, I began to see her interest in my class as an opportunity for

both of us; a collaborative project between my writing class and the computer center could meet each of our goals as well as serve the university. As chairperson for the university's electronic mail task force, Kathy wanted to encourage wider use of e-mail by staff and faculty. Two ways she wanted to do this were (1) to research the habits of current e-mail users and make recommendations for improvements in the system, and (2) to provide a good manual for e-mail users.

My goals as a teacher of technical writing are to prepare students for the kinds of writing they will do in their careers, including proposals, memos, and written and oral reports. In researching the e-mail system, making recommendations for improvements, and writing a manual, my students would obviously gain writing experience to help them function in the workplace.

And the Word Was Contract

When Kathy Wright visited my class and proposed a contract between my class and the computer center, the students were skeptical of committing themselves to such a project. I remember the look of anxiety on some faces, but the look of annoyance was more prevalent. I think my students felt a bit resentful about upsetting normal classroom routine—"Read a chapter and complete an exercise." Student resistance to the project was so strong that had I made "signing" the contract an option, I doubt many would have signed on. So, like Brando's Godfather, I made them an "offer" they couldn't refuse. I emphasized the word *contract,* hoping the connotation of the word would alter how students viewed their work. I hoped schoolwork would be perceived as a professional obligation rather than as one more academic hurdle to jump. At the start, students nervously sensed this project would require them to become expert researchers and consultants to the Microcomputing Center.

The only way to accomplish the work was to convert the classroom into a workshop, where we set deadlines that carried us toward completing the contract. The terms of agreement stated that my class would test the usability of the current e-mail user manual, make necessary changes, and retest the revised document; interview avid e-mail users and contribute profiles of these people to the Microcomputer Center's newsletter; and design and implement research on the current use of e-mail on campus and write a report advocating specific changes to the e-mail system in order to encourage a wider use of e-mail on campus.

At the beginning of the semester, students formed working groups; each chose a section of the manual to test and revise. Other groups formed to research and observe how students, faculty, and staff used the e-mail system. One group of computing "techies" decided to research and report on the technical limitations of the system. Each student agreed to interview an e-mail user and write a profile for the newsletter. I became the often-ignored general manager of the project.

Work to Learn and Learn to Work

I began each class period by asking several individuals and certain groups for extemporaneous oral progress reports, in which students informed each other of problems they were experiencing. Ensuing class discussions addressed how writing strategies could resolve these difficulties. In other words, we researched, proposed, wrote, revised, reported, and presented; the "daily lesson" in technical writing occurred spontaneously in response to individual student's concerns with the project. For example, one student, a wildlife major named Scott, was scheduled to interview the Vice Provost of the Division of Computing and Information Technology. Though the administrator was supportive of our project, his busy calendar posed scheduling problems for Scott. After a mutually satisfactory time was negotiated, Scott arrived at the office. The Vice Provost was gone. At the next class meeting, Scott knew he had to follow up with a memo requesting another interview, and write it in such a way that he did not offend the man who had "stood him up." Thus, the real-worldliness of this project let the students, like Scott, learn rhetorical principles that extended Moffett's real "communication dramas" beyond the four walls of the classroom (12).

At the end of the semester, we delivered our reports to the e-mail Task Force and presented to invited staff members of the Computer Center our work on the user manual and advocacy campaign. Over twenty-five guests attended the presentation. My students arrived in appropriate dress and comported themselves like the experts they had become, presenting their ideas and discussing their advocacy campaign with the computing staff. Aside from the obvious age differences, an observer would have had difficulty distinguishing my students from the professional university staff who attended.

Despite the fact that several students dropped the course early in the semester and several of those who stayed in the class experienced anxiety about the responsibility of fulfilling a contract with the university, the strong negative reactions disappeared by the end of the semester. At the end of the project, I asked my students to reflect on the experience, and nearly every comment was positive. What seemed most important to them was a change in their attitudes toward learning: They reported appreciating autonomy in learning; they enjoyed the opportunity to be experts; they valued collaborative working relationships; and they were proud that their work was going to be published and distributed to the university community.

The rhetorical exigency of our contract with the Microcomputing Center shifted traditional educational goals and values—from demonstrated skills acquisition in artificial settings to problem-solving strategies in workplace settings. In this environment, "communication dramas" offered a new method of collaboration among student, teacher, administrator, and staff. Thus, the student was constructed differently—from initiate or novice to expert or potential expert. I was gratified by this reversal, although I was disappointed that, curiously,

few students noted that they had learned to design a research plan and compose a technical report. I'm not so optimistic about the results of this project that I believe one experience in going public with their writing will change student attitudes about writing. These same students will likely offer resistance to similar projects in other classes that require student autonomy. Yet I am hopeful that the success of other projects like this one, which required students to go public with their writing, will inspire curriculum reform, providing students with more opportunities for students to use writing in professional contexts. The tide has already changed, and I see more and more writing teachers designing such communication dramas and going public with student writing.

Houses of Pain (Joan Latchaw)

"You want to write about what?"

It seemed a typical semester in my Basic Writing class: Many students had dropped out, behavior was disruptive, the better students were frustrated, and everyone was tiring of reading Lewis Thomas. (My course sequence for Basic Writing investigates writing processes, human development, and society through a series of assignments based on Lewis Thomas' *The Medusa and the Snail*.)

Then something happened that shocked everyone out of the doldrums: A date rape occurred on our campus. This shocking crime shook our small campus in rural West Virginia. The community seemed desperate for more information, hypothesizing possible motivations and constructing elaborate explanations. On one particularly frustrating occasion, students, faculty, and staff questioned an administrator about the procedures and facts of the case. As disturbing as the rape itself were the appalling attitudes and questionable procedures of the administration in handling the case. I soon found myself raising the issues and concerns in my classes. One day, my students confided that the alleged rapist had been a student in this very class; he had disappeared about two weeks earlier.

The incident so captured the students' energy and attention that one young man raised his hand and asked if we could forego Thomas' *The Medusa and the Snail* and write our own stories about rape and abuse. We negotiated on the spot. Being a proponent of critical thinking and reflective inquiry, I rarely assign purely narrative assignments. However, being an advocate of student-centered learning, I did not refuse their request. I asked that students include some research in their stories and essays. They agreed. We arose, en masse, walked over to the library, and descended on the reference librarian.

Thus, a bona fide rhetorical exigency was born—of student need and interest. The alleged rape certainly created a state of affairs among students on campus that could be "assisted by discourse," as Bitzer describes (1995, 304). From that first day at the library, my students—even my difficult students—suddenly began behaving as professionals. Some formed into work groups studying spousal abuse, rape, and addictions, defining their areas of interest,

assigning tasks, and setting goals. Like the students in Chris Benson's technical writing class, my students engaged in "communication dramas" as they negotiated with each other and outside experts. During one class session, each student reported on his or her project.

At some point early in the semester, another student asked, "Why not make this a class project—a book including all our essays?" Agreeing to that student's request, I believe, changed some of my students' lives; it certainly changed me as a teacher. What occurred was a social context for writing that would lead to planning, drafting, recursive thinking, writing, rewriting, and editing. Individual emotional responses, family backgrounds, interpersonal relationships, and societal tensions had a significant impact on the direction of our collaborative project. Thus, "the individual's writing [became] a mutual reshaping of author, culture, and text" (Fishman 1993, 323). Thus, the excitement was laced with complexity and confusion.

The project culminated in publishing *Houses of Pain,* a student publication about rape, abuse, and addictions, written for members of our university community. The project was extended over two terms, the second term offered as a one-credit independent study in which five students and I completed the book.

Embracing Chaos and Creativity

To their enormous credit, the students had more faith in the process and tolerated the chaotic stages (discovering and resolving issues) better than I did. They were not afraid to immerse themselves in the new ideas that affected their lives and community. Ironically, I became panicky (reminiscent of those early dissertation days and months) because I didn't "have" the process and couldn't yet imagine the resulting product. I had never interviewed anyone, followed a lead, worked on a magazine article, done a magazine layout, or contracted a printer. Through questioning and collaborating, I discovered that students, faculty, and staff had expertise I never dreamed of. Dina, a journalism student from one of my other Basic Writing classes, gave a presentation on interviewing techniques. In a highly professional manner, she answered a plethora of questions, followed by a lively dialogue. Our school counselor, active in media and public relations, talked to us about extending our "book" into the public domain. He envisioned a school publication. Afterward, he confided his astonishment at the students' interest and energy and placed his services at our disposal.

The excitement, although energizing, failed to allay my fears. The English faculty I had consulted said the project was too broad, that we had too many subjects and issues, and that we had better plan a narrower focus. Other faculty agreed. Ironically, it was the health counselor who advised "letting the creative process happen" and being "loose about the final results." All the articles that I read on process corroborated his view, but my discomfort level persisted. The students, following the counselor's advice, led with their instincts.

That process led to extraordinary professionalism and disciplinary behavior on the part of the students. They became experts, investigating unfamiliar territory. I, too, began following unimaginable suggestions and leads the counselor threw my way: a mini-grant application from the state, a prison psychologist working with rapists, newspaper articles about Carolivia Herron (a Yale scholar turned novelist after being plagued by horrific nightmares of abuse), legal documents on rape, and government officials.

Cross-disciplinary studies were in the making, and the students responded as real professionals. Embracing the process instead of trying to imagine the product led to productive collaboration. Linda, a psychology major, consulted with her psychology professor on issues of spousal abuse. Another student, Ron, suggested we go to a regional prison and interview sex offenders. This idea intrigued our counselor/advisor, who asked the students to draft a letter to the prison psychologist. Linda and Ron began to construct a campus-wide survey on rape, consulting with members of the sociology department. Ron, formerly a serious behavior problem in class, took the lead. A communications major, he began stopping by my office, setting deadlines on the calendar, contacting the college's public relations person, and discussing ways to raise money for printing and strategies for marketing. I learned that this "problem student" had worked on a newspaper for several years. He teased me that he had always been a good writer, but I just hadn't listened.

I slowly came to know my students as real people with exciting interests and intriguing pasts, some of which were heartbreaking. Gradually, the rhetorical situation expanded beyond disciplinary boundaries. These Basic Writing students began to find connections in the world with psychology, communications, education, and nursing. Identifying a "major" or establishing a career goal now had greater significance, because disciplinary knowledge could be practically applied. The students were treated as respected colleagues by other students, faculty, staff, and newspaper and TV reporters. Their efforts were valued by the academic institution and the townspeople because discourse created "positive modification," solving problems, helping others in the community, and adding to a body of knowledge.

Spiraling Out of Control and into the Community

What began as a private act (personal narrative) ended as social interaction, which featured "ineluctable tensions, what Dewey calls the 'doing' and 'undergoing' of all experience" (Fishman 1993, 316). Our unified experiences, learning about abuse, spiraled out into the surrounding community. The spiral progression was daunting in some ways—we felt responsible for others' lives and were unsure of our boundaries. And we felt the "ineluctable tension" from other faculty, who criticized the group for acting as politicians and psychologists. The boundary between text and culture was blurring. And it caused other tensions. The Office of Student Affairs asked us to talk to the Resident Advi-

sors (RAs), who would discuss *Houses of Pain* with their charges. When I came to the RA meeting to discuss the content and production of the book and how the leaders might use it, there was dissension. Some of the RAs wouldn't or couldn't engage with the sensitive material. Some denied such stories were possible. The rhetorical context had blasted assumptions about cultural values and individual beliefs, with all the accompanying tensions, conflicts, and controversies. It was finally decided that students could join discussion groups on a voluntary basis.

Houses of Pain reflected and responded to the community's pain. The book's statistics, art, essays, and personal narratives began to educate, heal, and help others. As a way to celebrate its completion, I organized a two-day symposium on rape and abuse for the college and the community. The first day, Carolivia Herron, author of *Thereafter Johnny,* a poignant, poetic novel of rape and abuse, gave a reading, followed by questions and answers. Of the nearly one hundred students who attended, many asked probing questions about racial, physical, and mental abuse.

Carolivia's session was followed, the next night, by a panel composed of Dr. Herron; Paul Kraedel, a prison psychologist; and Richard Kaspari, a labor-law attorney specializing in sexual harassment and rape on college campuses. The hour-long presentation was followed by a provocative, interactive, and controversial dialogue between panelists and audience. Some faculty in attendance reported that the panel was a highlight at our college.

The spiral progression outward from private to public sphere wound back upon my own life as a teacher and individual. I learned from my students about atrocities no persons should have to bear. I learned about the strength and courage of the human heart and soul, of the elasticity of the mind and body. As a teacher, I learned that novices can avoid marginality and assume expert behaviors by involving themselves in real rhetorical situations. The Basic Writer has gone public, and *Houses of Pain* is a testimony to the intelligence, motivation, and dedication of "underprepared" students.

Going Public: Transforming Classroom Culture

The students' work and presentation of themselves as experts in these two projects represent the culmination of a semester-long process: the reinvention of the classroom. For example, we learned a great deal about our students as we negotiated schedules and coped with deadlines. We acknowledged and celebrated our students' busy intellectual lives outside of our classes. Tardiness and absenteeism were no longer issues between the instructor and individual students: They became issues between collaborating peers.

The tricky business of grading became trickier: In one sense, grading was difficult in a workshop setting, because no individual's work belonged exclusively to him or her. After receiving editorial suggestions from many members of the class, a piece of writing, or the credit it earned, in a sense belonged to

more than one writer. How does one award proper credit? Such collaborative contexts seem at odds with the traditional grading system used by most universities, but collaborative peer review was one method with which we experimented to gain accurate assessment of student work. Another difficulty with grading the projects was that the grades might have seemed inflated to outsiders unfamiliar with the class structure. The student writing was much improved during the lengthy collaborative revision process, and by the time it was ready for publication, it was a good or excellent piece of work.

In another sense, however, the tricky business of grading became simpler: It was easier because the students recognized that publishing their work required them to maintain a high standard for the writing. As teachers, we no longer had agonizing debates with ourselves or with students in determining whether a student's work merited a C– or a B–. Very quickly we could see whether the work was publishable, and if it was not, we could communicate specifically what the student needed to do. Students seemed to appreciate our focus on a publishable standard rather than on a ranking of students against each other.

Finally, going public places student writing in an open forum; there are no secret "pacts" between the instructor and a student. When a student "blows off" an assignment, everybody knows, and everybody in some sense suffers, because that negligence delays the project. As teachers, we believe that going public with student writing represents a positive change in the academic culture; it represents an "opening up" of the learning process, which is beneficial to students, teachers, and institutions, and the communities they serve.

12

Composing Student Activists

Relocating Student Writing

Angela Hewett and Robert McRuer

What Marx seeks to establish beyond any shadow of doubt is that it is the appropriation of the form-giving fire of the labor process, the appropriation of all manner of creative possibilities and powers of the laborer (mental and cooperative capacities, for example), that allows capital to "be" in the world at all. But the internalization of these powers of labor as powers of capital at the point of production entails the transformation of the laborer into an appendage of capital, not only within production but in all spheres of mental, social, and physical activity. (Harvey 1996, 65)

As many neomarxist, "queer," feminist cultural studies scholars have argued, we are experiencing a late capitalist—or postmodern—shift in social relations that deeply affects the structuring of education. Such scholars have identified *flexibility* and *efficiency* as two keywords in the development of these new streamlined, hyperproductive relations, and we share their interest in interrogating how these terms now help to structure the problematic—or ideological framework—of education, particularly university education. Developing a rigorous critique of this problematic, we argue, begins by returning to some of the central insights of a cultural studies tradition. While we view "the university" as a fluid, heterogeneous entity (that we all have the ability to transform), we also recognize the ways in which many administrators, faculty, and students now constitute it as a "point of production"—reproducing the social relations necessary, to paraphrase David Harvey, to bring capital into the world. As many cultural critiques have underscored, we have to recognize the actually existing possibilities for transforming these sites of production, creating

openings for new social relations, "queer" relations that are not particularly productive for capital.

In this chapter, we discuss the ways radical teachers working within a cultural studies tradition (such as ourselves) work against the dominant ideological framework, encouraging the development of—and "going public" with—students' varied creative abilities, so that students and, crucially, teachers recognize themselves as more than appendages of capital. The larger vision that we hold to is of an educational process that would be liberatory for all involved. In this chapter, however, we concentrate more narrowly on discussing and analyzing what a cultural studies praxis is—how it contests not only dominant models of the university, learning, and teacher and student roles, but also understandings of the public spaces to which students might relocate their writing. Our main example—an annual composition and cultural studies conference for student writers, which we began to organize in the fall of 1997—is one of many possible practices teachers can develop to activate students' critical practices.

A feminist/queer cultural studies praxis, as we understand it, is very much at odds with the depoliticized and ideological notion of the university—and the university classroom—as private, protected space. Student conferences that build on the cultural studies tradition extend the modest yet important role that cultural studies classes already play in transforming the student body—generating students' control over the production of knowledge and building students' respect for their own creative agency. Throughout this chapter, we use the term *activist pedagogy* to describe teaching practices that promote agency, and we describe our students as "activist" when they develop that agency and take control over the production of knowledge. The space of the public conference—a space we will argue is contiguous with the classroom—allows for the emergence of such activism: It is a radically democratic space where participants can redefine the "point of production."

Cultural studies praxis immerses students and teachers in dialectical process, as they focus on "processes, flows, fluxes, and relations" and learn to recognize that "elements, structures, and systems do not exist outside of or prior to the processes, flows, and relations that create, sustain, or undermine them" (Harvey 1996, 49). In critically analyzing their own location (or positionality), it is useful for students to see their own identities as in process—open to creative and even pleasurable reconstruction and transformation. Without the developed ability to think in such ways (and we would insist that this is a truly critical literacy), students remain appendages to others' creative powers and they find it, understandably, difficult to imagine the creation of meaningful social change.

The "in process" knowledge that cultural studies teachers and students produce is, in many respects, nonconventional and even dissident, because it unsettles those educational relations that are most productive for capital. We

thus begin this chapter by critically describing the problematic that so deeply affects the university. We consider how this problematic seeks to restrict (and privatize) our creative agency and scholarly productions and how teachers and students are finding means to mobilize with others (in both the space of the classroom and "in public") to resist incorporation and exploitation. We then move into consideration of the specific ways student, teacher, and home community participants at the first annual Composition and Cultural Studies Conference for Student Writers produced activist knowledge and struggle.

Modes of Production in the Postmodern University

Working within the context of a so-called boom economy—that is, of seemingly ever-expanding productivity—teachers (especially adjuncts) and students are increasingly developing consciousness of the ways their campus/work experiences connect them with others, locally and transnationally. Students and teachers are increasingly agitated by their lived experience of gaps between the increased power and wealth for some (such as university presidents) and their own heterogeneous experiences of loss of control over the educational system. From multiple standpoints, they are describing, critiquing, and mobilizing against the contradictions within their environments, struggling to talk back to a dominant ideology that tells them (like all workers) that they must adapt to the "progressive"—efficient—changes occurring around them.

As activist-scholars committed to what Jeffrey Williams (1997) has called "the utopian prospect for education," we are very interested in forwarding students' and teachers' active critique of their lived experience of contradictions. The limits imposed on student and teacher creative agency are the logical extension of a dominant, late capitalist logic. Faculty, like other workers, are being effectively divided into skilled and "deskilled" groups, with certain scholars (such as composition instructors, a predominantly female group) being constructed as low-wage service workers. Thus, many in composition have difficulty being recognized as genuine shapers of an intellectual community. On the other hand, "skilled" faculty—those who are still (at least for now) slotted into tenure line positions—are constructed as efficient knowledge producers (an efficiency that is quantifiable). In our own English department, for instance, full-time faculty members are all subjected to a publication count at the end of the year. That count is made public, and "nonproductive" faculty members are exposed. Interestingly, part-time faculty and graduate teaching assistants, who are overwhelmingly responsible for the first-year composition classes, are not subjected to this surveillance. Not made accountable for the production of excellence in scholarship, they are—barred from faculty meetings and cut off from elite faculty benefits and salary—structurally unrecognizable as colleagues or even scholars.

Jill Blackmore (1997), in an article focusing on the crises in Australian

higher education, effectively outlines what we see as the central features of a
global, late capitalist educational system:

> The postmodern, market-oriented, flexible university is the result of "devo-
> lution." Its hallmarks are: intensification of academic labor; lack of job se-
> curity; surveillance techniques to ensure quality assurance; and quantifiable
> outcome-oriented performance management. Increased time and money are
> expended on quality assurance, while the capacity of staff to produce high-
> quality education is undermined by the under-resourcing of teaching and by
> time-consuming management demands for accountability. (91)

As Blackmore's description—with its emphasis on the loss of faculty control—indicates, the rhetoric of "flexibility" serves particular, market-oriented
goals. Flexibility, that is, does not signify a new curricular fluidity or a demand
that all conversations be as democratic as possible. Instead, *flexibility* is a syn-
onym for *streamlined:* It is educators and students who must be "flexible" as
the university works—much like other corporations—to administer efficiency.
Educators are thus being called on to be flexible as part-time and adjunct faculty work without adequate compensation and benefits, as job security in general is curtailed, as teaching loads and class sizes are increased, and as
teaching practices and curricular choices are more closely monitored.

Throughout the country, the commodification of knowledge and learning,
coupled with the withdrawal of state support for education, apparently work
against radical educators. Noting the "encroaching influence of the market-
place on all aspects of life," Patricia Hill Collins (1998) speaks eloquently of
the effects on oppositional scholarship, particularly the scholarship of black
women. Collins helps make visible the growing divide between being rewarded academic scholarship and the kinds of in-process learning and knowledge valued by home communities. To illustrate this divide, she reviews the
platform issues forwarded by the participants in the 1997 Million Woman
March; that platform called for

> A probe in the Central Intelligence Agency's relationship to the influx of
> drugs in African-American communities; the development of Black indepen-
> dent schools; new mechanisms that would help Black women when they
> leave the penal system; and better health care services. . . . Other platform
> issues included support for Black women who want to become profession-
> als, taking steps to curb homelessness and gentrification of urban neighbor-
> hoods and increased support for all Black elderly. (74)

Collins concludes that "none of these platform issues occupies a promi-
nent place in contemporary Black feminist thought," and she argues that this
is in large due to the pressures of the market—that is, the pressure to produce
knowledge as a commodity.

We see these pressures—to break from community ties and to concentrate
on flexibly negotiating market forces—reflected in ourselves, in our col-

leagues, and in our students. In this late capitalist context, in which students and faculty are produced as entities without, as Stanley Aronowitz describes us, "rights as a collectivity to retain sovereignty over the educational process" (quoted in Williams 1997, 306), it takes activist struggle to persist in producing ourselves and our students as, at least in some respects, oppositional entities. Clearly, the last thing our students need is another competitive public space to demonstrate and market their "skills." Within the problematic of late capitalist education, verbal "skill" may have been reduced to signaling a slick ability to pick up, try out, and apply the newest, most marketable scholarly framework. There are serious consequences, however, to such a deformation of scholarship. For all of us, learning should be more than a game. Participating in the construction of radical democratic traditions is not a matter of indifference: These are potential tools to survive and reshape exploitative, dehumanizing social relations (social relations that have real and often violent bodily effects). Indeed, the university must be reshaped to center on this mode of knowledge production.

The Composition and Cultural Studies Conference for Student Writers institutionalizes such a shift in our experience of literate practices and learning. Insofar as this is publicly accomplished, we certainly have put ourselves and our students in risky—that is, activist—positions. The intellectual exchange that students and teachers generate at the conference is not conducive to building late capitalist social relations. For one, the conception of teaching composition as service work is clearly troubled. Here, we need to say a bit more about the "special" relationship between composition teaching and other deskilled service work. As many activist-scholars have underscored, composition teachers are everywhere struggling with the ways in which their agency and abilities are diminished and are organizing to secure basic academic freedoms (such as a living wage and the right to define the content and method of their courses). Working against the dominant conceptualization of the composition teacher, our student conference—which is now organized by many adjunct faculty members—makes clear that composition teachers do not exist simply to serve the needs of other departments (producing efficient, polished writing). For students, teachers, parents, and others attending our public conferences, the work of composition is demonstrably central to the development of the student's intellectual agency and authority.

Institutionalizing such events is important (albeit risky) in the context of the flexible university. Given our problematic, we must design activist pedagogical practices that intensify the fight for "sovereignty" over the educational process. Student conferences informed by a cultural studies praxis help teachers and students "talk back" to and begin to reinvent the dominant university structure. And yet our goal in composing this chapter is not to advocate necessarily for this particular pedagogical innovation. Rather, we encourage our readers—teachers, students, activists—to locate the opportunities within their own contexts to construct such alternative publics.

The Composition and Cultural Studies Conference

Cultural studies draws attention to moments when hegemony falters and different voices, dialogues, and even means of communication emerge. The cultural studies pedagogy we employ aims to facilitate and proliferate such moments. We found our activist pedagogy on the feminist/queer belief that the open communication and exchange of written and spoken words between people can be both transformative and pleasurable. At the same time, we share the queer/feminist insight that such pleasurable, social uses of language are excessively regulated within the mass media and in many "public" spaces, such that most people rarely experience these pleasures or the potential for social transformation. In designing our classes, we therefore attempt, on multiple levels, to foreground the pleasures—and, with them, the atmosphere of hopefulness—that accompany the emergence of new and open forms of communication. This means, in part, that students see and hear ordinary people—for instance, a people's revolutionary theater in Kenya decolonizing culture or Damned Interfering Video Activists (DIVA TV) documenting AIDS activism—struggling together to create counter-discourses and narratives. To help students experience their own and others' uses of language as a social force, we feel that it is important to define topics or subject areas that will engage them in the contested processes of social change.

To that end, in spring 1998, we designed writing- and research-intensive seminars that focused on contemporary social formations: One of us worked with postcolonialism, neocolonialism, and hybridity; the other with contemporary lesbian, gay, and bisexual movements. Our own project in these courses was to move students away from conceiving writing and research projects as merely for oneself or for the teacher (and a grade) to conceiving such projects in terms of construction and potential transformation of communities. It was for this reason that we inaugurated the First Annual Composition and Cultural Studies Conference for Student Writers. At the first conference, scheduled at the close of the spring 1998 semester, students spoke about their critical research projects with audiences composed of many students (from our different sections), interested faculty and graduate students, the students' relatives and friends, and also a few members of the university staff.

We invited activist-scholars to moderate six panels that included papers focusing on a wide range of cultural studies projects. While three students from each of our classes presented at the conference (a total of eighteen presentations), all students worked throughout the semester at creating writing for this public forum. Additionally, although the students composed individual papers, those papers emerged from communal contexts. We both broke our classes into small research groups, in one case focusing on seven-year periods in bisexual, lesbian, and gay history and, in the other case, focusing on resistance movements in Africa, in the Caribbean, among indigenous peoples, and in the southwestern United States. Thus, students wrote individual projects,

but collectively researched the entire period or history of resistance. The group work in both classes provided students with a larger context and ensured that individuals speaking would have communities supporting them.

We want to discuss the final panel of the day—"Reading, Writing, Resisting the Right"—in some detail, because that panel both exemplified best and most obviously challenged the particular understandings of cultural studies and composition we had shaped with our classes over the course of the semester. The very title "Reading the Right" in fact named an activity central to cultural studies as we comprehend it. Dominant discourses are often naturalized as simply "common sense" or "truth," but a cultural studies pedagogy insists on interrogating how such discourses function as rhetoric—that is, as nonnatural, constructed discourses intended to work persuasively in particular cultural situations. For us, *reading* also had the queer/African American sense of "exposing" or "loudly calling out the inadequacies of." An activist pedagogy centralizes such reading strategies, moving them out of the street and into the university. Beyond that, an activist pedagogy identifies and interrogates in turn the competing rhetorics that come into play around and within hegemonic discursive formations.

The panel's title was appropriate, given the three student papers: Iris Victoria Allen's "Resistance Culture in South Africa: Before and After Sharpeville" explicitly detailed how the struggle against the Right's policy of apartheid in South Africa shifted in the early 1960s from nonviolent to violent means of defiance; Andrea Cerbin's "Can We As a Society Separate Church and State?: Legality, 'Morality,' and Same-Sex Marriage" critiqued the rhetoric of right-wing antigay commentators such as William Bennett; and Emily Henehan's "Anita Bryant's Rhetoric of Childhood" gave an historical overview of Bryant's late 1970s' "Save Our Children" campaign, which led to the repeal of gay rights legislation in Dade County, Florida. However, despite the unified focus on resistance and the Right, we were nonetheless aware that, by titling the panel as we did, we were going public with our own understanding of cultural studies and activism. As one of us jokingly suggested when announcing the panel to Henehan's class, "This is the sort of title that could get us written up in the conservative campus newspaper."

Such an article might presume a unified, "politically correct" leftist agenda or might even presume that views had been imposed on students by what conservative pundit Roger Kimball (in a notorious *60 Minutes* report attacking queer studies on university campuses) calls "a coterie of politically motivated people who are attempting to use the university as an ideological training ground." The unity staged by "Reading, Writing, Resisting the Right," however, was loose and contingent. We certainly had no guarantee that the papers themselves would be in agreement about what it means to "resist the Right," or that Allen, Cerbin, and Henehan would share political positions (in fact, we had not yet seen the final versions of the papers that would be presented, a few of which were completed only a short time before the panel).

In particular, we were well aware that religion complicated, or even threatened to expose completely, the supposed "unity" of "Reading, Writing, Resisting the Right." Both Allen's mother and her father, a Baptist minister, were to be in attendance at the panel, and Allen was to appeal directly to Christianity in her paper, including biblical quotations to illustrate some of her concluding points. Cerbin's paper, in potentially direct contrast, explicitly argued that religion, God, and marriage were not "natural" facts, but rather social constructs that have little place in civic and legal discourse, even though they currently dominate, in Cerbin's mind, the civic and legal discourse of the United States. Although Cerbin's paper was at times quite abstract and challenging, the point about religion as an "unnatural construct" came through quite clearly to the audience.

There was potential for contention around this panel, and we knew it. However, we were committed to composing student-activists—meaning not that we were committed to shaping student-activists into some prescribed activist mold, but rather that we were committed to understanding the writers and speakers with whom we had worked all semester as composing student-activists. Additionally, we were committed to relocating student writing in order to acknowledge more explicitly the ways in which students engage in numerous conversations with other communities located outside of our own contingent classroom communities. During the semester, our classes had collectively debated the ramifications of taking our writing to a larger, diverse audience. These conversations solidified the recognition that our classrooms needed to— and indeed already did—open onto other locations (the recognition, that is, of the contiguity of the classroom and the conference hall, or of the classroom and communities in Washington, D.C. and other places where students live).

Janice Radway argues that, within cultural studies, "contentiousness is productive, because it exposes the complexity of power and demonstrates that no single framework for analysis is wholly adequate to understanding, let alone for intervening in, that complexity" (Graff et al. 1994, 31). This productive contentiousness was evident as the students on the "Reading, Writing, Resisting the Right" panel presented their papers. Cerbin's reading of Bennett and other conservative commentators suggested that—contrary to American platitudes about separation of church and state—our civic and legal discourse is thoroughly imbued with ideas about God and religion. Henehan's paper, in contrast, used the separation of church and state as a wedge for questioning Bryant's tactics in the "Save Our Children" campaign. Henehan's paper stressed that we are supposed to have separation of church and state in this country, but after reading the section containing that argument, she reconsidered her position and suggested aloud that—as we had just heard from Cerbin—perhaps the problem is that we actually do not have the fundamental separation that we keep telling ourselves we do.

Multiple frameworks for understanding the complexity of power continued to emerge in the discussion following the papers. One of us asked Allen— who looked critically in her paper at the turn to violence in the struggle against

South Africa's policy of apartheid—whether it was possible to realize, in an irrational system, the rational dialogue she had advocated and whether the failure of activists to incite such a dialogue during Anita Bryant's campaign served as an example of the limits of rationality. (Henehan's main points were that Bryant had appealed to emotions rather than rationality by deploying a rhetoric of childhood, and that gay activists' attempts to counter with adult rationality had proven unsuccessful.) Allen not only defended her position but was seconded by Henehan herself, who pointed out that the majority/minority dynamics were different in the two cultural contexts: Blacks in South Africa were in the majority, but lesbians and gay men in Dade County faced different challenges because they were in the minority. An audience member challenged this reading of Dade County (or of the United States generally), asking whether such an understanding of majority/minority falsely set up another binary between those who would not support gay liberation (understood as the heterosexual majority) and those who would. This speaker suggested that many nongay people oppose antigay campaigns, and was thus reluctant to read such campaigns as "minority" concerns. A colleague of ours then challenged Cerbin in particular (and implicitly provided support for Allen's paper) by asking whether religion in general is too often ceded to the Right and whether progressive religious traditions were thereby written out of existence. Ultimately, the discussion was so productively contentious that the conversation could not be contained at the conference: Henehan, Cerbin, and another student at the conference went out to dinner with three other friends who had not been in attendance, and they reported to us later that the evening was dominated by discussion and debate of the ideas emerging from the conference.

"What is needed in cultural studies generally," according to Radway, "is a multiplicitous polyphonic, disputatious discussion of the complex ways in which cultural representation is mobilized in the interests of power" (Graff et al. 1994, 39). For that reason, we understand as positive what happened when we took our students' writing public: Students were extending (to the conference hall and other locations) the conversations they had already been having—because of their research, because of the numerous, overlapping locations through which they move—with communities beyond the walls of our classrooms, and they were seeing how their own ideas could be re-presented, re-membered, and mobilized. At the same time, we recognize that the event could have gone much differently (and certainly will go much differently as it continues to evolve annually). Even though Allen's father, the Baptist minister, clapped first and loudest after each paper (thereby challenging—or making multiplicitous—our own understanding of religion), other figures or forces (less tied, perhaps, to the liberatory African American religious tradition within which Allen's father is located) would be less likely to applaud as marginalized discourses were mobilized in newly constituted public space.

We are unwilling, however, to fix public space, to concede it to hegemonic discourses by containing student writing in a domesticated "private" space (a

space that the classroom, as we hope we've made clear, can never wholly be anyway). We want to articulate the writing and the speech produced in our classrooms to ongoing and collective demands that public space be understood otherwise, that public space not be understood as always and everywhere straight—that is, not simply that public space not be understood as always heterosexual and heteronormative, but also that it not be understood as "straight" in the sense of efficient, driven, focused only on greed and profitability. The relocation of student voices that an activist pedagogy encourages helps to stall the production of passive student bodies and of environments that can only protect monovocal, hegemonic speech. Student activists have composed, and can continue to compose, alternative publics. Their activism has the potential to disrupt the flexible university as they write into existence new ways of knowing and as they collectively and disputatiously write their way into new locations.

Works Cited

Anson, C. 1997. "The Role of Logs and Journals in Service-Learning Courses." In *Writing the Community: Concepts and Models for Service-Learning in Composition*, eds. L. Adler-Kassner, R. Crooks, and A. Watters, 167–80. Urbana, IL: American Association for Higher Education and NCTE.

Atwell, N. 1998. *In the Middle: Writing, Reading, and Learning with Adolescents*, 2nd ed. Portsmouth, NH: Boynton/Cook.

Bacon, N. 1997. "Community Service Writing: Problems, Challenges, Questions." In *Writing the Community: Concepts and Models for Service-Learning in Composition*, eds. L. Adler-Kassner, R. Crooks, and A. Watters, 39–55. Urbana, IL: American Association for Higher Education and NCTE.

Bakhtin, M. M. 1981. *The Dialogic Imagination*, ed. M. Holquist. Austin: University of Texas Press.

Bartholomae, D. 1985. "Inventing the University." In *When a Writer Can't Write: Studies in Writer's Block and Other Composing-Process Problems*, ed. M. Rose, 134–65. New York: Guilford.

———. 1995. "Writing with Teachers: A Conversation with Peter Elbow." *College Composition and Communication* 46 (1): 62–71.

Bauman, M. 1997. "Negotiating a Passage Among Readers and Writers on the Web." In *CMC Magazine* [on-line]. 1997 [cited 1 June 1998]. Available from World Wide Web: <http://www.december.com/cmc/mag/1997/jun/bauman.html>.

Beard, R. 1998. "Russia & the Internet." Course materials [on-line]. 1998 [cited 1 June 1998]. No longer available.

Berlin, J. 1988. "Rhetoric and Ideology." *College English* 50 (5): 477–94.

———. 1987. *Rhetoric and Reality: Writing Instruction in American Colleges, 1900–1985*. Carbondale: Southern Illinois University Press.

———. 1982. "Contemporary Composition: The Major Pedagogical Theories." *College English* 44 (8): 765–77.

Bernhardt, S. 1986. "Seeing the Text." *College Composition and Communication* 37 (1): 66–78.

Bishop, W. 1999. "Hint Sheets." *The Subject Is Writing: Essays by Teachers and Students*. 2nd ed. Portsmouth, NH: Boynton/Cook.

———. 1999. "Places to Stand: The Reflective Writer-Teacher-Writer in Composition." *College Composition and Communication* 51 (1): 9–31.

Bitzer, L. 1995. "The Rhetorical Situation." In *Rhetoric: Concepts, Definitions, Boundaries*, eds. W. Covino and D. Jolliffe, 300–10. Boston: Allyn and Bacon.

Bizzell, P. 1982. "Cognition, Convention, and Certainty: What We Need to Know About Writing." *Pre/Text* 3: 213–43.

Blackmore, J. 1997. "Disciplining Feminism: A Look at Gender-Equity Struggles in Australian Higher Education." In *Dangerous Territories: Struggles for Difference and Equality in Education*, ed. L. Roman and L. Eyre, 75–96. New York: Routledge.

Bleich, D. 1998. *Know and Tell: A Writing Pedagogy of Disclosure, Genre, and Membership*. Portsmouth, NH: Boynton/Cook.

Blitz, M., & C. M. Hurlbert. 1998. *Letters for the Living: Teaching Writing in a Violent Age*. Urbana, IL: NCTE.

Britton, J. et al. 1975. *The Development of Writing Abilities (11–18)*. London: Macmillan.

Britton, J. 1970. *Language and Learning*. London: Penguin.

Brodkey, L. 1989. "On the Subjects of Class and Gender in 'The Literacy Letters.'" *College English* 51 (2): 125–41.

———. 1987. "Writing Ethnographic Narratives." *Written Communication* 4 (1): 25–50.

———. 1986. "Modernism and the Scene(s) of Writing." *College English* 49 (4): 396–417.

Brooke, R., R. Mirtz, & R. Evans. 1994. *Small Groups in Writing Workshops: Invitations to a Writer's Life*. Urbana, IL: NCTE.

Bruffee, K. 1986. "Social Construction, Language and the Authority of Knowledge: A Bibliographical Essay." *College English* 48 (8): 773–90.

———. 1985. *A Short Course in Writing*. Glenview, IL: Scott, Foresman, and Company.

———. 1980. *A Short Course in Writing*. 2nd ed. Cambridge: Winthrop.

Calkins, L. 1983. *Lessons from a Child*. Portsmouth, NH: Heinemann.

Carter, M. 1990. "The Idea of Expertise: An Exploration of Cognitive and Social Dimensions of Writing." *College Composition and Communication* 41 (3): 265–86.

Cayton, M. K. 1990. "What Happens When Things Go Wrong: Women and Writing Blocks." *Journal of Advanced Composition* 10 (2): 321–37.

Collins, P. H. 1998. *Fighting Words: Black Women and the Search for Justice*. Minneapolis: University of Minnesota Press.

Cooper, M. 1986. "The Ecology of Writing." *College English* 48 (4): 364–75.

Cox, B. "Re: Student Web Page Survey." E-mail to the author, 9 May 1998.

Delpit, L. 1995. *Other People's Children: Cultural Conflict in the Classroom*. New York: The New Press.

DeWitt, S. L. 1997. "Out There on the Web: Pedagogy and Identity in the Face of Opposition." *Computers and Composition* 14 (2): 229–44.

Dixon, K. 1995. "Making and Taking Apart 'Culture' in the (Writing) Classroom." In *Left Margins: Cultural Studies and Composition Pedagogy*, eds. K. Fitts and A. W. France, 99–114. Albany: State University of New York Press.

Duin, A. H., & C. Hansen. 1994. "Reading and Writing on Computer Networks as Social Construction and Social Interaction." In *Literacy and Computers: The*

Complications of Teaching and Learning with Technology, eds. C. Selfe & S. Hilligoss, 89–112. New York: MLA.

Dutton, S.,& H. Fils-Aime. 1993. "Bringing the Literary Magazine into the Classroom." *College Composition and Communication* 44 (1): 84–87.

Ede, L., & A. Lunsford. 1984. "Audience Addressed/Audience Invoked: The Role of Audience in Composition Theory and Pedagogy." *College Composition and Communication* 35 (2): 155–71.

Elbow, P., & P. Belanoff. 1995. *Sharing and Responding*, 2nd ed. New York: McGraw-Hill.

Elbow, P. 1995. "Being a Writer vs. Being an Academic: A Conflict in Goals." *College Composition and Communication* 46 (1): 72–83.

———. 1998. *Writing with Power.* 2nd ed. New York: Oxford University Press.

———. 1973. *Writing Without Teachers.* New York: Oxford University Press.

Eldred, J. 1991. "Pedagogy in the Computer-Networked Classroom." *Computers and Composition* 8 (2): 47–61.

Ellsworth, E. 1992. "Why Doesn't This Feel Empowering? Working Through the Repressive Myths of Critical Pedagogy." In *Feminism and Critical Pedagogy*, eds. C. Luke and J. Gore, 90–119. New York: Routledge.

Finders, M. J. 1997. *Just Girls: Hidden Literacies and Life in Junior High*. New York: Teachers College Press.

Fisher, P. 1986. "Appearing and Disappearing in Public: Social Space in Late-Nineteenth-Century Literature and Culture." In *Reconstructing American Literary History*, ed. S. Bercovitch, 155–88. Cambridge: Harvard University Press.

Fishman, S., & L. P. McCarthy. 1992. "Is Expressivism Dead? Reconsidering Its Romantic Roots and Its Relation to Social Constructionism." *College English* 54 (6): 647–61.

Fishman, S. 1993. "Explicating Our Tacit Tradition: John Dewey and Composition Studies." *College Composition and Communication* 44 (3): 315–30.

Flower, L., & J. Hayes. 1981. "A Cognitive Process Theory of Writing." In *Cross-Talk in Comp Theory*, ed. V. Villaneuva, 251–75. Urbana, IL: NCTE.

Foucault, M. 1977. *Discipline and Punish: The Birth of the Prison.* New York: Pantheon.

———. 1990. *The History of Sexuality*, volume I. New York: Vintage.

Frankston, R. 1990. Interview: "Welcome to the Byte Summit." *Byte* 15 (9): 271.

Freire, P. 1970. *Pedagogy of the Oppressed.* New York: Seabury Press.

Frey, O. 1987. "Equity and Peace in the New Writing Class." In *Teaching Writing: Pedagogy, Gender and Equity*, eds. C. Caywood and G. Overing, 93–105. Albany: State University of New York Press.

Gere, A. R. 1987. *Writing Groups: History, Theory, and Implications.* Carbondale: Southern Illinois University Press.

Giroux, H., & P. McLaren, eds. 1989. *Critical Pedagogy, the State and Cultural Struggle.* Albany: State University of New York Press.

Giroux, H. 1995. "Who Writes in a Cultural Studies Class? or, Where Is the Pedagogy?" In *Left Margins: Cultural Studies and Composition Pedagogy*, eds. K. Fitts and A. France, 3–16. Albany: State University of New York Press.

——. 1988. *Schooling and the Struggle for Public Life: Critical Pedagogy in the Modern Age*. Minneapolis: University of Minnesota Press.

——. 1986. "Radical Pedagogy and the Politics of Student Voice." *Interchange* 17 (Spring): 48–69.

Godkin, E. L. 1890. "The Rights of the Citizen: IV. 'To His Own Reputation.'" *Scribner's Magazine* 8: 66.

Gore, J. 1993. *The Struggle for Pedagogies: Critical and Feminist Discourses as Regimes of Truth*. New York: Routledge.

Gradin, S. 1995. *Romancing Rhetorics: Social Expressivist Perspectives on the Teaching of Writing*. Portsmouth, NH: Boynton/Cook.

Graff, G., J. Radway, G. Rajan, & R. C. Davis. 1994. "A Dialogue on Institutionalizing Cultural Studies." In *English Studies/Cultural Studies*, eds. I. Smithson and N. Ruff. Urbana: University of Illinois Press.

Gramsci, A. 1987. *The Modern Prince and Other Writings*. New York: International Publishers.

Graves, D. 1983. *Writing: Teachers and Children at Work*. Portsmouth, NH: Heinemann.

Groening, M. 1998. "Sex Tips from Your Moral Superiors." *Life in Hell* (comic strip), In *The Valley Advocate*. Amherst, MA, Summer.

Gutjahr, P. 1995. "Constructing Arts&Facts: The Art of Composition, the Facts of (Material) Culture." In *Left Margins: Cultural Studies and Composition Pedagogy*, eds. K. Fitts and A. France, 69–82. Albany: State University of New York Press.

Harris, L., & C. Wambeam. 1996. "The Internet-Based Composition Classroom: A Study in Pedagogy." *Computers and Composition* 13 (3): 353–71.

Harvey, D. 1996. *Justice, Nature, and the Geography of Difference*. Malden, MA: Blackwell.

Haubitz, H. "Re: Student Web Page Survey." E-mail to the author, 23 May 1998.

Hawisher, G., & C. Moran. 1998. "The Rhetorics and Languages of Electronic Mail." In *Page to Screen: Taking Literacy into the Electronic Era*, ed. I. Snyder, 80–101. New York: Routledge.

Hawisher, G., & C. Selfe. 1998. "Reflections on Computers and Composition Studies." In *Page to Screen: Taking Literacy into the Electronic Era*, ed. I. Snyder, 3–19. New York: Routledge.

Hawisher, G., & P. Sullivan. 1998. "Women on the Networks: Searching for E-Spaces of Their Own." *Feminism and Composition Studies: In Other Words*, eds. S. Jarratt and L. Worsham, 172–97. New York: MLA.

Herzberg, B. 1994. "Community Service and Critical Thinking." *College Composition and Communication* 45 (3): 307–19.

Hofstadter, S., & G. Horowitz, eds. 1964. *The Right of Privacy*. New York: Central Book Company.

Hollis, K. 1992. "Feminism in Writing Workshops: A New Pedagogy." *College Composition and Communication* 43 (3): 340–48.

hooks, b. 1989. *Talking Back: Thinking Feminist, Thinking Black.* Boston: South End Press.

———. 1994. *Teaching to Transgress: Education as the Practice of Freedom.* New York: Routledge.

Howard, T. 1997. *A Rhetoric of Electronic Communities.* Greenwich, CT: Ablex.

Hunt, K. 1997. "A Plea for Visual Literacy." In *CMC Magazine* [on-line]. 1997 [cited 26 February 1998]. Available from World Wide Web: <http://www.december.com/cmc/mag/1997/jun/last.html>.

Jarratt, S. 1991. "Feminism and Composition: The Case for Conflict." In *Contending with Words: Composition and Rhetoric in the Postmodern Age,* eds. P. Harkin and J. Schilb, 105–23. New York: MLA.

Johnson-Eilola, J. 1994. "Reading and Writing in Hypertext: Vertigo and Euphoria." In *Literacy and Computers: The Complications of Teaching and Learning with Technology*, eds. C. Selfe and S. Hilligoss, 192–219. New York: MLA.

Jones, D. 1997. "An End to the Curious Social Construction of 'Expressivism' and the Pragmatist Tradition of Peter Elbow." Paper presented at the annual meeting of the Conference on College Composition and Communication, Phoenix, AZ, March 11–14. ED420875.

Lawlor, R. 1991. *Voices of the First Day: Awakening in the Aboriginal Dreamtime.* Rochester, VT: Inner Traditions.

LeFevre, K. B. 1987. *Invention as a Social Act.* Carbondale: Southern Illinois University Press.

Lewis, M., & R. Simon. 1986. "A Discourse Not Intended for Her: Learning and Teaching Within Patriarchy." *Harvard Educational Review* 56 (4): 457–72.

Lewis, M. G. 1993. *Without a Word: Teaching Beyond Women's Silence.* New York: Routledge.

Lowenstein, S., E. Chiseri-Strater, & C. Gannett. 1994. "Re-envisioning the Journal: Writing the Self into Community." In *Pedagogy in the Age of Politics*, eds. P. Sullivan and D. Qualley, 139–52. Urbana, IL: NCTE.

Lu, M. 1998. "Reading and Writing Differences: The Problematic of Experience." In *Feminism and Composition Studies: In Other Words*, eds. S. Jarratt and L. Worsham, 239–51. New York: MLA.

Lu, M., & B. Horner. 1998. "The Problematic of Experience: Redefining Critical Work in Ethnography and Pedagogy." *College English* 60 (3): 257–77.

Macrorie, K. 1970. *Telling Writing.* Rochelle Park, NJ: Hayden.

———. 1970. *Uptaught.* New York: Hayden.

———. 1968. *Writing to Be Read.* New York: Hayden.

Mahgoub, Y. 1998. "Re: Student Web Page Survey." E-mail to the author, 1 June 1998.

Malinowitz, H. 1992. "Construing and Constructing Knowledge as a Lesbian or Gay Student Writer." *Pre/Text* 13 (3–4): 37–52.

Mansfield, M. 1993. "Real World Writing and the English Curriculum." *College Composition and Communication* 44 (1): 69–83.

Martin, N., et al. 1976. *Writing and Learning Across the Curriculum 11–16*. London: Ward Lock.

Mauriello, N. 1997, August 1. "The College Writing Peer Response Project." [English course web site]. Retrieved September 1, 1999, from the World Wide Web: http://www.iup.edu/~nickm/peer.htm.

McBride, K. 1998. "Re: Student Web Page Survey." E-mail to the author, 9 May 1998.

Mensel, R. 1991. "'Kodakers Lying in Wait': Amateur Photography and the Right of Privacy in New York, 1885–1915." *American Quarterly* 43 (1): 24–45.

Miller, R. 1994. "Fault Lines in the Contact Zone." *College English* 56 (4): 389–408.

Minter, D., A. R. Gere, & D. Keller-Cohn. 1995. "Learning Literacies." *College English* 57 (6): 669–87.

Mirtz, R. 1997. "The Territorial Demands of Form and Process: The Case for Student Writing as a Genre." In *Genre and Writing: Issues, Arguments, Alternatives*, eds. W. Bishop and H. Ostrom, 190–98. Portsmouth, NH: Boynton/Cook.

Moffett, J. 1968. *Teaching the Universe of Discourse*. Portsmouth, NH: Boynton/Cook.

———. 1983. *Teaching the Universe of Discourse*. Boston: Houghton Mifflin.

Moran, C. 1998. "Review: English and Emerging Technologies." *College English* 60 (2): 202–09.

———. 1994. "How the Writing Process Came to UMass/Amherst: Roger Garrison, Donald Murray, and Institutional Change." In *Taking Stock: The Writing Process Movement in the '90s*, eds. L. Tobin and T. Newkirk, 133–52. Portsmouth, NH: Boynton/Cook.

Murray, D. 1968. *A Writer Teaches Writing*. Boston: Houghton Mifflin.

Negroponte, N. 1995. *Being Digital*. New York: Alfred A. Knopf.

Nelson, J. 1990. "This Was an Easy Assignment: Examining How Students Interpret Academic Writing Tasks." *Research in the Teaching of English* 24 (4): 362–96.

Newkirk, T. 1997. *The Performance of Self in Student Writing*. Portsmouth, NH: Boynton/Cook.

———. 1993. "Locating Freshman English." In *Nuts and Bolts: A Practical Guide to Teaching College Composition*, ed. T. Newkirk, 1–16. Portsmouth, NH: Boynton/Cook.

O'Reilley, M. R. 1993. *The Peaceable Classroom*. Portsmouth, NH: Boynton/Cook.

Orner, M. 1998. "School Marks: Education, Domination and Female Subjectivity." *Foucault's Challenge: Discourse, Knowledge, and Power in Education*, eds. T. Popkewitz and M. Brennan, 278–94. New York: Teachers College Press.

———. 1992. "Interrupting the Calls for Student Voice in 'Liberatory' Education: A Feminist Poststructuralist Perspective." In *Feminisms and Critical Pedagogy*, eds. C. Luke and J. Gore, 74–89. New York: Routledge.

Pagnucci, G. S., & N. Mauriello. 1999. "The Masquerade: Gender, Identity, and Writing for the Web." *Computers and Composition* 16 (1): 141–51.

Peck, W., L. Flower, & L. Higgins. 1995. "Community Literacy." *College Composition and Communication* 46 (2): 199–222.

Popken, R. 1995. "Student Publications and the Acquisition of Research Genres." *InLand* 18: 15–20.

Pratt, M. L. 1996. Me llamo Rigoberta Menchú: Autoethnography and the Recoding of Citizenship. In *Teaching and Testimony: Rigoberta Menchú and the North American Classroom*, eds. A. Carey-Webb and S. Benz, 57–72. Albany: State University of New York Press.

Reynolds, N. 1998. "Composition's Imagined Geographies: The Politics of Space in the Frontier, City, and Cyberspace." *College Composition and Communication* 50 (1): 12–35.

Rhodes, K. 1994. "Thinking Expressivist, Cultural Studies and Spiritual Pedagogies (and Feminism) Together: The Search for a New Term." Paper presented at the annual meeting of the Conference on College Composition and Communication, Nashville, TN, March 16–19. ED373340.

Rief, L. 1992. *Seeking Diversity.* Portsmouth, NH: Heinemann.

Romano, T. 1987. *Clearing the Way: Working with Teenage Writers.* Portsmouth, NH: Heinemann.

Sandercock, L. 1998. *Towards Cosmopolis: Planning for Multicultural Cities.* New York: John Wiley & Sons.

Schaafsma, D. 1993. *Eating on the Street: Teaching Literacy in a Multicultural Society.* Pittsburgh: University of Pittsburgh Press.

Schutz, A., & A. R. Gere. 1998. "Service Learning and English Studies: Rethinking Public Service." *College English* 60 (2): 129–49.

Sedgwick, E. K. 1990. *The Epistemology of the Closet.* Berkeley: University of California Press.

Selfe, C., & R. Selfe, Jr. 1994. "The Politics of the Interface: Power and Its Exercise in Electronic Contact Zones." *College Composition and Communication* 45 (4): 480–504.

Shalit, R. 1998. "The Man Who Knew Too Much." *Linguafranca* 8 (1): 31–40.

Shor, I. 1980. *Critical Teaching and Everyday Life.* Boston: South End Press.

60 Minutes/CBS News. 1998. "Sexuality 101."

Sladky, Paul. 1997. *Free Falling and Other Student Essays*, 3rd ed. New York: St. Martin's Press.

Smith, C. 2000. "Nobody, Which Means Anybody: Audience on the World Wide Web." In *Weaving a Virtual Web: Practical Approaches to New Information Technologies*, ed. S. Gruber. Urbana, IL: NCTE.

Spear, K. 1988. *Sharing Writing: Peer Response Groups in English Classes.* Portsmouth, NH: Boynton/Cook.

Spigelman, C. 1998. "Habits of Mind: Historical Configurations of Textual Ownership in Peer Writing Groups." *College Composition and Communication* 49 (2): 234–55.

Sullivan, P. 1991. "Taking Control of the Page: Electronic Writing and Word Publish-

ing." In *Evolving Perspectives on Computers and Composition Studies,* eds. G. Hawisher and C. Selfe, 43–64. Urbana, IL: NCTE.

Taylor, D. 1997. *Many Families, Many Literacies: An International Declaration of Principles.* Portsmouth, NH: Heinemann.

———. 1996. *Toxic Literacies: Exposing the Injustice of Bureaucratic Texts.* Portsmouth, NH: Heinemann.

Thomas, B. 1992. "The Construction of Privacy In and Around *The Bostonians.*" *American Literature* 64 (4): 719–47.

Tobin, L. 1996. "The Personal Narratives of Adolescent Males." *College English* 48 (2): 158–75.

Tuman, M. 1996. "Literacy Online." *Annual Review of Applied Linguistics* 16: 26–45.

Turkle, S. 1997. *Life on the Screen: Identity in the Age of the Internet.* New York: Simon and Schuster.

Walker, N. 1988. "'Wider Than the Sky': Public Presence and Private Self in Dickinson, James, and Woolf." In *The Private Self: Theory and Practice of Women's Autobiographical Writings,* ed. S. Benstock, 272–303. Chapel Hill: University of North Carolina Press.

Warren, S., & L. Brandeis. 1890. "The Right to Privacy." *Harvard Law Review* 4 (5): 289–320.

Watkins, S. 1996. "World Wide Web Authoring in the Portfolio-Assessed, (Inter)Networked Composition Course." *Computers and Composition* 13 (2): 219–320.

Whitney, G. 1998. "Re: Student Web Page Survey." E-mail to the author, 24 May 1998.

Williams, J. 1997. "Renegotiating the Pedagogical Contract." In *Class Issues: Pedagogy, Cultural Studies, and the Public Sphere,* ed. A. Kumar, 298–312. New York: New York University Press.

Woodlief, A. 1997. "Changing the Paradigm: Hypertext and Interactive, Student-Centered Learning." In *Technology Tools for Today's Campuses* [CD-ROM], ed. J. Morrison. Seattle: Microsoft 1997 [cited 1 June 1998]. Available from World Wide Web: <http://horizon.unc.edu/projects/monograph/CD/Language_Music/Woodlief.asp>.

Yancey, K. B. 1998. *Reflecting in the Writing Classroom.* Logan: Utah State University Press.

Yaro, R. D., & T. Hiss. 1996. *A Region at Risk: The Third Regional Plan for the New York–New Jersey–Connecticut Metropolitan Area.* Washington, D.C.: Island Press.

Contributors

Jonathan Benda, lecturer in the Department of Foreign Languages and Literature at Tunghai University in Taiwan, has presented papers in Taiwan and the United States on teaching Internet research concepts and skills to students of English as a foreign language. He is currently working on a Ph.D. in Composition and Cultural Rhetoric at Syracuse University.

Chris Benson, research associate and publications coordinator at the Thurmond Institute, Clemson University, is active in a variety of programs in education. He is editor of the *Bread Loaf Rural Teacher Network Magazine* and an associate of Write to Change, a nonprofit agency that promotes action research and writing in a variety of schools and communities. Chris has numerous publications in such journals as *Teacher Magazine* and *Education Week*. His co-edited collection, *Electronic Networks: Crossing Boundaries/Creating Communities*, was published by Heinemann in 1999. Another co-edited book, *Writing for the Community: Methods, Model, and Motives*, is forthcoming from Calendar Islands.

Wendy Bishop, a professor of English at Florida State University, is the author and editor of a number of books, essays, and articles on composition and creative writing pedagogy and writing research. Her recent collections include *Mid-Passage, Touching Liliana, My 47 Lives* (poetry chapbooks), *Thirteen Ways of Looking for a Poem: A Guide to Writing Poetry, The Subject Is Reading: Essays by Teachers and Students*, and *In Praise of Pedagogy: Essays, Flash Fiction and Essays on Composing* (co-edited with David Starkey). She lives in Tallahassee but spends as much time as she can with her family at Alligator Point, Florida.

Sara Daum is a graduate student in Medical Sociology at the University of Alabama at Birmingham. Although her current research interests include medically oriented topics such as adaptive responses to Type I diabetes, social demography, and power relationships in eating disorders, her ongoing interest in Symbolic Interactionism and qualitative research led her to collaborate with Jason Palmeri on the chapter contained herein about peer response groups at New College of the University of South Florida.

Amy Goodburn, associate professor of English and Women's Studies at the University of Nebraska–Lincoln, teaches courses in composition, rhetoric, and literacy studies. She has published in the *Journal of Advanced Composition, English Education,* and *Composition Studies* and the collections *Feminism and Composition* and *Race, Rhetoric, and Composition*. Her research focuses on critical and multicultural pedagogies, ethnographic/teacher research, and school/community literacy practices.

Angela Hewett, assistant professor of English at George Washington University, has delivered many conference papers on Virginia Woolf, and published the article, "The 'Great Company of *Real* Women': Modernist Women Writers and Mass Commercial Culture," in *Reading Modernism: New Directions in Feminist Criticism* (Garland, 1994). Formerly associate director for the Writing Program at Rutgers University, Angela is also active in composition studies.

Emily Isaacs, assistant professor of English and Freshman English Coordinator at Montclair State University, has most recently written an article for *Writing on The Edge,* "Restarting a Life: Building a Home without a Bulldozer." She was a co-editor of *The Composition of Our"selves"* (Kendall Hunt, 1994) and an assistant producer and contributor to *Teaching in Process: Multimedia Resources for Writing Teachers* (CD-ROM, Houghton Mifflin, 1996).

Phoebe Jackson, visiting assistant professor of American Literature at William Paterson University, was a co-editor of *The Composition of Our"selves"* (Kendall Hunt, 1994) and a contributor to *Teaching in Process: Multimedia Resources for Writing Teachers* (CD-ROM, Houghton Mifflin, 1996).

Joan Latchaw is an associate professor at the University of Nebraska at Omaha, specializing in rhetoric and composition. After two stints as Director of First Year Writing at Shepherd College and North Dakota State University, she is focusing on the scholarship of computer-mediated communications. She co-edited *The Dialogic Classroom: Teachers Integrating Computer Technology, Pedagogy, and Research* with Jeffrey Galin. Latchaw and Galin have co-authored articles on intellectual property and have designed and taught joint graduate seminars, using MOOs, listservs, and other technologies. Graduate education is another vital interest which Latchaw is exploring in her work on affective factors influencing critical thinking.

Amy Lee is assistant professor of English and co-director of the writing program at the University of Minnesota's General College. She teaches basic writing and community-action learning courses. Her book *Composing Critical Pedagogies* was published in NCTE's "Refiguring English Studies" series, and she is collaborating on a series of articles on teacher development with Shari Stenberg.

Nicholas Mauriello is an assistant professor of English and the director of the Comprehensive Writing Program at Spelman College in Atlanta, Georgia. He has published articles in *Computers and Composition* and various book chapters. With Gian S. Pagnucci, he is co-editor of *The Future of Narrative Discourse,* a two-book series to be published by Hampton Press.

Robert McRuer, assistant professor of English and associate director of the Human Sciences Program, George Washington University, is author of *The Queer Renaissance: Contemporary American Literature and the Reinvention of Lesbian and Gay Identities* (New York University Press, 1997). He has written articles for the collections *Critical Essays: Gay and Lesbian Writers of Color* (Haworth, 1993) and *Enabling the Humanities: A Disability Studies Sourcebook* (MLA, 2000), and for *Genders, the Journal of Homosexuality,* and the *Children's Literature Association Quarterly.* He is currently completing a book on the intersections of "queer theory" and Disability Studies, tentatively titled *De-Composing Bodies: Cultural Signs of Queerness and Disability.*

Charles Moran, professor of English, University of Massachusetts, Amherst, and National Writing Project Site Coordinator, has published in such journals as *Computers and Composition, College English,* and *College Composition and Communication,* and in numerous collections. Moran is co-author (with Hawisher, LeBlanc, and Selfe) of *Computers and Teaching of Writing in American Higher Education 1979–94* (Ablex, 1996), co-editor (with Anne Herrington) of *Writing, Teaching, and Learning in the Disciplines* (MLA, 1992), and co-editor (with Elizabeth Penfield) of *Conversations: Contemporary Critical Theory and the Teaching of Literature* (NCTE, 1990).

Derek Owens is assistant professor of English and director of the Writing Center at St. John's University (Queens, New York City), and lives with his wife Teresa Hewitt and son Ryan on Long Island. He is the author of *Resisting Writings (and the Boundaries of Composition)* (Southern Methodist University Press, 1994) and *For a Threatened Generation: Composition and Sustainability* (NCTE Press, forthcoming). His articles have appeared in *Works and Days, Readerly/Writerly Texts, Composition Studies,* and the collections *Into the Field: The Interdisciplinary Site of Composition Studies* (MLA, 1993), *Ecocomposition* (SUNY Press, 2001), *Keywords in Composition Studies* (Boynton/Cook), and *Literacy Theory in the Age of the Internet* (Columbia University Press, 1999).

Gian S. Pagnucci is an assistant professor of English at Indiana University of Pennsylvania (IUP). He teaches courses on Narrative Theory and Technology and Literacy in IUP's Graduate Studies in Rhetoric and Linguistics program. He has published articles in *English Journal, Computers and Composition, Theory into Practice,* and *Works and Days.* Gian has also published chapters in books by NCTE and Heinemann. He has just guest-edited, with Nicholas Mauriello, a special issue of *Works and Days* on "The Future of Narrative Discourse." Additionally, Gian has published short stories, poems, and a collection of children's folktales. His web address is http://www.english.iup.edu/pagnucci.

Jason Palmeri recently received his B.A. in Literature from New College of the University of South Florida. His article, "Transgressive Hybridity: Reflections on the Authority of the Peer Tutor," is forthcoming in *Writing Lab Newsletter.* Jason has given presentations at the National Conference of Undergraduate Research and the Florida Council of Teachers of English. Drawing on his experience as a peer writing tutor, Jason assisted in the development of a writing center and WAC program at New College.

Shari Stenberg is an assistant professor and director of composition at Creighton University. Her research interests include composition studies and critical–feminist pedagogies. She is currently collaborating with Amy Lee on a series of articles about teacher development and critical pedagogy.

Andrea Stover, assistant professor of English at Belmont University, specializes in composition, autobiography, and basic writing. Her article, "Using Student Publications: Developing Audience Awareness," was published in *Notes in the Margins* (Spring 1995). She was an associate producer of "Teaching in Process: Multimedia Resources for Writing Teachers" (CD-ROM, Houghton Mifflin, 1996).